ATTRACT
MORE PATIENTS
IN THE NEXT 6 MONTHS
THAN IN THE PAST 6 YEARS

COLIN RECEVEUR

ATTRACT
MORE PATIENTS
IN THE NEXT 6 MONTHS
THAN IN THE PAST 6 YEARS

COLIN RECEVEUR

SmartBox Web Marketing

819 Mount Tabor Road Suite 8, New Albany, IN 47150
Toll Free: 888.741.1413 - Fax 502.371.0659
Email: colin@smartboxweb.com
Website: www.SmartBoxWeb.com
Facebook: www.fb.me/SmartBoxWebMarketing
Twitter : @creceveur
YouTube : www.youtube.com/SmartBoxWeb

Contents

Advance Praise

"I've done dental marketing in the past with the big dental website guys, and right now, **there's no one better than Colin.**"

~ Avi Weisfogel, D.D.S.
Cosmetic, Implant, and Sedation Dentist in Old Bridge, New Jersey

"Some of you dentists out there may be doubting if they actually deliver. I'm here to tell you that **they deliver.**"

~ Saj Jivraj, D.D.S., M.S.Ed.
Prosthodontist and Implant Dentist near Los Angeles, California

"**Colin is our secret weapon** that we deploy for our best member practices all over the country."

~ James McAnally, D.D.S.
CEO, Big Case Marketing and President, Master Dentists Academy

"Colin puts it all together in **a way that gets results** and saves me time."

~ Robert Matiasevich Jr., D.D.S.
Cosmetic Dentist in Santa Cruz, California

"**Colin basically is a genius** on all types of marketing, is the CEO of SmartBox Web Marketing, and he has various products and DVDs that dentists across the country are using."

~ Woody Oakes
President, The Profitable Dentist and Excellence In Dentistry

"Our biggest referral source is the Internet."

~ Donald Plourde, D.M.D.
Cosmetic Dentist near Boston, Massachusetts

"Today, many patients are online and they're looking to research the background of the professional they're going to choose. 50% of my patients come from online."

~ Saj Jivraj, D.D.S., M.S.Ed.

*"The one thing I like about Colin is **he comes through with the stuff that he says;** he's ready to back it up. He's going to work for you, get you the results that you need."*

~ Avi Weisfogel, D.D.S.

"Colin diversified me, getting me exposure in all my different dental niches."

~ J.D. Murray, D.D.S.
Cosmetic Dentist in Atlanta, Georgia with two office locations

*"I've started working with SmartBox, I would say about a year, year and a half now, and I will tell you that **it's changed my practice.**"*

~ Saj Jivraj, D.D.S., M.S.Ed.

"You can be the best, most highly trained dentist in the world, but without the ability to SELL the patient on needing the treatment, it's just not going to happen."

~ Sean Tarpenning, D.D.S.
General Dentist in Eau Claire, WI

"I'll keep on working with them and highly recommend anyone to do the same."

~ Andoni Guisasola, D.D.S.
General Dentist in Spain

"I think the benefit that we saw right away was the fact that now we had somebody that could take over."

~ Robert Matiasevich Jr., D.D.S.

"I wanted to have the ability to have the telephone number monitored, which you offered. I wanted to have that. I wanted to have the ability to get better placement on search engines. I wanted to have video capabilities of our own staff and do that on our own, and I wanted to be able to communicate quickly, as far as changes in the website."

~ John K. Argeros, D.M.D.
Sedation Implant Dentist near Boston, Massachusetts

"Colin really seemed to be able to put that together in a way that made sense – in an orderly fashion, so it wasn't something that was going to take up time every week for me to do, because that's the way I had been doing it."

~ Robert Matiasevich Jr., D.D.S.

"The biggest reason for engaging Colin and SmartBox was to be able to have more patients around our area know of the procedures that we can do. To know about the options in one dentistry visit of walking into an office with a denture and leaving with permanent teeth, if that's what they choose, or being able to have fillings done without a shot and without drilling anymore."

~ Steven J. Sutherland, D.D.S.
Dentist/Owner in Los Angeles, California

"Talking on the phone, it was nice to get Colin's passion for what he does. It was something that really interested me. When he said he could help and solve the problems we were having, there was a nice reassurance there."

~ Robert H, Klein, D.D.S.
Implant Dentist in Kansas City, Missouri

*"Colin started his own company 12 years ago, which is 72 years in Internet time, so don't let his youthful looks fool you. He owns a slew of certifications with Google, Microsoft, Cisco – they all come with lots of little important letters after them. More important than those letters is **his intimate knowledge of what we're up to as dentists** and his ability to tie all of the pieces together on the web. The fact that he gets it is why he's rapidly become known as a 'Google God' for dental professionals."*

~ James McAnally, D.D.S.

"He has some really great products. His father is a dentist and is one of the three dentists in town I would trust to do my own dentistry. The unique thing about Colin is since his father is a dentist, he has this ideal playground to test new ideas and marketing before rolling it out to the rest of his clients."

~ Woody Oakes

About The Author

Colin is the Go-To Guy for Dental Web Marketing

Word Count: **1255**
Approximate Time to Read: **2.8 minutes**

To know SmartBox Web Marketing, you have to know founder and CEO Colin Receveur, the dynamo that powers this marketing machine. Even though SmartBox was incorporated in 2001, it began inside Colin during his childhood.

Colin's experience helping dentists predates search engine optimization (SEO), Google, websites and even the Internet. No, Colin's experience goes back to when he was a 7-year-old boy helping in his father's dental office, filing records for a dime apiece.

He worked almost every day in his father's office – and spent almost every night on the family's Compaq computer (remember those?) in the early morning hours learning how to design and code websites in the Internet's infancy.

Though his dad is a dentist, Colin's mom was a top sales executive with a Fortune 100 healthcare organization. So it was only natural for him to want to monetize his interest in websites.

"In the 8th grade, my mom became concerned how I came into several hundred dollars, and she worried I was into 'something bad,'" Colin said. "I was doing affiliate marketing, selling banner advertising space on my website and getting commission checks!"

Colin's love of websites only grew from there. He launched a business designing websites for local businesses as a sophomore in high school (all while still working in his dad's practice).

Ultimately, he combined all of his loves into SmartBox Web Marketing. He built his father's first website in 1997. By 2006 he had partnered with Dr. James McAnally to service his Elite clients' web-marketing needs, and in 2010 began working with Dr. Michael Abernathy and his clients. SmartBox now works with more than 360 dentists on three continents.

"My background in dentistry, working in the office from a young age, managing my dad's and hundreds of other practices, gives me a unique perspective into what dentists really want and how to leverage the tools available to help them reach their goals," Colin said.

While it's not unusual to receive an email from Colin at 5:30 in the morning, it's not just because he's a workaholic. His young son Benjamin is an early riser – and that helps dad get an early jump on the day.

When Colin's not working with clients, he's a voracious reader of non-fiction, especially books on marketing. But don't think Colin is all work and no play.

Colin loves to scuba dive shipwrecks, collect shot glasses (which he started at the precocious age of 10) and learn about World War II. Both of Colin's grandfathers served in the big one, one as a paratrooper and the other as a medic who landed on Iwo Jima.

Since this makes Colin sound like he can leap tall buildings in a single bound, it's only fitting that his favorite superhero is Superman. But there is no hiding his secret identity as a man who can get you more of the clients you want faster than a speeding bullet.

"Many marketing firms just get marketing. Website design firms know how to design pretty websites. SEO firms can do SEO. The problem is, when all you have is a hammer, every problem starts to look like a nail," Colin said. "As a dentist, you don't want marketing or websites or SEO, You want NEW PATIENTS in your chair. At SmartBox we know how to maximize every tool to make that happen."

Foreword

Dr. Michael Abernathy

Word Count: **599**
Approximate Time to Read: **1.3 minutes**

Over the past 40 years, dentistry has changed tremendously.

But most of us who practice are prepared for that.

We stay current by reading the latest articles, going to continuing education and attending workshops and seminars to learn new methods and techniques.

As a dentist, you're prepared for that. You **expect** that.

But what nobody tells you or prepares you for is how to get patients to walk in the door to see your expertise and all of these new things you can do.

When I first started my general dental practice in McKinney, Texas, back in 1974, all you had to do was put up your sign and get a listing in the Yellow Pages and you'd get patients.

Those patients would tell other people, and they'd become patients.

When I sold this practice, we were collecting $8 million per year with two associates and eight hygienist when most people were grossing half a million. We had a 50 percent profit margin and brought in 200 new patients per month with no managed care.

In fact, people started calling what we did the **"Gold Standard"** for dental practices.

But the world has changed. The Internet has changed the way we have to market our practice.

We live in a web-centric world. No matter how someone hears about you, online and offline, they look to the Internet to validate who you are and find out if you're the right dentist for them. That's why they go to your website.

Still, just having a website isn't enough anymore. How are you attracting people to it? Are you attracting the right people to it? Are you ranked at the top in a Google search in your area? Are you leveraging the latest technologies or just chasing "shiny objects"?

And if you have a website, but how old is it? Does it work with the mobile devices? Once someone comes to your site, do they stay and read? Do they actually make a phone call or email for an appointment?

Because that is really what marketing effectiveness comes down to – **getting new patients**.

In 1991, I teamed up with Max Gotcher and founded Summit Practice Solutions to coach other dentists on the business side of dentistry. Since then I've published more than 250 articles and three books, and given who knows how many lectures and presentations around the country and world.

As you can imagine, my reputation means a lot to me. I've worked hard to hone what I know into replicable systems that other dentists can benefit from. So I don't give out endorsements lightly or very often.

So I can say with all confidence that Colin Receveur knows what he's doing to leverage the Internet to help dentists attract more and better patients.

We use him, and probably the greatest endorsement I can give is that we encourage our clients to work with Colin. We want them to be successful.

If his system of website development, search engine optimization, telephone tracking and drip marketing didn't work, I wouldn't write this.

But it does work.

His systems guide you on how to attract potential patients to your website, what kinds of blogs, videos, content and pictures to put on your website, and how to keep your name in front of **potential** patients and turn them into **paying** patients.

You're really getting a lot of good information from Colin, and if you follow his system, you'll get results.

To Your Success,

Dr. Michael Abernathy

Co-Founder, Summit Practice Solutions
Owner, Dental Success Seminars and DDS Partners
Author, The Super General Dental Practice

Preface

Word Count: **564**
Approximate Time to Read: **1.3 minutes**

How to Attract More Patients in the Next 6 Months Than in the Past 6 Years

Now that would be exciting wouldn't it?

I haven't met a dentist yet whose eyes don't perk up when you start talking about results like that.

Just think about what that could mean for your practice.

More patients in six months than in the previous six years.

Is that possible?

I can tell you this:

Once you experience it, your eyes will be opened forever. And you will **never** go back to the "take what you can get" daily grind that most dentists endure.

Please understand this type of patient attraction is not something your "average" dentist is going to be able to do. If you're reading this, I'm assuming that you're not average and that you have no desire to ever be average.

The path to attracting more patients in the next six months than you have in the past six years is a journey that requires two specific steps:

The first step is to understand the **process and structure**. You have to understand how a system capable of this actually works. It's a very specific structure you need for results.

The second step is to commit to the **execution**. But I don't mean that you're actually going to do the work. You've got to be leading the business so you can't get stuck operating in it. If you do, you go nuts.

The most valuable use of your time is treating patients. There's simply no way around it. And the future success of your practice is dependent on how many of your available hours you invest doing just that.

We've broken down the book as much as we could. There is still a lot of information here so we've given you some easy ways to work through it. As with every instructional book you read, you like to know the person who wrote it is credible. We've inserted some of our testimonials from clients that have worked with us through the years, who are some of the most highly regarded dentists in the country. These give you a true idea of what our clients think of us and our work.

Also included are podcast and radio show transcriptions that give you a better feel of what kind of people we are at SmartBox, further explanations on specific Internet marketing tactics as well as knowledge from some well known and highly thought of people in the dentistry world.

We know you're busy and don't have a lot of time to spend reading book after book on how to grow your practice. That's why we've included all you need to know in one book and have broken down the book into short chapters that you can quickly read, digest and put into action in your practice.

The mid to high-scoring college graduate reads from 450 to 800 words per minute. We have based the amount of time needed to read each chapter on if you're reading at 450 words per minute. You'll find an estimate at the beginning of each chapter so you can work through the book a little at a time throughout your week and not have to spend your off time working on your practice.

Make sure not just to read; consume and digest. Whether you're a note-taker, highlighter, page-corner-folder, note-scribbler-in-the-white-space or just have a photographic memory, this book is worthless if you don't take action. You can't take action without remembering what you read here.

Remember, Rome wasn't built in a day and your marketing campaign won't be either. Don't try to implement everything we discuss in this book in a week. Develop a plan of action and steadily implement the ideas we outline.

Reading this book is a first step in commitment to marketing. Even with technology making it easier and less expensive to reach your target audience, too many practices only advertise when sales are down, costing them tens of thousands of dollars in lost opportunities when the sales are up. Develop a consistent marketing strategy you can keep going in good times and bad.

Keep Moving Forward,

Colin Receveur

Introduction

Word Count: **3882**
Approximate Time to Read: **8.6 minutes**

Will You Become Invisible To New Patients Looking For a Dentist?

Little could James Marshall have known in 1848 that finding a single gold nugget in a sawmill ditch would make him important to dentistry.

Marshall's discovery touched off the California Gold Rush of 1848-1858 that saw more than 90,000 people race to find their fortune in the first two years. The final tally was 300,000 when the rush was over – or 1 in every 90 people in the U.S. at the time.

California is a big state, so some of those arriving first may have had a chance of finding gold. But what chance did those who showed up late really have?

More importantly, what does this have to do with **giving you and your family the lifestyle you dream of?**

"Gold Rushes" Are Occurring All Around Us

This "Gold Rush" cycle has repeated itself plenty of times in many different markets. Here's how it works:

Something new like the Internet comes along and there's a limited time where it's just like the Wild West. Results are easy, things are good. A few people are getting BIG pieces of the pie and the gettin' is good!

But then the masses start to get wind of what's going on. Pretty soon, they come to get a piece of the pie, too. They tell their friends and now the pieces of the pie start to shrink. Pretty soon, that "first mover advantage" disappears and results plummet.

Eventually, you have so many people cutting up the pie, **each person only gets a few crumbs!**

Don't Settle for Crumbs!

Right now, 94 percent of new patients use the Internet to research and find a doctor. In previous years, putting your practice directly in front of those searchers and potential patients has been relatively simple.

In fact, getting new patients online was so straightforward that you could get results even with one of those cookie-cutter dental websites.

The first mover advantage made up for a lot. I hate to start off with so much bad news but ...

Those Days Are OVER

As more dentists discover the power of attracting new patients online, more and more are flocking to the Internet – fast. There's a lot of money flowing online as dentists all over the country try to get the attention of new patients.

When a few dentists are doing smart things online, it's possible to create amazing results. But when thousands of them are all doing the same things, those "smart things" quickly become invisible and worthless.

You see, along with all of those marketing dollars comes noise. From buying Facebook fans to Twitter followers to banner ads or directory listings or other paid advertising – there's a lot of money creating a lot of noise. That noise is making it harder and harder for your next potential patient to find you online.

What we know is this:

More Patients Than Ever Are Looking For You Online

Do you have a plan to stand out and make sure they end up in your chair?

Think about it like fishing: Five years ago, only the smart guys had a "net," a website. These days, **everybody** has a net. So if you show up with just a net, you'll have absolutely ZERO advantage over everybody else.

That's not a good recipe for success.

The exact same thing is going to happen online. For the dentists that don't make a move now, they are going to find the Internet to be extremely unprofitable.

The fact is, you can still "get by" online with the basics even without differentiating yourself. You might get a few patients online even with the most basic website.

That's not going to be true by the end of this year. The dentists who are trying to attract patients online with "the basics" are going to find themselves **without** a steady stream of new patients.

If all you want is a new website, save yourself some time and **stop reading**. What I have isn't for you. But if you're looking for a next-level strategy to absolutely **DOMINATE** online, then keep reading, because I'm going to share more about getting that done.

Notice I didn't say you need a better website. You probably do, but that's just the beginning!

The Only Way to Attract Patients Online Over the Long Term is To Build a Better Patient Attraction System Than Anyone Else

Let me repeat that:

Consistently Attract Patients Online by Building a Better Patient Attraction System Than Anyone Else

Without a system, you're going to be invisible. Dr. Raleigh Pioch knows this. He's a dentist in Salem, Oregon. You can read what he said on the right of this page.

Getting found is becoming hard enough. And it's easy to think that's the whole battle. But it's just the beginning.

A lot of dentists complain about patients being so price-conscious. I'm talking about the "does insurance cover this?" type of patients. Every dentist has had them. No one wants them forever. Patients like that just want a "dentist."

The secret is to create a system that makes them want **YOU**. And to make that attraction they feel to you and your practice **so strong** that they'll do whatever it takes to be your patient – even pay higher fees.

This is the type of system that the guys who know what they're doing online already have working.

Most dentists are losing out on 50 percent of their case acceptance simply because they don't have a real **patient attraction system**. They're missing Step 3 of the strategy, and they have no idea. They probably have a "website," but that's about it.

Read that paragraph again carefully. If you don't want to forfeit 50 percent of the revenue that ~~could have~~ **should have** been yours, then you won't want to make this mistake.

Without a System Like This, You Can Spend a Ton of Money to be Invisible Online.

So what does a complete patient attraction system look like? Keep reading

There are four steps to this that you need to understand. Skip any step and your results tank.

STEP 1: ATTRACTION

Your prospects must be able to find you on the web, no matter if they search on Google, Facebook, local search or on their mobile phone!

The alphabet soup of "buzzwords" you've heard (SEO, SEM, PPC, SMO, etc.) are simply the tools to achieve a top ranking visibility. Being found at the top of the search engines is just the first step of any successful web marketing strategy.

STEP 2: CONSUMPTION

Your prospects must understand the types of dentistry you offer. Remember, patients are searching for answers to their problems. You do this through informational reports, packets of information, templates and written books. All of these resources help you achieve "celebrity status." We do this for our clients. You've got to have resources like this working for you or you'll lose out to the dentist who does.

Would you choose the dentist with a firm handshake and kind word, or **the one who literally "wrote the book?"**

You want to be the "top guy to see" in your niches of dentistry (emergencies, cosmetics, Invisalign, implants, dentures, etc.). You may offer a wide array of services, but you can build your marketing and web presence to look like you are "the only guy" doing the procedures that bring you the patients you want.

STEP 3: FOLLOW-UP

Potential patients may stumble across you online now, but 85-90 percent of your website visitors are NOT ready to immediately call you. By offering to send them valuable information in exchange for their contact information, you can answer all of their questions and become their "expert," all the while keeping your name in front of them until they are ready to buy.

STEP 4: PHONE TRACKING

All your time and effort is wasted if you can't figure out exactly what works and what doesn't. With our proprietary Zetetics® Phone Tracking system, we can tell you down to the penny, which marketing works and, which doesn't so you **don't waste your marketing dollars.**

This is the type of tracking you need to make your money accountable for results.

The Bar Is High and Getting Higher

As you can see, a system that attracts new patients online is pretty comprehensive. It's way beyond a "website."

More than that, you can't really have too many doctors in one area using the same **patient attraction system**. If you do, everyone suffers!

Just look at those dentists still using the cookie cutter websites. To think that you're going to attract a steady stream of new patients online using the same type of website and strategy as thousands of other dentists is just nuts. It's not going to happen.

So there's a little bit of secrecy required here if you want the maximum effect. Once you get something that works, the best thing to do is keep it to yourself.

You are protecting your investment by doing this. It IS an investment you know. And when you're investing, the only thing that matters is your return on that investment. So here's what you have to pay attention to:

How Much Are You Putting Into Attracting Patients And How Many Dollars Are You Getting In Return?

It's really hard to tell from the outside looking in whether all of the gizmos and promises to help dentists actually work or not. I don't envy your position if you're trying to figure out, which solution is right for you.

But I can tell you that most of what I see out there aren't really "solutions." They're more like "**partial**" solutions.

They probably do **one** or two things really, really well. So well, in fact, that when you look at them, they look really impressive.

But that won't get you patients.

● The latest Internet tricks and gizmos might get your website

---

ranked highly, or they might get your site to look good on a mobile device.

- Getting a #1 ranking on Google isn't going to fill your chair either. It's a start, but it's just a start.

- They might even get you a bunch of clicks and hits on your website. Traffic certainly is exciting when it happens. Unfortunately, you can't **fund your retirement** with clicks!

- There's no way most of the "solutions" you see out there take complete strangers sitting in front of their computers at home and transform them into **new patients**.

- Getting a boatload of "likes" on Facebook isn't going to fill your chair with the patients **YOU** want.

But that's **exactly** what you can expect from a complete online **patient attraction system**.

Does It Work? Does It Attract the Patients YOU Want?

It's exciting to talk about strategy and about systems of attraction and everything. You get caught up in putting yourself in the driver's seat of one of those systems. That's the picture you paint in your head.

You can FEEL how great that would be. And it is. It's a beautiful thing to witness really. Even better if you're the one that's benefiting from the results.

There Are Some Results I Can Share With You

Of course I only know the results my clients have gotten. These are the results that come from an online patient attraction system built right. One built with the four steps needed to **attract the patients YOU want.**

You'd think that the most valuable thing about having a system like this working for your practice would be the new patients that it attracts into your chair.

On one level, that's the case. But there's something else that's even better.

Once you have something like this working for you, you can stop chasing the latest and greatest Internet gizmos. You can focus on doing what you do best (treating patients) and still sleep well at night knowing the patients are going to keep coming.

Differentiation is the Key

You may be asking yourself, "If it works so great, why isn't everyone doing it?"

Because we don't offer it to every dentist in every market.

You can't have too many doctors in one area using our patient attraction system. If you do, the result is rapid dilution.

It is like thinking you can take a pint of jet fuel, dilute it with a tanker truck of water and still expect combustion in the jet to get off the ground.

When strategies that normally work very well on the Internet get diluted by having too many dentists in one market using them, the result is so weak that competing, less complex strategies win the day. It is for that very reason that any expert you rely on cannot be working with more than a couple of dentists in your market.

Exclusivity for Results is a Very BIG Deal

Otherwise, your efforts will be a waste of time and money as your competitors will be doing the same things and watering down your results.

Chapter 1

Web 3.0 and Your Dental Practice

Word Count: **10,105**
Approximate Time to Read: **22.5 minutes**

"I know that the Internet is the wave of the future, but it IS the future – it is now."

~ *Raleigh Pioch, D.D.S.*
General Dentist in Salem, Oregon

*"Right now, everyone wants to be contacted or stay in contact and it's not the way that we used to do it before. Everything now is either text or digital – Internet, that's what people want. Remember now, we're building this practice not only for my age and older, but for my partner's age and younger, to keep the practice going. Those people look at the Internet, they look at things coming to them continually: being notified about this, they like that – they want to be kept abreast of things and they want it in the format they want it, which is not really in the mail or anything anymore – **it's all on the web.**"*

~ *John K. Argeros, D.M.D.*

*"One of Colin's fortes is the use of the Internet to market the office. **I've always relied on Colin** for his overviews and expertise in the Internet and the technology of the office."*

~ *Tom Gibbs, D.D.S., F.A.G.D., F.D.O.C.S., F.I.C.O.I.*
Cosmetic and Implant Dentist in Chicagoland

"The level of competition we have is astronomical. The odds are against us so I just need you to put everything in my favor. I wanted to cover it all, I wanted to cover all my bases and so that's why I picked the Elite package. I didn't want to leave anything on the table, I wanted to go for it and I had faith from what I'd seen from the other websites, I was confident that I was doing the right thing and was excited about doing it."

~ *Raleigh Pioch, D.D.S.*

*"I think that currently, one of the biggest referrals for us – for dentists now – is becoming Internet related. **People are searching***

the Internet for their healthcare providers *to find out more about them. That's why we contacted you: to make sure that we had a website that answered a lot of people's questions and hopefully helped them make a decision to make an appointment here."*

~ Donald Plourde, D.M.D.

"SmartBox will paint you in a light, which is favorable and which patients can relate to. They've done all the research from a marketing perspective, they know what buttons patients press in order to get the results they're looking for, and with their expertise in the dental marketing business, they will actually guide the patients toward your practice."

~ Saj Jivraj, D.D.S., M.S.Ed.

Make the Web Work for You

The online world has certainly changed in recent years. You may think that changes only happen every few years and the Internet has plateaued and stalled in it's progression, but I'm afraid this is not the case. The web is constantly changing and, therefore, anyone who wants to get ahead with the great benefits the web has to offer their dental practice has to stay abreast these changes and always be on the lookout for new developments. The next big change that is coming is what is known as Web 3.0. This upgrade will take the online environs and transform them from a static place to a dynamic environment where users are the focus. In addition, those same changes will make it vital that companies adapt and grow at the same time.

The modern Internet offers tremendous advantages for almost everyone, including benefits for your practice, your ROI, and your profitability. However, knowing what tools to use, how to implement various strategies, and where to turn for help can be enormously frustrating for dentists.

This section is designed to help you come to terms with Web 3.0, how it affects your practice, and how you can use tools like social media marketing and Search Engine Optimization to not only grow your business, but to ensure the most success as well as stay ahead of your competition.

This portion offers vital information about new systems and options online, new marketing methods that have emerged in recent years, and how you can harness their potential. In short, this is your guide to the Internet and making it work for you.

What Is Web 3.0 and Who Benefits?

Before we can delve into how the various components of Web 3.0 can be of use to your practice, you need to understand a bit more about what it actually comprises. What is Web 3.0, anyway?

Actually, this is a difficult subject to define – it means many different things. Web 3.0 is a term used to separate user-centric designs from static web designs and systems used in the past. At its heart, Web 3.0 is about giving users access to information and allowing them to share it. This is what makes it so incredibly valuable to you and your practice! It's also about attracting attention through different means.

There are quite a few different components to this topic, as well, including:

- SEO (Search Engine Optimization)
- Paid Search and AdWords
- Local Search Optimization
- Social Networking and Marketing
- Online Video
- Mobile Marketing
- Blogging

In addition, successfully putting these components to work for your dental practice will require some specific knowledge.

Each area mentioned above requires special steps and techniques in order to ensure that you reap the utmost benefits. However, it can be almost impossible to "go it alone" here. This section will help you understand the processes involved, as well as the benefits that you can see.

Who benefits from these tools and techniques? Actually, it's a win-win situation for all involved. Consumers/patients benefit because they are able to find the information that they need more easily, while dental practices (and all other businesses) benefit from the increased exposure, better conversion on websites, better brand recognition, and higher ROI.

What are the Benefits to My Practice?

Can Search Engine Optimization, paid search, AdWords, social networking, mobile marketing, online video and blogging really be of benefit to your practice? Yes! These techniques give you several advantages that you cannot find in any other way:

- Attract search engine spiders (an automated way that your website's content is included in search results)
- Boost search engine page rank
- Attract visitors through natural search results
- Encourage current patients to share about your practice with friends, family, and coworkers
- Encourage interaction between current (and potential) patients and your practice
- Make patients aware of new services and techniques offered
- Inform patients by showing procedural videos, pictures and engaging in discussions
- Highlight your practice's culture, ethics and character
- Set your practice apart from others in the community
- Make patients aware of special saving programs/discount programs and encourage them to share that information with others

As you can see, Web 3.0 can help you achieve many goals, all of which are vital to your profitability, stability, and overall success. How does this work, though? Here is a brief overview of each component and how it works. We'll also dig into each of these in greater depth later on.

SEO (Search Engine Optimization)

Search Engine Optimization is a seemingly simple term that applies to myriad different subjects. There's a whole host of different processes involved in optimizing your website and your online efforts, but they all boil down to these key points:

- They make your site/content more visible to search engines and increase your page rank through natural search results.
- They make your site more visible to web surfers/potential patients looking for specific information on important dental topics.

Paid Search and AdWords

Paid search programs have been around for quite some time. These are paid advertisements that appear along with natural search results when your customers search through Google or another search engine for your targeted keywords. AdWords is Google's pay-per-click (PPC) program, and is one of the most popular out there. However, there are other paid search options, including those used on Facebook.

Local Search Optimization

Local search optimization is perhaps the best branch of SEO for your practice. This allows you to target your specific keywords, but decrease the level of competition you face from national and international services. Local search optimization is really just the process of integrating your geographic location in your keywords, but has proven to be enormously important for local businesses just like yours.

Social Networking

Social networking is not new, and chances are good that you already use it on a personal basis. However, it can also be of immense benefit to your practice. More and more businesses (of all types) are using social networking to their advantage and it's actually been compared to SEO in terms of effectiveness. There are also different social networks that you need to utilize, as they're geared toward different audiences and uses.

Online Video

Online video has become one of the most interesting phenomenons of the modern age. Consider the rise of YouTube – once a simple video sharing site. When it's popularity soared, Google purchased it and today it's one of the most heavily used websites in existence. Using online video sharing sites can be a great idea, but there are many other ways that you can put this technology to use for your practice, including integrating it with your social media efforts and even in a blog.

Mobile Marketing

Few things have changed the way that people interact with the Internet more than mobile technology. Today, it's become the norm to find information online via a smartphone or to look up directions and information about local businesses on portable devices. However, mobile technology presents some unique challenges to business owners. For instance, how do you ensure that your website displays correctly on small phone screens? Mobile marketing also requires several other considerations, but it is immensely effective.

Blogging

Blogging has been around for several years (it's one of the original Web 2.0 components) and it is still a vital and effective tool for businesses large and small. Using a blog can give your practice a "personal" face and help you connect with your patients on an intrinsic level, something that is impossible with even the best website. Your practice's blog can also be used for other purposes, including integrating all of your online efforts (it's better to use a blog than a website as your online marketing hub).

The following sections will expand on each of these topics and help you understand exactly what you need to do, and why you need to do it.

Who Doesn't Benefit from 3.0?

At this point, you might be wondering who doesn't benefit from Web 3.0 elements like blogging, social networking/marketing and Search Engine Optimization. The answer here is a bit murky and will require some explanation. For instance, let's say that a particular dental practice did not want to develop an online presence. This hypothetical practice has all the patients they can handle, and there's never a shortage of new patients or returning patients in need of help. Obviously, this business wouldn't benefit much from any of these components. However, such practices don't exist in reality – there is no practice, no matter how well-established, that can predict with utter certainty that they have all the patients they will ever need.

While the question of who doesn't benefit might seem to have several answers, there's really only one – everyone benefits. Any dental practice, regardless of location, size, or type, can enjoy better profitability, patient retention, and growth with the help of these tools and techniques. However, it should be noted that there are times when you need to benefit, but won't. Most notably, this applies to using "black hat" SEO – unethical practices that attempt to mislead search engine spiders and real users. Black hat SEO techniques must be avoided at all costs, or you will find that your site is blacklisted and banned from search engine results completely.

How To Win The Marketing Game

with Colin Receveur, Jonathan Moffat & Max Gotcher

Jonathan Moffat: Hi and welcome to another episode of Dental Doc Talk Radio. My name is Jonathan Moffat, and with me, as always, is Max Gotcher. Today we are excited to have a special guest with us. He's a bright young man named Colin Receveur, and Colin's company is called SmartBox Web Marketing. You can find Colin's company at www.SmartBoxWebMarketing.com

Now, you may be asking yourself, there's a lot of marketing guys out there, a lot of website guys out there. Why Colin? Well, I met Colin a few months ago in April in Destin, Florida, and was very impressed with his depth of knowledge in web optimization, and not only web optimization, but how to optimize your website and drive new patients at a very affordable rate.

Me, as a business owner, that was something that I thought was pretty impressive. But what's more impressive is Colin actually does what he says he can do. So, like I said, I just met Colin in April and have been very impressed. But Max, you've known Colin for quite a while. Is that correct?

Max Gotcher: I guess I first met Colin 10 or 12 years ago. His dad actually is a dentist and we did some work with his dad back years ago. I think on one of my visits to his dad's office I was having some computer problems and he said, "Let my son Colin take a look at it. He can probably fix it." Sure enough, he did in about five minutes, I think. He's been not only involved in all things Internet for a long time, but again, growing up in a family with his dad as a dentist gives him, I think, a little bit different perspective from maybe a lot of his competitors out there doing what they're doing with websites and Search Engine Optimization and all of those kind of things.

Colin: Thanks for having me, guys. I appreciate your time.

Jonathan: So, Colin, when you sit down and talk to guys, where are you seeing these doctors, these dentists, need the most help? When you are talking to a new dentist, not a client, maybe they have a website up. Maybe they're doing a little bit of marketing. But where do you see that these guys need the most help?

Colin: Great question. A lot of guys have a lot of successful aspects already in place in their marketing campaign. A lot of dentists have a good website. Maybe they've had phone training in their office, and they have a lot of successful aspects already rolling. But they're just not happy with the results they've been getting.

Generally, what we find when we're looking at a web marketing campaign that maybe they've done some Search Engine Optimization on, they've built a website in the past, and they've got a few of the aspects and they are just missing some pieces along the way. There are cracks that these patients are falling into that keeps them from moving from the search engine to their website, turning them into a phone call, and, of course, into a paying patient.

That's the biggest complain we get is, "Hey, I've got this website. It just doesn't generate any results. It's not doing anything for us." That's where we are able to help lots of dentists, is turning what they have or taking them from the ground up, in many cases, from Zero to Hero as we call it, from wherever they are to wherever they need to be with using their website as a true marketing tool that is going to pull in patients.

You know, not just selling them a shovel but actually doing the digging for them and showing them how to use it as a marketing tool to leverage it to get an ROI. That's what it comes down to – marketing is about ROI. It's not an expense. When done properly, of course, it is an investment that pays for itself several times over at minimum.

Max: Colin, I tell you what I see a lot of, and I know you probably do as well. Let me preface this by saying if I go back 12, 15 years ago, I was getting the question a lot from dentists: do I need a website? That went on for maybe five years or so.

I rarely anymore find a practice without a website. But what those websites look like and what they do for the practice varies all over the map. But what I still see a lot of is an office that they've jumped in, they get a website, say anywhere from 5-10 years ago, but they haven't really done anything to it since then. Yeah, it's a website. But like you said, it's not really generating any business for the practice.

Colin: The landscape is constantly changing. I know that's a theme that all of the marketing companies drive home, but it's really the reality. Ten years ago most docs didn't even have a website. The few that had a website – the fast movers – were the ones that were taking the lion's share – the market share – of the patients that were searching online 8-10 years ago.

Nowadays, most docs have a website of some sort. We see a lot of docs that have 3, 4, 5, 6, 10 websites, even, and are doing all kinds of aggressive marketing with it. Ten years ago, if you just had a website you were ahead of the curve. Nowadays, that's almost the status quo. Everybody has a website. The technology has evolved so far that there's even tools out there that you can build your own website in a short period of time without even hiring a marketing person.

With that, with the expansion of the technology and the ease of setting all that up, well now you have to find a way to go one step above that. Ten years ago you went one step up and you had a website. Now, well, what's the next step? You have to find some way to differentiate yourself, because patients are searching out there and they see 25 doctors in their area that have a website. Well, what is it that makes that patient choose Doctor X over Doctor Y?

So you have to have the mechanics, have the system in place, not just a website that talks about what you do, but have something that makes you stand out in the patient's mind to appeal to that patient.

There's lots of different ways to do that. But it's evolved that simply "just having a website" is the accepted standard. People go to the web to find your contact information. Take a look at Google: several years ago they started with their Local Places initiative. Essentially, what Google did was they went to the Yellow Pages and they copied everything that's in the Yellow Pages and they plugged it into their Google Local Places.

So they have the largest "Yellow Pages" phone book directory that is always changing, always updating. And they essentially created 160 million websites for every small business in America. If you go to Google, whether you know it or not, whether you have claimed it, whether you have gone to Google and said, "That's my business. Let me edit that information. Let me soup up that listing," you have a webpage out there on Google that's floating around. It might have your correct information, it might not.

And Google is not the only one that's done that. You've got Google and City Search and Yellow Pages is online now. All the Yellow Books are online. That's where people search. People look online to find resources they need. People look online to look for the answers to questions that they have, whether it's looking for a local provider or if it's looking to educate themselves about what kind of provider they might need or what options are best for them.

Jonathan: Colin, you made a comment earlier when you were talking about doctors' websites and good websites. What makes a good website? What does a good website look like? What should a good website have and what should a good website not have?

Colin: In terms of being Google friendly, in today's world you've got to have lots of content. There's different definitions of good. I'll start with Google-good because you have to be friends with Google if you want to be found on the Internet. Patients don't know who you are. They have to have a way of finding you.

In the past, they had a little book that sat in their drawer that they opened up to the dentist page and flipped through there, and the guy with the cutest ad or the biggest ad or the first ad, in some cases, was the guy they called. Now people go to Google. So you have to play ball with Google. Google wants to see websites that are going to keep their people happy.

So if you turn the tables, Google is a company. Google is a business. Google makes their money through selling advertising. If you break it down to very simple terms, Google sells advertising on its search pages. When you search Google, you see those sponsored listings at the top and down the right-hand side. And that is by and far the vast majority of Google's revenue.

And if you want to appear in those places … now, of course, you can do Pay-Per-Click and you can hop to the top very quickly. But it gets very expensive very fast. I'll circle back on that a little bit later.

But playing ball with Google – Google wants to keep their searchers happy. The more people it satisfies, the more times the consumer is going to come back to Google versus their competition: Yahoo or Bing or any of the other search engines.

So Google strives to deliver a high quality result. And Google says that from what it sees, websites that have lots of content – lots of original, unique content, websites that are updated regularly, websites that have lots of multimedia components – Google says statistically that when it delivers a search result, when it puts a website #1 that has a lot of good content, all those things I listed, that that consumer is happy.

So that's essentially what you have to do. Google wants to see its customers happy, like any good business would do. So playing ball with Google means giving them what they want: putting out a lot of content, multimedia and video on your website. That is what the modern consumer wants to see online. A good, successful website has those features, those aspects that are done well.

When Google sees new content and it's well optimized – it has all the keywords that people are searching for – then they're going to rank you higher and show you to more people. You get more exposure. And it's a compounding effect.

Jonathan: You made a comment that marketing is all about ROI, right? I agree with you. I don't know that there's anyone that wouldn't agree with you. In fact, many would say that's the business we're kind of all in, right Max? Same thing with you. If we don't produce results as a consultant, if we don't produce results as a financial planner, then we are going to lose clients. So it's all about return on investment, and I think that's where it needs to be.

You made the comment that new patients should be generated from the website and the online marketing these guys are doing whether it's through Facebook and some other mediums. How many new patients should these guys be getting with their website and online marketing? If you want to break those up into two separate pieces, that's fine. But how many new patients should these guys be getting from their websites?

Colin: That brings up a number of good points. The first thing that sticks out in my mind is how are you tracking what's successful? There's a lot of companies out there that when they do the optimization and they build you a website, the only report you get at the end of the month is, "Hey, you had 300 visitors on your website." Many dentists, maybe not knowing any better, have accepted that as acceptable.

But the truth is – the reality is that dentists, whether you are a corporate dentist or a privately owned dentist – across the board in the service industry – you are not an Amazon.com selling little widgets. There's not a "Buy It Now" button on your website. Hits and clicks on your website, while it does give you a marker for whether you are getting traffic or you're not getting traffic, it doesn't really show you what kind of ROI you have. People in the service industry, myself included, we produce ROI when our phone rings. Dentists aren't getting any new patients if their phone is not ringing. So that's how we judge our success: based on how many phone calls we can send to a particular dentist.

We have several packages. Some dentists are more aggressive than others. But generally speaking, we have an intro package, our Web 3.0 package. Within 3-6 months we see anywhere from 30-60 phone calls in a given month coming from the web marketing that we do.

Going forward with that, we had a client last month who has been with us for about 18 months on our Web 3.0 package. He had 164 phone calls from his website and his web marketing last month.

So as you continue to do things right online, as you continue to use what's called a White Hat tactic – that's a buzzword in the industry – do things the way Google wants to see it done, the right way, Google continues to promote you. You get your website elevated to more #1 positions. It's that compounding effect. The better Google ranks you, the more patients see you, the more patients call you.

One of the biggest metrics that Google looks for is when they deliver a search result and a consumer clicks on, say, your website, if that consumer clicks back right away, Google looks at that very negatively. And it makes sense. They obviously didn't deliver a good search result if that person clicked back and went back and researched again.

So as you get more #1 rankings, you continue to move up the totem pole, so to speak, and Google looks upon that more favorably and more favorably. Does that all make sense?

Jonathan: Absolutely. Do you have a number of a benchmark that you kind of say to a doctor, "Hey doc, if you are not getting 10 new patients a month or five new patients a month from your online marketing efforts, then it's time to rethink the strategy." Is there a number? I know you said there's a couple different ways to measure that. But, bottom line, these guys are going to measure it as how many new patients are walking through that door that came from some sort of spiel from their online marketing efforts.

Colin: A lot of it depends on what kind of patients the doctors are looking for. There's a lot of different tactics. Some dentists are just looking for the bread and butter and they are wanting a lot of new patients coming in and a steady flow that they can move through. They have maybe one, two, three doctors in their practice.

That type of marketing obviously is going to have more new patients than, say, if you are a specialist or if you are only looking for Invisalign or implant cases. If you are drilling down into a niche, you are going to have a higher case size, a higher value per patient, but a lower volume. So it's really going to depend on specific situations. If you are spending a couple thousand dollars a month, three, four thousand dollars a month on your online marketing and you are not generating ...

Let's look at the numbers. The overhead in your practice being somewhere from 50-60, maybe even higher than that, depending on how optimized your Internal processes are, if you are not getting 3 or 4 to 1 on the money you are spending, you are not covering your overhead. If you are just getting 2 to 1 on your money, you are just paying your expenses. So sit down and look at your own numbers. A lot of times an unsuccessful marketing campaign doesn't mean that you are doing everything wrong.

A bucket does have some solid walls on it, but you have a hole on one side that's leaking water out. Using good tracking methods – using call tracking so you can narrow down and find out where the leaks are in your marketing campaign, you can stick a plug in it. Sometimes docs will have several marketing campaigns going. One or two of them are going great, and they've got maybe another one or two that are just draining money. And it looks like overall that their marketing is not working. But you drill down and you refine your target market, you refine your advertising methods, and you can make them profitable across the board.

Max: You know, Colin, you said one thing there a minute ago that I totally agree with, and I tell it to dentists and team members in dental practices all the time. I think we've talked about it before on the radio show, too, here, Jonathan, is that the reason you do any type of marketing is to make the phone ring. Dental offices don't get a lot of walk-in business. I mean, 99 out of 100 people are going to call before they come in.

One thing that I see, and I'm guessing that you see this as well, lots of times practices put up barriers there at the front desk, the person who is answering the phone, or the person at the phone just is doing a bad job of it. And so, you might have a very nice campaign running and they may be getting – like this guy that you said here got 164 calls last month, but what's really key is how many of those turned into appointments?

So that's something else that the practice owner needs to be aware of. Like you say, if you've got three, or four, or five different campaigns going with different things, you need to be sure you are tracking each one of them to see, which ones … don't get mesmerized by the fact that you've got a lot of new patients. You've got to really pay attention and keep track of this.

Yeah, the 3:1 return on investment, I tell people all the time that's just a bare minimum. If you are not getting at least 3:1, something needs to change.

Colin: That kind of segues into another interesting point. The phone call tracking is more than just seeing numbers of what's generated. It's the bridge between your marketing and your practice. We record all of the phone calls that come through our Zetetics phone tracking system.

I'll give you an example. We are working with a new client we brought on about a month and a half ago. A couple weeks ago during our first monthly review call, looking through the call tracking we found about 15 phone calls during normal business hours. The majority of them were between two and three in the afternoon. They were flat out not getting answered. We could pull this up in a nice pretty report on our system.

We said, "What's going on here? You are missing all these phone calls right in the middle of the afternoon." We were on a conference call with the staff and the doctor goes, "Well, we try to stagger our lunches. Shirley goes to lunch at 2:00 and we've only got one person at the front desk answering the phones." Well, that's when you've got volume coming in. They had one person at the desk trying to juggle too many phone lines and they were missing calls.

Max: They need to put Shirley on a diet.

Colin: Yeah. New patients aren't going to leave messages. Maybe some, but they are looking for somebody right now. You have to have a way to – boom! – respond and turn that into an appointment or they are going to the next result down the search page.

Max: A minute ago you said something about Pay-Per-Click and you said you'd circle back to that. What did you have in mind?

Colin: It's been a big transition. Like everything, marketing tactics change. Markets become saturated. Costs go up. It becomes less efficient. You've got the same pie that's being split ten ways instead of five ways. That's kind of what's happened with Pay-Per-Click. 2007, 2008, 2009 – even some markets a year or two ago you had a few doctors that were running Pay-Per-Click marketing. You take a pie and split it three ways and everybody is fat and satisfied. Then you have all these marketing companies that are pushing Pay-Per-Click and promising these results.

And now, compared to three or four years ago, you've got 15 marketers in a given market area that are all doing Pay-Per-Click. The population hasn't grown that much. You are splitting the pie that many more ways.

I'll give you a real world example. You take a doctor that, for the last several years, has been spending, $1,000, $2,000, $3,000, whatever the number is a month just on Pay-Per-Click. They've seen their returns diminishing because where, in 2009/2010 they were buying clicks for a quarter or 50 cents or a dollar a piece, now they're paying two or three dollars per click, or maybe more. You know, you go to San Francisco or Chicago, you can hardly even get into the race for less than five or ten bucks a click, which is just insanity. Keep in mind, that's not a phone call. That's a single click to your website. Fifty cents to $5 is a tenfold increase or decrease.

So you take a $1,000 marketing budget, where you used to be getting 2,000 clicks a month to your website, now you are at $5 a click and you are getting 200. That's a huge swing in the amount of traffic that you are buying. So, in a lot of markets what we see, guys who have been doing that Pay-Per-Click, it kinda reminds me of the Yellow Pages. They did it for so many years they are scared to cut back because it used to work, and they know it used to work because they proved it. But now that things have changed, they are a little timid, a little gun shy to try new things and they are blowing this money.

It varies by market. I feel confident saying that in most markets right now, Pay-Per-Click is not the best return just simply because every marketing company in the country has been pushing it for the past three or four years – it's just saturated. It's like anything, it gets saturated, the costs go up, and it's a bidding war. That's essentially what your Google AdWords – your Pay-Per-Click, is.

Jonathan: I have a question on that Pay-Per-Click, because, Colin, you and I had a conversation about that back when I saw you in Destin, Florida, a few months ago. This is probably a two-part question here. But the first part is a lot of emphasis, it seems like, on … when I'll talk to doctors, I'll be meeting with some clients and they'll say, "Yeah, Jonathan, I'm not on the first page of Google. I'm on the fifth page of Google." The first part of the question is how big of a deal is it for these guys to be on the first page of Google? When they search, for example, "dentist Carlsbad California," how important is it for them to show up on the first page of that search result? And the second part of that is how difficult is that to do without doing Pay-Per-Click?

Colin: I'm going to break that up into a three-part question because it's somewhat of a game. I'll start with kind of explaining how the game works. Getting to the first page of Google is paramount. 90%, 92% – I've seen different statistics but overwhelmingly, consumers do not click to page two. You are going to have about a 65% distribution of clicks going to the first three or four results on the first page.

So not only do you want to be on the first page, but you want to be at the top of the first page, because that's where the action is – that's the first thing people see – that's where everybody is going to be clicking.

So, first and foremost, you've got to be at the top of the first page if you want to be found. If you don't want to be found, yeah, page two is great.

Max: Colin, to that point, too, I think what Jonathan was asking is about page ranking in terms of your generic ranking, if I'm using the right term there. I'm seeing pages now where there is so much of the paid stuff at the top, where I used to see 10 or 12 generic listings on a page, now there is so much of the paid stuff at the top that you are down to maybe only 3, 4, or 5 generic listings on the first page. Correct me now, if I'm not using the proper terminology there. But when you search for something on Google and that comes up, there's that little shaded box at the top, kind of yellowish. That's all paid listings.

Colin: It is. And Google has experimented so much that for some people, it's a yellow shaded box, some people it's a blue shaded box, some people it's purple. They test unbelievable amounts of data. But that brings up another good point.

Let me circle back to the game I was chatting about. Showing up #1 on Google is paramount. But what are you showing up #1 for? You have to understand kind of the psychology of how patients search to understand what you want to show up for. A lot of dentists think that if a patient within 50 miles of them searches for "dentist," they want to show up #1 for that and that's the holy grail. And that's generally not true.

Patients, when they search, they are going to start out with a very general term: "dentist" or "dentist in Dallas." As they learn more about the field they are searching in, they search for "dentist in Dallas." They look at the search results and they scroll down the page, and they go, "I don't just want a dentist. I want a pediatric dentist," or, "I want a dentist that specializes in dentures," or, "I'm looking for a dentist that has a special offer right now that I can take advantage of" or maybe they are looking for a family dentist. Maybe they know they have a root canal that they're having trouble with – an old root canal – and they want to know who is best to fix that kind of problem.

So, the consumer is very educated. And they're going to drill down into what they are looking for. So they might search, look at the results, maybe click on a couple pages, and then go back to Google and search again and search for "pediatric dentist Dallas." Now they are getting somewhere. Now they are starting to find what they want, or "Family dentist in Dallas," or whatever it is that that consumer is looking for. They want to find exactly what's available. And with the Internet, it is really available at their fingertips. So they drill down and they drill down, and finally they find a result that fits this idea that they have in their head, and they pick up the phone and call.

So getting to the search terms that people are actually ready to call is where you want to focus your money. "Dentist in Dallas" is a term that you'd be lucky to get in the game on the Pay-Per-Click side for $5 or $10 a click.

On the organic side, you've got 5,000 dentists that are fighting for that term. Organically, it's going to take a lot of time and money to get into that and, of course, a lot of time and money to stay – to maintain – a ranking in that kind of market. As you go into the subsections, you know, going into what's called a long-tail keyword, three or four word search terms, you can get into those games for a lot cheaper, a lot less competition, and the ROI is just as good – typically better because you are not spending as much to get there.

The interesting thing with Google is Google has really gotten a lot smarter. As you optimize for different terms, say you optimize for "pediatric dentist" and you optimize for "family dentist" and then you optimize for "cosmetic dentistry," Google will realize that you are focused on those three terms and they will start to intermingle the search terms. So as you get ranked for more three and four word search queries, it now becomes easier and cheaper for you to rank for one and two word search queries that people are searching for.

So it's kind of a blurring effect, if you will; it all gets blurred together. And Google sees, "Hey, this website is ranked well for these three terms. Now let's try them out and try them in some one and two word search terms." And if you've been working at it and you've got a killer website, the consumers are going to respond to that.

Max: I know one thing that you are doing with your clients, and I think this is something that maybe a lot of dentist out there, especially ones that I was referring to earlier, that put their website up five or ten years ago and haven't done much to it since then. But talk to us for a couple minutes about having your site optimized to work on a smartphone – a mobile device.

Colin: Mobile devices are huge. The boom has already exploded. Just ten years ago, websites were the new craze and guys were jumping on that bus. For mobile websites, the bus has already left the station.

There was a statistic on Google over the summer sometime, June/July-ish, August maybe even, that 52% of all local … let me make sure I get this right. It was 52% of all local services were searched for on smartphones versus on a desktop computer these days. So, consumers looking for plumbers, electricians, dentists – any kind of local service are searching now on mobile devices: iPads, iPhones, Androids, iPods, instead of on desktop computers.

Max: I remember even as recently as maybe eight or 10 years ago, you know, you'd be going through your day doing whatever you are doing, and if you thought of something you wanted to look up later when you got home on your computer, you'd make a note of it on something. I'd get on some days and I'd have two, three, four things on there. Some days I'd have eight or ten things that I'd want to sit down at the computer later that evening and look up. And now, if a thought flashes through my head, I'm immediately on my phone looking it up.

Colin: Gary Vaynerchuk, the social media icon, I followed him quite a bit, and he was talking at one of his lectures. I saw him in person in Arizona earlier this year. He made a joke about billboard advertising. He said, "Who looks at billboards these days?" He said, "People are barely watching the road in front of them over their mobile phones. They don't have time to look at the billboards."

It's the truth. We've shifted to an instant gratification society. We have a thought, it's translated instantly by our thumbs on this little touchscreen device, and boom!, up pops the answer. Your mobile website not only needs to pop up first when people search there, but you need to have a click-to-call button on your website. Your website pops up and they take their thumb and they push "call" and it automatically dials the number on their mobile phone for them and calls your office.

So once they pull up your mobile site, they don't even have to thumb the number in anymore. This generation of iPhone and Android users just clicks on the button and it does the rest for them.

Max: What about reviews, Colin? I know good reviews and all play some part in your page ranking, right? Part two of the question, what about the negative reviews? It seems like in most practices, even asking people to go on and write reviews, there's still not a big percentage of people that will go on and do that for you.

But I mean, you make somebody mad and they are instantly telling everybody in their circle of friends through Twitter, Facebook, and everything else, not to mention the fact that they can go on and put a negative review on a web review page. Do you see much of that going on?

Colin: Oh, all the time. I read DentalTown's online forums. I keep an eye on it. A couple days ago, you may have heard, and this has happened a couple times, and it makes national headlines every time it happens. There's a dentist up in New York that is suing a patient because they left a bad online review. There was a dentist out in Washington that did it last year and ended up going bankrupt. It baffles me that dentists think they can fight fire with fire on this topic because every time it happens, it just makes national headlines and it's horrible PR. As I'm going through this thread on DentalTown, there's a good number of docs that are responding and saying, "I don't do the online reviews. I don't participate in that. I don't do that. I don't recommend it. I don't want any part of it. It should be illegal. They shouldn't be allowed to post that stuff online."

I kinda chuckle. I made a post. Basically, it's the way our society is going. The online reviews are here to stay. Whether you are on the bench or you are in the game playing, the game is happening. The game is being played whether you are on the sidelines or you are included, or whether you include yourself. It is a huge part. It plays into the ranking factor that Google figures sites are ranked on. Good reviews, you rank higher. Lots of reviews, you rank higher.

In fact, Google actually had a bug in their algorithm about a year ago – a year and a half ago where they only counted the number of reviews a business had received to determine their ranking. It wasn't a dentist, it was just some random business out in California that had like 20 horrible reviews and he was appearing #1 because he had 20 reviews and nobody else had any. Since then, Google has fixed that. Now you have to get good reviews to rank up top.

But yeah, very critical importance to be playing that game. I think one of the cracks in the floor is that when you get a bad review, another big complaint I hear is that the dentists can't respond to it because it might violate HIPAA or it might violate some kind of confidentiality with the patient.

But that's not what online reviews are about. It's not about proving who is right or wrong. Online reviews are a way that, you know, if a patient didn't have a favorable experience, if they didn't feel like they were treated right, they are going to talk about it online. Then all of your prospects are going to see it when they search for your name or your business name.

Dentists need to be out there responding but not in a way to prove who is right or wrong. You are not out there to strut your shoulders and prove that that patient – that insurance deal that got fouled up – that was the patient's responsibility, and they signed a release form that says they're responsible for getting reimbursed from their insurance.

That's not what it's about. It's all about customer service. In some ways, I feel like maybe my grandparents' generation is more equipped to deal with this oncoming social media and review revolution that my generation is because my grandpa understood customer service. He understood that it's not about what you do, it's about how you handle and how you set expectations.

You get a negative review online, okay. You don't have to prove you are right. Your front staff probably already tried to prove they were right, and that's why you are getting the bad review. It's all about customer service. Get on there, make a nice post. Say you are really sorry. "Come back. Give us a second chance. Call my cell phone directly." Or if you know who the patient is, pick up the phone after work one day and call the patient.

I'll use my own experience here. I got married almost three years ago, two and a half years ago, and we used a local tux place – well known. Rented from them before, had a great experience. For whatever reason, all the tuxes we rented fell apart. I mean literally: buttons were popping off, the little adjustment thing on the side of my pants broke and I had to use a paperclip for my own wedding to hold my pants up. It was a horrible experience.

When I went to drop the tuxes off I said, "This was horrible." The girl at the front desk was kind of snotty and she was like, "Oh, well sorry about your experience." Well, that didn't satisfy me. So I left them a negative review online.

A couple days later I get a call from the owner. He wanted me to come back and talk about it. I met with him. He made it right in my mind. He fixed the problem. He made it right. That's what it's about. It's not about proving who is right and wrong. It's about customer service.

Did I answer that completely for you, Max?

Max: You did, yeah. I would just add one thing to that, Colin. And I don't think there are many doctors out there thinking about this yet. But I've seen it in some of the practices I deal with. Let's say the practice is seeking to hire a new front desk person, or a new dental assistant, or a hygienist or maybe even looking for an associate dentist to come in and go to work for them.

Those people now are searching to see what kind of reviews you and your office are getting. I know of some specific cases where people have said, "No. I'm not even going to bother to go there for an interview because they've got all these negative reviews. I don't want to work in a place like that."

I think for the better, really, long term, if people really get their heads out and get with it on this that this is going to improve customer service, hopefully. And it's certainly going to be a way to separate practices, so to speak: the good ones that get all the good reviews from the ones that get the negative reviews.

I would say that those people that are getting negative reviews are going to probably have to spend more and more and more dollars to keep new patients coming in.

I think we're about out of time. I just wanted to ask you one other thing, Colin. I don't know how prepared you are to talk about this. Certainly, I think we've shown here that there's plenty that we can talk about. Maybe we will have you on again someday. Without going into a lot of detail, I think you are starting up a program – and I don't think you are even advertising it yet – where you are going to give a little bit of a special break to a young dentist or a dentist that hasn't been in practice very long. Give us a thumbnail view of that and then maybe when we have you on the show again, you can go into detail.

Colin: Yeah. In fact, we're not even launching it till, really, next month. But I know I sent you over some details on it. It's our "No Smart Dentist Left Behind" scholarship program. What we saw was that a lot of dentist getting started: coming out of school with debts and buying practices, starting practices, and equipment purchases – you know, all the insanity. I don't need to talk anymore about that. I think that's enough said. But they're looking at their marketing and they oftentimes will choose a marketing place based on what they can afford in today's world. It's like patching a broken water line versus replacing the section. It's oftentimes not the best in the long run.

What we are going to be offering is a way that young dentists – new practice owners – can get the solid marketing advice, get a website that is going to grow with them, that is going to be something that they can expand on and is going to be a platform that …

I'll give you one example. A lot of dentists, they come out and they buy a little cheap template website for $50 a month, whatever it is, no setup fee. What they find is after they've been in practice for a couple of years, the template website doesn't have any ranking. And yeah, they have a webpage, but it has no SEO. And yeah, you can spend Pay-Per-Click and drive a bunch of traffic to it, but like I said earlier, the ROI isn't there in a lot of markets.

So what we want to do is we want to get new dentists into a website – into a marketing platform – that is going to grow and is going to scale with them as their practice scales. We want to get in at the ground level. We are going to be offering a package, our Web 3.0 package, only for new docs/new practice owners on our scholarship program for … I don't have all the specifics hammered out just yet, but over a 50% discounted rate.

Basically, it's at our direct labor cost. We're not even paying to keep our lights on so that we can get docs in at ground level. We can get them in a system that two years from now, they are going to have a kick-butt ranking instead of two years from now, they are starting from scratch again because they bought a cheap template website because that's all they could afford. We want to get them into a solid platform. So yeah, that's on the horizon.

Jonathan: That's great. Sounds great. Well Colin, we appreciate having you on. Are there any last words you'd like to say before we sign off here? Also, I want to make sure that you give everyone your phone number, email address, and website information for them to contact you. We'll also have Colin's contact information on the description of the radio show on the website as well. So you can click directly on that link to get to Colin's website. But Colin, why don't you give us a few closing remarks and then your contact information for everyone to get in touch with you?

Colin: If you are a doc that is not getting results from your website or you don't know what results you are getting, or you are not happy with the results you are getting, give us a ring. We offer a no obligation, free consultation: just a 15 minute chat to see what you are doing, where you are at, and where you are trying to get to.

My direct line is 888-741-1413. That will ring right here at my desk. I can't always answer all the calls live, but I do promise to get back to you within 24 hours. So if you have any questions about your website or marketing or are looking for some direction on how to find the patients that you want to attract, feel free to give us a call.

Max: And that's SmartBoxWebMarketing.com. Is that correct?

Colin: That is correct.

Jonathan: Great. Colin, we really appreciate you being on the show with us. I know you've done a lot of work with Max. You and I have spoken several times. You are one of the good guys, so we're happy to have you on the show. Again, we'll have links to Colin's website in addition to his email address and contact information on the description of the show page. So please check that out and give Colin a call.

Max, anything else you wanted to add before we sign off?

Max: Nope. That's it for me.

Jonathan: Alright. We appreciate you for listening and we'll talk with you guys next month. Thanks guys.

Colin: Sounds great. Thanks for your time, guys.

Chapter 2

Web Design

Word Count: **3673**
Approximate Time to Read: **8.2 minutes**

*"More and more dental websites are accessed through mobile applications. **Older dental websites don't do that.***

*"The types of branding that your practice would have are reflected in the photographs, the pictures, the marketing – the things that you have in your website. But even more than that, **your marketing ties really intimately into your website.** You're driving people there; there needs to be a consistency, a continuity with external marketing, internal marketing, and your dental website. **Colin is able to put the whole package together and that's probably the biggest difference in this company and some of the companies that we've worked with before.***

*"You know we see this a lot when we talk to dentists all around the country: they put their dental website together 10 or 12 years ago, whatever it was, and then time gets by and you don't update it. They begin to look dated and people notice that when they go to your dental website and look at it. I guess there's good news and bad news in that; if they're still going to your dental website and you haven't done anything to it in a lot of years, that's a problem. **Very few dental websites actually generate business for the dentist, and that's the kind of thing that Colin and SmartBox are able to accomplish for your dental practice."***

~ Michael Abernathy, D.D.S.

"I knew that I wanted video, I already knew that and had been researching it for some time but how do you get there? I was not satisfied with a local company that didn't understand dentistry because the experience I've had with marketing in the past, when people really know dentistry and really have experience with marketing and there are other people who have used it and it's worked well for them, well it probably is going to work for me too.

"When I found your website it was a referral from some other trusted practice management person. I started researching more

*and more and it just made sense what you were doing. I already wanted to go there but you're just so far ahead of my thought curve – I was ready to click; **I was ready to move and ready to do something, knowing I was about five years behind on updating my website."***

~ Walter Hadley, D.D.S.
Cosmetic Dentist in Kennewick, Washington

*"I have to say this, I actually had people say our website kind of sucked. It doesn't suck anymore. We're as guilty as the next person; it's easy to get comfortable. No matter how you dice it, while certainly not a cure-all magic marketing bullet, **every practice must have and incorporate the web as part of that marketing puzzle."***

~ Michael P. Abernathy, D.D.S.

*"**Colin has made my websites produce.** Even when I do display ads or radio campaigns, many of the patients that I see say, 'Yeah, I heard your ad or saw your ad in the paper and then I went to your website, and that's what really impressed me: how much effort you put into your website and I figured that if you put that much time and effort into your website, you must really make a commitment to your profession.' I think that a website with tons and tons of information tells people that you're serious about what you do."*

~ Ron Receveur, D.D.S.
Implant and Cosmetic Dentist near Louisville, Kentucky

"The thing I like most about SmartBox's marketing is the results that we're getting."

~ Robert H, Klein, D.D.S.

*"Your dental website must open quickly and address the things that patients are really concerned about. Colin has done so many with so many doctors. It's funny because it seems like every time you turn around, there's somebody that will do dental websites. I don't care if it's your 12-year old or a college graduate, but **this is different – this is an investment.***"

~ Michael P. Abernathy, D.D.S.

"People, when they're searching for a provider, they usually have a lot of questions and we try to have a comprehensive website that

---

will answer most of those questions for them."

~ Donald Plourde, D.M.D.

"You guys are nice guys, but at the end of the day, it has to be successful and it has been. So, the best thing is it seems like monthly **we're getting a couple big cases – implant driven, large implant cases a month from the website** *or the web stuff that we're doing with you guys."*

~ Robert H, Klein, D.D.S.

"Some cool news for you: we have just hooked up with SmartBox Web Marketing to give my Killer toothache members awesome websites. Colin and I hooked up after the last The Profitable Dentist meeting with Woody Oakes and thought we could put our brains together and give dentists something cool to play with. He's got a neat package of a website, and he can hook you up with a membership program."

~ Yar Zuk, D.D.S.
Marketing Expert and crazy celebrity tooth collector

"The one thing that I got out of most of the Internet guys is they were all very similar. It was all very generic – kind of the same exact thing.

"I could go to one website and it would look the same as the other website, which looked the same as the other one. They would all promise the same things; we'll get you on the front page of Google, we'll do this. Most of them haven't come through on any of their promises.

"The one thing I like about Colin is he comes through with the stuff that he says; he's ready to back it up. He's going to work for you, **get you the results that you need.** *He's going to talk to you and explain everything that's going on and he's going to help you with the different parts of Internet marketing to really make your website work."*

~ Avi Weisfogel, D.D.S.

"I'm basically looking to put all my competition out of business. I'm looking for web domination, that's what I want. I want the dominant web presence so that my competition isn't even an afterthought, it's Dental West Associates, that's what people, when they're looking for a dentist in Salem, when they're doing their keyword searches, I want to be the one that comes up, that's what I'm looking for. It's

---

total domination and destruction of all my competition so that they'll work for me one day.

~ Raleigh Pioch, D.D.S

"Since we've been using SmartBox Marketing, we've had great success.

Last month, we had 160 leads or something from just the website.

*"Recently, with the expansion into surgical things such as implants and things of that nature, the majority of our larger cases are coming from the web-based stuff that we're doing with SmartBox. So, I've been very happy with the success. Before, I'd have to look back at the numbers, I don't even know how well it was tracked, but it was maybe 10 or 20 a month. And now, **we're up to averaging 80-100 phone calls a month.** Last month was 160 leads, which is a great response. **The amount of traffic, the bigger cases, the implant cases that we're getting, are 90 percent driven from the website."***

~ Robert H, Klein, D.D.S.

Do You Know Where Your Dental Website Is Failing?

How to design your dental website to get you the best results possible for the least amount of money

One of the biggest myths in dental marketing is that by just building a website, new and qualified patients will flow into their office like water out of the hose when you turn on the spigot. Some dentists bought template cookie-cutter websites while others built customized ones, but regardless, the mindset of "If you build it, they will come" could not be farther from reality.

The First Impression Might Be Your Last

This is the #1 cause of why many dental practices failed with their web marketing in the past. The reality is you have less than three seconds to convince your potential patients that they should do business with you. What does your dental website say in those first few critical seconds?

To understand better, let's go back and start at the very beginning to

---

see your website from your patient's eyes:

1. First, for a prospective patient to even find your website, you have to be seen where they are searching. Remember, these prospective patients are searching for a dentist – they don't know your website address. You have to be at the top of the SERPs for the keywords THEY are searching for.

2. Once a prospect is on your website, they need to be pre-qualified so you both know they are a good fit for your services. **Skipping this step will explode your schedule with unqualified leads that never move forward with case acceptance.**

3. Then your prospects must be compelled to call and schedule a consultation. **Do you just want "hits and clicks" on your website or do you want phone calls, new patients, and accepted cases?**

4. You must follow-up and keep in touch with your prospects until they are ready to buy, **otherwise, you're missing 50% of your case acceptance.**

5. And THEN they turn into paying patients!

You can have the best office, staff, equipment, and expertise, you might be "Dentist of The Year" with all of the right credentials and certificates, but if you don't have the right systems in place to not only "be seen" but also to pre-qualify, follow-up, and close the cases, your prospective patients (that you've spent lots of time and energy to attract) are not going to buy your services. Once in place though, you can count on your systems to work for you for the rest of your professional career.

The Core Tenets of Convertibility

Website design is one of the most important considerations. The design of your site will affect everything from your users' experience to the ability of search engine spiders to index it properly. Ensuring that you build a website that encourages conversion of its visitors is not terribly difficult, so long as you adhere to the core tenets. A website that enjoys a high conversion ratio has the following qualities/attributes:

- It gives visitors what they want – immediately. High conversion websites don't beat around the bush, but give visitors the information they need up front.

- It loads quickly in all browsers. A website with high conversion is easily accessible to all visitors whether they're using Chrome, IE, Firefox, Safari, or something else.

- It is easy on the eyes. This goes far beyond color schemes and graphics. A website with high conversion rates is easy to read using a simple, elegant font and good color combinations. Information is clearly delineated with titles and headers, and visitors have no difficulty reading the content that appeals to them.

- It is accessible via mobile devices like smartphones. Ensuring that your potential patients can view your website from anywhere is vital.

- It is optimized for both search engine spiders and real people, using the concepts discussed in the chapter on SEO.

Ease of Navigation

The first rule you need to adhere to is you must provide your visitors with a website that can be easily navigated. There are several considerations that you will need to make here. A website that cannot be easily navigated by a first-time visitor will not be successful. In fact, you'll actually drive away potential patients.

The navigation menu for your site is the key to easy navigability for your visitors. The menu used should provide direct access to all pages of your site that you want visitors to be able to access. In addition, it should do so in a logical, streamlined way. One popular way to do this is with a drop down menu that expands when the user clicks or hovers the mouse cursor over the link. This gives them the ability to move from one page to a related page very easily.

The location of your navigation menu is also important. It should be clearly visible, but it should not detract from the visual appeal of your site. Therefore, you should stay away from menu systems that don't integrate with the rest of your website. For instance, in the past it was relatively common to see DHTML menus that floated along as the visitor scrolled down the page. The problem with these types of menus is it distracts the visitor from your content, which is not something that you can afford to do. The best option is to build menu systems that integrate with the style of the site, complimenting your design and content, while still making navigation a simple, effortless thing. For instance, WordPress menu systems are often elegant, simple, and effective, whether located at the top of the page or along the left or right side. Doing so can still provide your visitors with the ease of navigation they demand and can do so in a way that most of them are familiar as well.

Graphics and Optimization

The graphics used throughout your website are another consideration here. If you go too "graphic heavy," you will alienate your visitors. You'll also slow the page load time to a crawl if your graphics are not optimized. It is important that you ensure that your graphics are of the highest quality possible but optimized to load quickly, even for visitors with slow Internet connections. Recent studies have shown that the majority of Americans connect to the Internet at 3 MBPS or less. Many people in your area might not even have high-speed Internet like cable or DSL – dial up Internet still exists and more people still use it than you might think.

There is also the consideration of making your site available for mobile users. Mobile access has become enormously popular – just think of how many people use smartphones or tablet computers today to access the Internet on the go. Obviously, even a full 3G signal is not as fast as a standard DSL connection. This means you need to build your site with mobile users in mind as well. The best option here is to actually rebuild your website to be completely responsive so that no matter what kind of smartphone or tablet the visitor is using, it looks great.

Website Readability

In addition to optimized graphics, you will need to make sure that you also optimize your fonts and the colors used. Too often, websites use text and background colors that blend together or clash horribly. This makes for a jarring experience and will drive away your visitors. Instead, use complementary colors throughout your site – make sure that readability is high.

Ensuring maximum readability goes far beyond the colors you choose to use though – it extends to the fonts themselves. Ideally, you want a stylish, modern font that is highly readable without eyestrain. You want a font that offers beauty, but that does not detract from your content. That can be hard to find, but a wide range of high-readability fonts have been designed for use on the World Wide Web. If all else fails, you can always fall back on time-tested favorites like Arial. The key is to use a simple, easy-to-read font in a size that appeals to your readers. You should avoid flowery script fonts for anything other than embellishments within graphics

---

and similar uses. These are very hard to read and will detract from your visitors' experience.

Optimization for Mobile Users

As mentioned, mobile access is growing by leaps and bounds. Today, it's common to see people using their iPhones, Blackberrys, or Android devices to search the web, visit websites, check email and interact through social networks. What does this mean for you? Simply put, it means that more and more of the visitors coming to your website will be using a mobile device. It also means that you need to take some very specific actions here to maximize your site's value to this growing percentage of potential patients.

Streaming Video for Mobile Devices

Video will play an essential role in the success of your website. However, it requires that you take different steps to display those videos for mobile users. You will need to use the right video widget on your site. There are quite a few different options out there including Brightcove, YouTube, Vimeo, and many others. Having a good video widget on your mobile-optimized site ensures that all visitors can access the information that you have and offer.

GPS Enabled

GPS technology has changed the way that people navigate, as well as many other things. For instance, it's now common practice to use GPS technology within websites to help users. The most obvious example of this technology in use is the provision of maps that use a visitor's GPS information to identify their location in relation to your office. For example, GPS information can be used to create maps to give potential patients directions from their location (wherever that might be), right to your office doors. This can be a very handy feature for users (and a valuable one for your practice). For instance, if a patient loses a filling or crown while at work or shopping, they can use these maps to easily locate your practice to have the problem fixed.

Click-to-Call

Click-to-call implementation is also important here. Mobile users rarely have the time or ability to write down a phone number when they locate your contact information. Instead, you should use click-to-call technology. This allows mobile users to simply click your phone number via their smartphone screen and make the call. It offers convenience and saves time as well. The same technology can be used with other communication tools, such as email addresses. When you enable click-to-email, you provide similar convenience to click-to-call features. This allows visitors to click your email address and immediately open their email client with a new email properly addressed, ready for them to type their message and hit send. This is an excellent option for questions and concerns that are not time-sensitive such as emergencies.

Chapter 3

Search Engine Optimization (SEO)

Word Count: **8885**
Approximate Time to Read: **19.7 minutes**

"I can tell you too that it's made a big difference just in the last four or five months. We've actually had people buying things through the website. We've actually had people calling and asking questions because **they're able to find us now on the website, and they weren't able to find us before."**

~Maxwell R. Gotcher

"Colin diversified me, getting me exposure in all my different dental niches."

~ J.D. Murray, D.D.S.

"The other side of things: the Search Engine Optimization. I know doctors are bombarded with that from all corners of the earth, and since they're confused and since there are so many options out there, what most of them end up doing is nothing – which is a mistake.

"We never endorse anything. The only time we ever endorse anything is when we get feedback from our own clients and it's doing well; that, or we try it ourselves. Colin started working on our website maybe four or five months ago and it went from unrecognized in a Google search to now: we're on the first page and working our way up on the first page. That's another thing that doctors and dental practices need to recognize is **it's really not enough just to have a dental website, because people won't search very long for your website.** *It's important to have it highly ranked so that it comes up on page one, and is as close to rank number one on page number one as you can get. That's certainly something that Colin and SmartBox are able to accomplish for dental practices.*

~ Michael P. Abernathy, D.D.S.

*"**A warm thank you to Colin Receveur for bringing our practice into the 21st century with Google SEO, which is proving to be very successful.** I thought I'd take this moment to*

thank you, Colin, for building our website and getting us to the point that we're actively promoting our practices on the web and through Search Engine Optimization."

~ Randy Schmidt, D.D.S., M.S.D.

A Brief History of SEO

Search Engine Optimization (or SEO) is probably one of the most talked about subjects on the modern Internet, but the least understood at the same time. It's a complex subject experts can spend years studying to master the various techniques used. Does that mean it's impossible for you to understand and implement? Not at all – there are some simple, effective SEO techniques that can be easily applied to benefit your practice. As you can gather from its name, SEO is purely strategically including information to get the best ranking on searches that relate to your practice so you are easily found online. Each of the myriad techniques used in SEO is designed to help with search engine rankings – the higher the better!

In order to understand SEO and how to use it for your dental practice, you have to first understand the World Wide Web. We will not delve into a deep history of this issue, but will skim the surface and explain it in brief. **Stay with me here, I'm giving you the "10,000-foot overview" as quickly as possible ...**

The Internet and the "Web" are Not the Same

It helps to view the Internet as a large collection of servers (massive computers) that house all of the web's contents: websites, data, images, videos, and more. Everything you see online is stored on a server somewhere around the world.

These servers are independent and need some sort of connectivity to allow them to be accessed by people around the world to view their "contents." That connectivity is the "web," which is a massive network that allows the servers to talk to each other. Think of this like a spiderweb, deriving from one location that connects to lots of other locations farther out. This is where search engines come into play. Google, as an example, looks at all these servers, indexes their contents, and then allows people to search for and easily access whatever is available. Basically, Google organizes all the information on the Internet and uses the web to connect you with results for what you're searching.

Without search engines, the Internet would be like a library without a card catalog or a librarian – you would never be able to find what you're looking for.

Google is your GPS

Here's a quick example: You are a dentist located in California but you want to find a dentist in New York City for your friend that needs a crown. You open up your browser on your computer, go to www.google.com, and search for "Dentist NYC." Because Google has indexed most of the websites in the world, it can show you a list of dental practices specifically in New York City. Think of Google as a GPS device – it doesn't actually control the content, it merely helps you find your way when you are searching.

Once you click on the result you like, your computer will download information hosted on another computer thousands of miles away and display it on your screen, all thanks to search engine indexing and the structure of the web.

But how does that apply to my need for SEO?

Let's start by reviewing what SEO means: Search Engine Optimization. This is describing what a dental website owner is doing in order to ensure that he or she gets a very high position, or "rank," in the search engines like Google and Bing. If you have a dental website, it is going to contain a lot of information about your dental practice and services. All this information is loaded into your website using a series of structures and codes to create everything from the images, videos, contact forms, and links. Pretty simple, right? Keep reading …

Web Page Contents

You will want to fill your dental website with the kind of content that is relevant to your dental practice. This takes careful consideration, compelling calls to action, a good eye for design, and more. You can fill your web pages with good information and images but you may miss the opportunity for a higher SEO ranking without first considering implementing keywords into your content. **"Keywords" are the most common phrases and terms people actually use when searching for your dental services.** For instance, you might offer teeth whitening, so your keywords would include "teeth whitening," "deep bleaching," "smile whitening," and other related phrases. Of course, you can fill your website

---

with these terms and still not appear at the top of the SERPs (Search Engine Result Page). Why not? Let's hop in the Delorean and take a quick trip back in time to understand …

Back to the '90s

The idea of SEO was first mentioned in the late 1990s when webmasters had grown a bit weary of the standard protocols. These early search engines were in their infancy and had a very limited set of features (by today's standards). The ranking would be calculated based on keyword density and HTML coding (which was all open to a lot of abuse), so the relevance of results was not always that great.

Soon, website owners understood the need for a higher ranking when a web user went looking for information in the different search engines. This created the first instances of website owners implementing SEO, some ethically and others using the dreaded "black hat SEO" (more on that later).

PageRank, Google, and a New Era

By the late 1990s and early 21st century, the quality of any search engine was determined by its capabilities in producing relevant results that were not "false" or the result of some sort of word "stuffage" and/or fraudulent "blackhat" tactics. This is why the algorithms began to get far more complicated and began looking at new outside factors that could not be manipulated easily, if at all. This led two students, Larry Page and Sergey Brin, to create the "backrub" format search engine that used math to rate web pages. Though the two would later go on to create Google, during the 1990s they were focused on PageRank instead.

Named after Larry Page, PageRank is a number that is calculated by their proprietary algorithm and has the capability for looking at the strength and number of inbound links websites have. This is the proprietary algorithm used by Google. Because Google seems to be the world's preferred search engine (with around 70% of all searches beginning there), it makes sense to do your SEO according to their models (and using all of their tools).

Link Building is the Foundation for High-Quality and Effective SEO

By creating links that point to your website from others, you are creating a system that gives your website a tremendous level of authority through a variety of valid links. Later in this book, we are going to take a very close look at SEO and Google, and how you can overcome recent "Panda" changes to this now famous algorithm.

Why SEO is Critical to Dentists

As a dentist, you are a professional with skills that are needed by EVERYONE. Yet, you are finding it tough to get the number of patients and generate the amount of income you need to be as successful as you have hoped. What is the problem? More importantly, what is the answer? You know there are plenty of people with the need for your care or treatments, so where are they?

They are out there BUT most of them are NOT using old-fashioned Yellow Page directories and/or phone books to find their dental practitioners. Those printed phone books are quickly becoming obsolete and only being delivered to homes and offices with landlines. Unfortunately, in the current era, fewer than 60% of households even have landlines. This means that those ads you are paying for are probably not steering many patients to your door. If you want to really know how much these old methods are generating, pay $30 a month for one of our Zetetics trackable phone lines and track and record all your calls for a 12 month period. With the use of this separately listed phone number, you'll be able to track what the Yellow Pages is producing and figure EXACTLY how many dollars that ad is generating in your practice, down to the penny.

Consider also that Nielsen reports 86% of consumers looking for local services will use the Internet, as opposed to the traditional phone book to get names and numbers, and more than 80% of the searches are followed up with offline action. To "drill down" even further, over 50% of all those local service searches occur from a mobile device (but that's another topic in itself).

Clearly, all of this adds up to one thing: it is of major importance for you to be able to rank highly in Internet searches. This is most often done through the process known as Search Engine Optimization, or SEO.

Intro to SEO and SERPs

If you head to the Google homepage and type in something as basic as "dentist" along with the name of your hometown and state, you will generate a list of returns or results that the search engine believes is the best fit for the information you provided. If you are in a place as massive as New York City, you are going to see a huge number of listings. The search results are broken down into the "top" choices that appear on the first two SERPs (Search Engine Result Pages), as well as the rest of the results in the pages beyond.

You should know that almost all SEO campaigns are working to see results that put the website in question on those first two pages. Why is it so important to be there? It is due to the simple fact that around 90% of Internet users abandon their searches after the first page.

To conduct a successful SEO campaign is not a simple thing. It takes conscious effort to discover the best keywords to use. These are the terms "traffic" you want is going to enter into a search engine when looking for your niche of dental care. For example, "dental implants New York" or "gingivitis treatment Poughkeepsie," etc.

How to Crush the Competition with Web Marketing

With Colin Receveur & Dr. Woody Oakes

Woody: Good evening everybody. This is Woody. And tonight it's my pleasure to be with you and our guest, Colin Receveur with SmartBox Web Marketing. Colin, how are you doing this evening?

Colin: Doing well. How are you, Dr. Oakes?

Woody: Doing good. I enjoyed your cover on the issue of "The Profitable Dentist" as Superman.

Colin: [laughs] Well, that's what we try to be is a superhero for our dentists that we work with.

Woody: You are built exactly like that, right?

Colin: Exactly like it, muscles and all.

Woody: Well, I envy you then. That's quite a cover. I thought it turned out well.

Colin: I did as well.

Woody: I read it before, but this morning I looked at the magazine and reread the interview we did. Anybody who is on the call tonight who hasn't gotten that particular issue of the magazine with Colin in his Superman outfit on the cover needs to read that little three-page interview. I think it will be really informative to you.

Colin, one of the first things I want to talk about, because you do so many things, SmartBox Marketing is not just another website design company. As people will learn in the interview, you do tracking, you do video, I mean just dozens and dozens of things that we're going to be talking about.

One of the first things I wanted to talk about that kind of differentiates your company from other companies is something you call the mirror effect. Can you kind of tell our listeners tonight what exactly that is?

Colin: The mirror effect is all about what kind of patients you really want to attract. Let me give you an example. I talked to a prospective dentist earlier this morning who had called in, and one of his big complaints with his website was he was getting all the patients that were coming in looking for discounts and coupons, and they were price shopping for the cheapest service provider.

When I went and looked at his website, his website was full of discounts and coupons and free everything. The mirror effect is when your patients are out there looking, when your prospective patients are searching for a service provider, when they look at your website, they see themselves in the reflection.

If you put out there that you have the best prices in town, and coupons, and discounts, and free everything, that's going to be type of person you attract. They are going to see themselves reflected in your website or in your marketing.

If you put on your website that you have the best service in town and you provide tremendous value, not necessarily the cheapest price, then the patients that are looking for a higher level of service – a higher level of care are going to see their reflection in that website, and they're going to choose a service provider that fits the model that they're looking for.

Woody: That's a good point because oftentimes, a website company will talk about, "We get 150 new patients a month," or, "We get 200 new patients a month." Oftentimes, that's kind of a misnomer because what kind of patients are you getting? Are you getting the shoppers?

Kind of a good example, or maybe a good analogy, is kind of like dating, for example. If you are a four and you are trying to attract tens, it's probably not going to work. If you want to attract nines and tens, then you probably should get yourself as close as you can to a nine or ten.

Kind of the same thing with a website. The way the website looks, performs, functions – the message it sends is kind of what you are going to get back. If you throw up one of the discount websites like we see in Dental Economics and some of the trade journals, then you are going to get a certain type of patient back. It's not going to be the quality that you might want.

Whereas, if you are giving an image of value and it just shows from the website that, "Hey, I'm not the cheapest in town, but we are pretty doggone good and you are going to receive high value."

Colin, one thing I wanted to talk about, and we might be getting ahead of ourselves a little bit, I wanted to talk about your father, who is a dentist. I think one of the best dentists in town. I think I've told you before one of the three dentists in town I would actually let … well, one of the two dentists in town I would let touch my own mouth. One of them just retired.

Tell us a little bit about how SmartBox got started. We might be going backwards a little bit, but growing up in a dental family and seeing your dad and the high quality of dentistry that he does, how did you get started with SmartBox?

Colin: Well, I guess it was just kind of my generation. I remember back as far as I can remember I was kind of tinkering around on the Internet and building webpages back when I was in grade school. I remember my mom screaming and yelling, wanting me to go outside or get off the computer, and all I wanted to do was build webpages, play on the Internet, and build things online rather than building things out in the driveway.

My dad's idea of daycare growing up was I would get off school and come to the office and file charts. So I guess it was just kind of the merging of two worlds. I always enjoyed the web design aspect, being online, marketing and having Dr. Ron as a father: being a dentist, growing up in his office and learning from the ground up what drives a dental practice not just in the front office, but also in the backend – marketing, how he positioned himself to attract patients. Now we run all of his marketing campaigns for him. We have for the past six or seven years now exclusively.

Woody: Yeah. And Ron is not paying me to say this, but he's known as one of the high-end dentists in town, known as somebody. If you really want quality, this is where you go. But he's also known as being a little bit more expensive than the other dentists in town. But that combination that we talked about of value with high quality dentistry … So, do you think that's where you kind of got this concept of, "Let's market for a certain kind of patient, but let's market for the kind that my dad, or Ron, would want?"

Colin: It is. Well, with any marketing you have to find a way to differentiate yourself. When that consumer is out there looking on the Internet or looking in the Yellow Pages – if anybody actually still uses that – wherever they are looking, that consumer is trying to choose who's going to be their dentist. There has to be something that makes you stand out from the crowd, either the best price, or the best service, or the best value, or that you are the most pain-free dentist in town. There has to be something that that consumer can chew on, can bite into, and say, "This is my guy. This is the guy I'm going to choose to be my dentist."

Because, you know, dentistry is a personal thing. It's not a plumber. It's somebody that's working in your mouth. It's not something that a consumer does one search on Google and goes, "Okay, this guy looks good. I'm going to go to him."

So yeah, there has to be a way to differentiate yourself. If you don't want the price shoppers and the bargain shoppers, what do you do? Well, you go toward value. You go toward offering great service, and great results, and a very high level of service and product, which is the direction that Ron went.

You might know better than I do. I know of one other dentist in town that has a Galileo CT scan machine in his office. So when he is doing reconstructions and implants, they don't have to go to the hospital. They can get it all done in one place.

As far as dentists that are actually placing implants and restoring them in the Louisville market area, how many dentists are doing that? There's the one guy out on Dixie Highway that does only mini implants. There's a couple of periodontists around town that will place the implants but they won't do the restorative.

So he's positioned himself in the market as the go-to guy, all in one place, the expert, so to speak, for the Louisville market. That's what differentiates him. That's what we want to help dentists do, is to find your niche in the market. Maybe that's not it – the way Ron has gone, but there is a way to differentiate every practice to make them more appealing to the consumers.

Woody: Another point that a lot of dentists don't know, or maybe they know it and don't really think about that much: most of the really good dentists I know have multiple websites. I don't know how many Ron has now. Probably, what, four, five, or six?

Colin: He actually had 12 up until a few months ago, and we went in reverse and we merged them down into four or five, which he has now.

Woody: A lot of dentists have one website and they wonder, "How come I'm not getting any implants?" Here's a dentist that has one website devoted just to implants that eventually directs traffic to his website.

So there's a whole lot more to it than most dentists realize. Colin, the next thing I want to talk about is dominating the first page of Google, why it's so critical. Everybody has heard that you need to be on the first page of Google. A lot of people have heard that you need to be #1 on the first page of Google. So let's talk about that a little bit. I think everybody knows what Google is, but let's talk about getting on the first page of Google, what ranking really counts, some of the things you need to know about that.

Colin: There was a study done a few years ago by a large … kind of like the Nielsen of the Internet … a large statistical company that found that if you are not in the top three search results, you are simply not really going to be found. The #1 search result is taking roughly 50% of the clicks, the #2 result 25%, and the #3 15%-16%. By the time you get back to #4-#10, you are splitting that amongst a market share of 10%-15% of the overall searches on that term.

Now, that study came out in '07 and '08 and things have changed a lot since then. The search results have become a lot more intertwined – a lot more complex. If you go right now to Google and search for "'your town' dentist" or "'your town' implant dentist" or "'your town' Invisalign," you are going to see all kinds of different search engines within Google. You are going to see their AdWords, their Pay-Per-Click engine – which is

going to come in on the side or the top (or both). You are going to see the local search engine, which is the maps and the addresses. You are going to see the organic search engine, which is the traditional area in the middle bottom.

They also have YouTube videos that they are now showing right on the first page of Google. And then they also have their latest search engine, Google AdWords Express, which is a Pay-Per-Click advertisement, but if you go search and you see that some of the Pay-Per-Click advertisements have two or three lines and others have six, seven, or eight lines, it's the same cost in most cases but Google is allowing you to have a bigger ad on the front page.

So when a consumer is on there searching, dominating the search engines simply means that you are going to be found in multiple positions. The old days of having a website that has one position ranking … you know, you have a website listed in the organic results, and maybe its #1, and that's great. But in today's Google, you have search results that are all around you: below you, above you, to the left, to the right.

Dominating the search engines means that your patients can find you everywhere: you have a Pay-Per-Click ad that's running, you have a local search page that's been optimized and you are showing up, an organic search page, you have some YouTube videos that we've optimized and are showing up right there on the first page. It goes back to the old branding. The more times your consumers see you and hear your name, the more you are recognized and the more comfortable they are moving toward calling you, making an appointment, and becoming a patient.

Woody: And Colin, if you are on the third page of Google, what are your chances of somebody calling you?

Colin: Oh, I would say zero, but there's always that one in a million chance, I think.

Woody: Right. And I'll tell you one thing I've noticed, because I did some research before this interview, and looking at your dad's practice, I mean he's just all over the place. [laughs] You do all these different searches and his practice pops up all over the place. So you've obviously done an excellent job of putting him everywhere.

Colin: That's what it's all about. He pulls in 15-20 large cases – you know, the implant-specific types of patients that he's looking for – the

Internet is sending him 15-20 new patients a month with everything that we're doing online.

Woody: One of the things we talk about is getting in front of your tribe. "Tribe" is simply a term for your followers. In other words, at "The Profitable Dentist," we have maybe 25,000 dentists who are in our tribe that follow us, get our magazine, and so on. So what are some ways of keeping your name as a dentist in front of your tribe? How do you do that?

Colin: There's all kinds of ways. A lot of dentists are doing newsletters. And that's a fantastic way to reach out and touch people. Make sure that you are putting some kind of compelling content in the newsletter. I've seen some pretty bland ones come out that I'm not sure patients even open. But newsletters are a very traditional way of staying in front of people.

Going online, we have automatic communication systems called autoresponders. We partnered up with Infusionsoft to offer a phenomenal autoresponder system that you can reach out and automatically stay in front of your patients for two or three years after they've visited your website.

Woody: You think about an autoresponder as simply technology that does what we used to do by hand, and the sheer numbers are just incredible when you think a person goes to your website, maybe they order a free report, and then they are in that sales funnel for two or three years without you doing anything. It's all done by the software and, in your case, Infusionsoft.

Colin: We've had dentists come to us and they've had these spreadsheets that they have one of their front office staff … you know, they have columns: send direct mail piece one. Send direct mail piece two. Send email three or A, B, C. And they have these huge spreadsheets that they are using to track every patient and what marketing piece they're received.

They're dedicating tremendous resources in terms of labor to this. It's something that we can literally automate for pennies per marketing piece that goes out. If you have 100 prospects that opt in on your website in a month and each of those prospects is going to get 30 pieces of information, whether it be an email or a postcard in the mail or a text message, they get 30 pieces over the next two years and you've got

100 a month, you are at 2,400 contacts over two years times 30 pieces apiece is 72,000 pieces of information that you've sent out over a two-year period.

To do that without technology and automation, you could have a whole team of people working on that. And we can automate that.

Woody: It would be totally impossible if you think about it. Colin, the other thing is, once you are sending out all this information to people who have kind of raised their hand that they have an interest in your practice, and they click onto your website or they make some move in a positive manner, how do you convert those clicks to phone calls?

Colin: You have to give them a reason. You have to answer their question and tell them why you are the best person for their needs. The general rule is when somebody comes to your website, you want to talk 70% about how you can help them and 30% about who you are.

We do these Swift Kick web critiques where I get on their website – and kind of like when you are watching the Super Bowl on TV, you've got the guy with the marker drawing the plays on the screen and showing you what's going on – we do this for prospective clients and show them what's going on with their web marketing.

When we're going through these videos with clients, we show them, "Hey, here's what's missing. Here's the piece that is why you are not getting patients to call you." We go on their website and they are talking about how great they are, and they have a list of everything they do clinically. Or we go on their website and they've got pictures of implant surgeries and flapping gums and all kinds of stuff that patients don't want to see. It's like when you go to the mechanic. You don't want to see pictures of how they change your head gasket or fix your transmission. You just want to know it's going to drive when you pull it out. That's the same thing patients want. They just want to know that you are the guy to fix it, you are not going to hurt them and you are going to do a good job.

Woody: I continue to be amazed at people who put periodontal surgery on the homepage of their website. I mean, all the blood, guts, and glory there and somehow they think that's going to attract patients. It's just incredible.

Colin, another thing I wanted to ask you about is actually quantifying your results and something you call Zetetics phone tracking. Can you explain what that means and how it works?

Colin: Well, Zetetics, by definition, is the quantification of something that's unknown; it's an algebraic term. So we named our new patient phone tracking system after it because that seemed appropriate. So many dentists do marketing or they have a website or they are spending money out there in any marketing field whether it's billboard, radio, TV, newspaper, the Internet, Pay-Per-Click, SEO or local search and they're spending money every month cranking out these marketing campaigns.

And when I ask them, "How many patients did that send you last month? How many dollars did that generate?" they stutter. They don't know the answer. So that's the basis of what Zetetics does, is we can take any marketing campaign you are doing, put one of our trackable phone numbers in it, and this isn't just a phone tracking system. This isn't just something that we tell you, "Hey, you got 32 calls with this last month." This is a system that we can show you how many calls you got, how many cases you presented, how many dollars were generated. We record the calls for you so we can review them with your staff.

So the marketing funnel doesn't end when that phone rings. The marketing funnel ends when they write you the check. And we want to make sure that with our dentist clients, the ball doesn't get dropped as that patient moves through the funnel from the search, to the website, to the autoresponders, to actually picking up the phone and calling once they've developed that level of trust. Passing them off to the front desk, we want to make sure that transition is there. Because otherwise, again, the dentist is spending money, and more money, and more money is going out, but nothing is coming back in.

Woody: And again, you can track all that basically automatically?

Colin: All done for you.

Woody: That's incredible. When I think about how it used to be done and all the man and woman hours taken to do that, to know that this all can be done this way now is totally incredible.

Another point I want to make as we go through the interview, a lot of dentists think that they can practice dentistry plus keep up on all the Internet stuff, too. I'll tell you as somebody who has tried real hard, you can't do it. [laughs] There is way too much going on out there. That's why you need to bring in an expert like Colin who literally has been doing this since grade school and keeps up on this all the time.

Your main goal is to be a dentist – to be productive. You are the most productive when the bur is on the tooth or you are doing implants, doing grafts, whatever. It's not trying to learn the latest and greatest about the Internet. So if you learn nothing else from this teleseminar tonight, learn the fact that you cannot do this. You have to have somebody who does this all day long to be successful.

Colin, the next thing I wanted to talk to you about was how to optimize videos to be #1 on Google. One of the things that happens sometimes is people will do a search for "dentist" in, say, New Albany, Indiana. They might pull up two or three websites. They look at the websites and then they make a decision based on those websites, which one or two they are going to call.

Oftentimes, or the way it used to be is that – say a dentist had a video of testimonials that was very engaging. I would watch one video and say, "That's kind of interesting." And then you are kind of drawn into it and you watch another one. And then you watch another one. And after hearing the social proof of two or three people talking about how great this dentist is, then you are tempted to call.

I remember a video that your dad had a number of years ago where he talked about the reason he got into dentistry and it was very, very compelling. I think he was one of the first dentists in our area to do a video.

Talk a little bit about how you can optimize videos to be #1 on Google.

Colin: Google, in many markets, is putting videos right there on the first page. Sometimes at the top, sometimes at the bottom. It depends on how well-optimized your videos are. Just like your website, we can promote your videos organically right up to the first page.

You hit a number of killer points, Woody. Videos humanize you – every dentist in today's market. I can look in any market area in any state of this country and I will find ten dentists that are "painless" and "cosmetic." And if that is the niche – if that's your niche – there's nothing wrong with that. I have a lot of dentist clients that are extremely successful with those two keywords. But you have to find a way to, again, set yourself apart from every other dentist that's a cosmetic dentist and everybody else that does painless dentistry. No matter how many times you say you are the most painless dentist in town or you have the best cosmetic results in town, there is absolutely no way you can put into words what a video can do on your website.

For instance, just like you said, Dr. Ron talking about how he got into it – his passion. Or you put a patient in front of the camera that never smiled at family events before, so they always had their hand in front of their mouth because they were so embarrassed. You put that person in front of a camera. When we're doing interviews with patients, the camera is sitting off to the side. This isn't a process where we stick the camera in their face and tell them what to say. It's a process that we want to evoke emotion out of them – a conversation that we have with them and the video camera is just running on the side.

When that patient goes on camera and says, "He changed my life with these implants, or these veneers, or this partial he made for me, or he was able to fix my denture so I could eat comfortably again," whatever it is, it goes back to that mirror effect – you are going to attract the patients that message resonates with. When they see your patient testimonials that talk about how you, as a dentist, changed their life, you are going to attract more of those kind of patients.

Woody: You are right about the quality of the video. I've watched a lot of these. When they start out, the patient is obviously kind of nervous because they are on camera. But after the first 30 seconds, they relax, forget about the camera, and it's kind of like they are just talking to you. That's the part that is really powerful. That's the social proof that a prospective client needs to pick up the phone and call that office.

Colin: And something else that should be said is I see a lot of dentists these days doing their own video. They buy a flip-cam. I think that's fantastic. I think there is definitely a place and a purpose for that.

But what you don't see on a lot of the videos we produce is – you know, you see the person with the emotion spilling out. We did a video shoot up in New Jersey last month and one of the ladies had a young daughter that had just died of cancer. This dentist – honest to God, true story – this dentist had gone out of his office with his front staff and helped carry this little six-year old girl with cancer up the stairs and into their office to do dentistry on her.

I don't know. I'm going to be a father here in a few months and that has ...

Woody: Oh, congratulations. Didn't know that.

Colin: Oh yeah. January we are expecting our first. I don't know. I guess that kind of resonates differently with me with that perspective. This lady was on video and at the time we were filming, her daughter had passed away from the cancer. All this emotion just ... it was an hour-long interview that we edited down to three minutes. It was just incredible.

When you talk to somebody, you talk to them as a person, not as, "Here. Talk into my camera." The quality and the energy and the emotion that goes into stuff like that.

Woody: Yeah, it really comes through on a video. I mean you can't write copy that can even come close to video that's done well.

Colin, one of the questions I wanted to ask you too, and this is kind of an open-ended question, but what is it that makes SmartBox different from any other provider? Because there are a lot of providers in this niche.

Colin: There's a lot of web designers out there. And by web designer, I mean somebody that is good at designing websites – the graphical aspect, the aesthetically pleasing aspect. There's a lot of companies out there that only do piecemeal marketing. They only do Pay-Per-Click or they only do local search. They will give you this little one piece of the puzzle – one piece of the puzzle here and there. The difference between us and those guys is we put the pieces together. We don't just design websites. We design beautiful websites – aesthetically pleasing websites also with functionality in mind.

I'll give you a perfect example. The two biggest things we see on dentists' websites these days that are killing their new patient flow, their results, is they are using Flash. Flash isn't compatible with Google. Flash isn't compatible with any Apple product. So if you have a patient on an iPad, an iPhone, an iPod trying to look at your website and you've got Flash on it, they can't see that. Google can't read Flash. So if you have a Flash website, Google is looking at your site and they're going, "What are these big holes everywhere?" Or, "The whole website is missing." Well, it's a big Flash file.

And the second thing is, these are extremely popular, the rotating banners on the front page where they have the pictures that scroll around in circles. We've done dozens of tests with those – studies – where we have taken out the scrolling pictures and put in an offer, such as "Get our free report" or just put in a static image that doesn't change. Every time we do it, the results go up.

I can't read people's minds why a patient searches and they see that rotating banner and they don't call, click, or contact you. But I think people get kind of mesmerized by it. You have five or ten images that rotate every five or ten seconds and they just sit there and watch it and they don't do anything. So my guess is as good as yours on that.

Woody: Yeah. I've seen that. We had a couple years ago in our coaching program – probably one of the highest producing dentists in the country, a guy out of Texas. His website had Flash and had that little rotating banner like you are talking about. We went back and forth about, "You got to get rid of that." He said, "Well, it looks good." I'm like, "Well, it looks good but it's killing you." To this day I think it's still up there. Well Colin, we're running out of time, but I did have a couple other things I wanted to ask you. What is the "No Smart Dentist Left Behind" scholarship program?

Colin: Woody, what do you think it costs right now for a new dentist to go through school, pay for school, and open his own practice?

Woody: Well, I've heard all kinds of numbers. I've heard, at the low end, $300,000.

Colin: Whew! Man, you'd be on a bargain if you got it done for $300,000. But yeah, $300,000. I've heard $500,000. I've heard a million bucks by the time you get through school, you pay for the equipment, you sign the lease, you do the remodeling …

Woody: I've heard the worst thing you can do is marry one of your classmates. That doubles your debt.

Colin: That's probably a good point! The "No Smart Dentist Left Behind" scholarship program is a way that we can help out, that we can get onboard with these new dentists and new practice owners. Not necessarily new graduates; maybe it's a dentist that is going out on their own, leaving the corporate world or leaving being an associate somewhere. It's a way that we can get on board with these guys and get them the tools that they need to succeed. What we see a lot of is these guys go out and they buy a template website or a cookie-cutter website. The next year, they've got a little bit of money left over so they spend a little bit of money on Pay-Per-Click and they're driving Pay-Per-Click traffic to this template website, and it's like flushing it down the toilet.

We want to help dentists to get the real tools they need. You know, a comprehensive website built on our SNAP platform or a WordPress platform that is going to be scalable, is going to grow with them, and it's going to work.

So what we've done is you can actually go to www. NoSmartDentistLeftBehind.com and you read all about it there. We're offering our services at a steep discount: 50% off. We're essentially just paying for our direct labor costs, not even paying to keep the lights on to help these new docs with their incredible debt loads and still get them access to websites and video and Search Engine Optimization and all of these items at our cost. We can help you succeed. And when you succeed, we're going to have your business for life. That's what we're looking at is we're playing the long game, hoping that these docs will stay with us after we've helped them get off the ground.

Woody: Sounds like a great program. By the way, fascinating interview. I learned a couple things I didn't know. Anytime I learn something from an interview, I consider it worthwhile. Anybody on the call, how can they learn more? How can they get in touch with you? What are the next steps?

Colin: For anybody looking for more information, you can go check out www.BestDentalWebsites.com. And for anybody that is looking to find out more specifically about how we can help them, I'm going to extend an offer to anybody that's on this call tonight.

We have our Swift Kick critiques where I personally spend 30-45 minutes developing a marketing plan. I talked about that Super Bowl marker drawing on the screen, showing you what we can do to improve your web presence, how we can help you to find those new patients, attract them and get them to call your office. So for the first ten people that respond to this call, we're going to waive the $250 fee for our Swift Kick critique. You can go to www.DentalSwiftKick.com and just fill out that form on the page. There's no obligation, no commitment. If you decide you like our ideas and you can find somebody that's a better fit for your needs, feel free to take it and run.

Woody: And Colin, any phone number if somebody would just like to call and bounce a few ideas off of you?

Colin: They can reach me at **888-741-1413**.

Woody: Sounds good. Once again, thank you for a very informative evening. And congratulations on that new baby coming in January. Catch up on your sleep is the best advice I can give you.

Colin: [laughs] Well thank you. I appreciate your time, Dr. Oakes.

Woody: OK. Take care.

Chapter 4
Keyword Implementation

Word Count: **2555**
Approximate Time to Read: **5.7 minutes**

Does good SEO automatically mean that you'll be placed in the #1 spot for Google search results? It's possible, but in order to achieve that top rank (or even a spot on the first page of results), you need to ensure that you have dotted all the i's and crossed all the t's. Most Search Engine Optimization techniques hinge on one thing – keyword implementation. Therefore, you need to know what a keyword is, how it's used, what they can do for you, and how to identify those that apply to your practice.

All About Keywords

Keywords are the foundation for all of your Search Engine Optimization processes, from on-page optimization to article marketing and everything in between. Without the right keywords, your patients will not be able to find you. Moreover, search engine spiders will not be able to index your website correctly. As you can see, they're pretty important. This section will detail what keywords are, how to use them and how to identify the best options for you.

Keywords are actually very simple. They are nothing more than terms or phrases that your patients might use to locate services similar to those you offer. For instance, if your practice was located in Atlanta, Georgia, then a possible keyword phrase your patients might really use in Google or another search engine might be "dental cleanings Atlanta." The potential combinations are almost limitless, but you only need to focus on those phrases that your patients are most likely to use.

In reality, the most frequently used keywords are service types or names (teeth cleaning, teeth whitening, Zoom whitening, laser whitening, teeth bleaching, etc.). Other keywords that are likely to be used are geographic references – the town or city in which your practice is located. Local search terms are the best option for you in many instances, as they are far less competitive (a topic that will be touched on shortly).

To sum up, a keyword phrase is nothing more than a word or words that your patients are using to try to find you online. They're usually pretty logical and often descriptive. That makes them somewhat easy to identify, particularly for dental practices. Other businesses, those that deal with a wide range of products or services, often have to target dozens or hundreds of keywords. Your practice can benefit from targeting only those that actually apply to what you offer.

Identifying Your Keywords

Now that you know a bit more about what keywords are, let's move on to the problem of identifying those that apply to your business. What makes a good keyword? This can be a bit confusing. There are quite a few factors that go into making a good keyword that actually does what you need it to do. It's important to note here that the wrong keywords are not going to generate the traffic you need (website visitors that convert to patients). In fact, targeting the wrong keywords is really only wasting time, effort, and money.

Obviously, dental practices differ – you might offer completely different services than an office on the other side of town. Your office might focus on a specific type of clientele, or you might prefer to accept a high rate of referrals. The point is, your situation is going to be unique, and your keyword selection needs to reflect that.

The single best course of action here is to choose keywords that are evocative of your particular practice. For instance, if your office focuses heavily on offering cutting-edge whitening procedures, then keywords like "laser whitening," "laser teeth whitening," "teeth bleaching," "dental tooth bleaching," and the like are going to be more applicable to your practice than others. If your practice focuses more on preventative care, then you might target keywords such as "dental teeth cleaning," "tooth cleaning (your location)," or something similar.

Competitive Keywords

It's also important to understand that not all keywords are created equal. While many phrases and individual words will apply to your practice, chances are good that they apply to every other dental office out there. These are considered "highly competitive" keywords, and need to be avoided. What's wrong with a little healthy competition? There are several problems here, all of which will reduce your results, increase your costs, and slash your visibility. First, if you are targeting highly competitive keywords, you are going up against other dental offices, dental providers, and other businesses, all of which have a more established base than you do. The more competitors target a particular keyword, the harder it will be for you to rank with it in search engine results. Obviously, there is no point in targeting keywords that are not going to boost your visibility.

In addition, should you choose to use those keywords in your paid online marketing (PPC campaigns and the like), then you'll be paying far, far more per click than you should be, simply due to the immense saturation. Therefore, it's really best to make sure that you target keywords that are applicable, but are not supersaturated in the market already.

Determining Your Keywords

As you can see, finding the right keywords is more than important. While you might have a very good idea of what words and phrases your customers are using to find services similar to those offered by your practice, it's important to be thorough in your evaluation.

To help you accomplish this, you can use a keyword search tool. Google has an excellent one, and it's free to use as well. You can access the keyword tool through your AdWords account at https://AdWords.Google.com. This tool (and the others that are available) will be very helpful to you in determining the best keywords to choose.

One of the first things that you can do is determine just how frequently used your keywords are. For instance, at the time of this writing, the search term "dental cleaning" receives 22,200 global searches per month, but the competition level is only moderate. On the other hand, "dental cleaning tools" receives only about 1,300 searches per month, but the competition is high.

You want to target keywords that are frequently used in user searches, but have a moderate to low level of competition. The Google keyword tool can help you find those. In addition, this tool will suggest alternative keywords based on the word or phrase that you are targeting. For example, if you search for "dental cleaning," Google offers alternative keywords that include:

- Ultrasonic dental cleaning
- Cost of dental cleaning
- Dental deep cleaning

- Free dental cleaning
- Dental cleanings
- Laser dental cleanings

Each of these could be a viable alternative keyword for your practice, depending on the competition, the number of searches and, of course, what you offer in your practice as well.

All of this begs the question of just how many keywords you should target. The answer here will differ from practice to practice, but it's best to focus on a handful of highly relevant keywords for the core of your website content and marketing materials.

You can use alternative keywords and keyword phrases in supplemental marketing and content: blog posts, article marketing, and the like. First, you need to create a list of highly targeted keywords that offer the best mix of searches, competitiveness and applicability to your practice. Next, you need to know what to do with them. Where do you use those keywords?

Implementing Your Keywords

Your chosen keywords will form the foundation of your online presence in almost all regards. They should be used everywhere you can, from the content of your website to the internal HTML code (H1 and title tags, for instance) to your blog posts, your social networking efforts, your article marketing, and your PPC campaigns. Simply put, your keywords should be used in everything that you do online.

While using your keywords in every online application possible is vital, you also need to ensure that you implement them with the correct frequency. This is referred to as "keyword density" or the number of times a keyword or phrase appears within a certain number of words. There are two main schools of thought here: specific density and natural use.

Specific density is an artificial way of making certain that your keywords appear X number of times within a specific piece of content. Some websites shove keywords into their content willy-nilly, hoping that a high keyword density will make their site appear more legitimate to search engine spiders. This approach can work, at least for a short time. However, an artificial keyword density often makes your content unreadable for real people – you will actually alienate visitors rather than encouraging conversion. Consider this content:

"If you want to find the best teeth whitening in Southern California, then we are your best choice. We offer teeth whitening services that get the job done. Teeth whitening is an important process, so it's vital that you choose the right teeth whitening procedure for your needs."

This is an example of "keyword stuffing." While it might seem like it gets your point across while using your keywords to their best advantage, it's not good content. You need to ensure that your content appeals to both search engine spiders and real people. After all, the real people visiting your website are those you hope to convert into patients – putting your best foot forward here is vital.

Natural keyword density is very different from artificial keyword implementation. This practice simply relies on the natural frequency of keywords within your content. While it results in a lower keyword density, it's far more readable to real people (encouraging conversion) and also connects with search engine spiders (for search engine page rank). Good content should be readable and optimized with keywords, so a natural keyword density is your best option here.

More on Keywords

You will have to spend time learning about keywords and how to use them most effectively, which is not a simple matter. The Internet is packed with information that can help you, including places such as Google AdWords, Keyword Spy, SpyFU, and many others. When you have developed the strongest list possible, you can incorporate them into your videos, blogs, and social networking sites. Let's take some time right now to learn a few valuable details about keyword selection for websites and videos.

The Search Type

In the process of selecting your keywords, it helps to know to know most web experts see searches as falling into one of three possible types or categories:

- **Information** – This is the sort of search that indicates that a consumer is looking for specific information, such as "symptoms of Gingivitis."

- **Transaction** – This is a search for details that will help the consumer complete some sort of activity, such as "dental implant dentist in NY."

- **Navigation** – This is a search that really has only one possible result. For example, when the user types "Dr. Receveur's Dental Office" in the search terms, its because they are looking specifically for that office.

How can knowing or identifying the searcher's intention help a dentist to choose the best keywords? Knowing that your patients may have a different need is going to help you really optimize the text and the way it applies to the videos that you begin to use.

Though it may be very difficult to integrate all three types of searches into a list of keywords, it can help when optimizing a video for SEO performance. You would simply make a point of avoiding a particular "slant" to the keywords chosen. For example, you could use "Dr. Receveur's Dental Office.com – Tooth Whitening Techniques" as a title for one of the videos you optimize.

Avoiding Popular or Competitive Keywords

Let's also not forget that you don't want to rely on keywords or terms that are already heavily in use, usually referred to as "saturating the market." This is the time when a local SEO concept is going to work in your favor. Relying on keywords that include your geographic location and identifying the unique factors about your practice will increase the success of your SEO campaign. For example, consider you might seek to attract patients of a specific type. This might mean that you are offering services for those who are fearful of dental work, someone looking specifically for cosmetic solutions, or children only dental services. Your keywords must be unique and an accurate reflection of this.

At the same time, you need to remember that a lot of the words that just pop into your head are going to apply just as equally to your practice as they would to the practice on the other side of town and all of the offices in the county. While it might seem like a "no brainer" to use those terms, it could end up backfiring because a lot of other dentists and specialists thought of them too. This can often make it very difficult to choose terms that are not too competitive. For example, just as you might sit there and wrack your brain to figure out terms that would be used to conduct searches for your services and products, a patient would use the same approach. This means you might easily come up with the same sets of words or phrases as millions of other dentists; you actually want to avoid this.

Again, we suggest that you turn to a site like Google AdWords to research the popularity of specific terms and to find the combinations of dental terms that have a reasonable rate of competition, rather than the fiercest levels. This site is also a great way to find a bunch of useful and workable alternatives too.

What should all of this accomplish? When you are going to do video marketing, it means that you are going to be using the strongest keywords for the titles, tags, and descriptions of the videos (we'll look at that in a moment), but it also means that you are going to be able to keep the highest quality of your website content. Rather than forcing yourself to create text, articles, blogs, and other content that contains high numbers of your chosen phrases, you can focus on creating lots of high-quality videos that contain the terms in their descriptors, which boost search engine results just as effectively. For example, let's say you are thinking about the ways to optimize your videos in order to have them appear on the first page of Google search results. You would want to fill the title, description, tags, and backlinks with the most effective keywords. What you don't want to do is fill them with the most competitive terms. It is only by heading to a site like Google AdWords and running a comparison that you can determine how to make the best choice.

In this example, we'll say that the video is about teeth whitening with lasers. Your keywords need to include the most frequently searched terms, but also need to avoid those that show the highest competition. This could mean that "laser whitening" is far more competitive than "teeth whitening lasers," but they both receive a relatively similar amount of searches. It is always best to stick with the least competitive keywords when optimizing in order to get the most visibility in the SERPs.

Chapter 5

Creating Quality Content and Backlinking

Word Count: **5519**
Approximate Time to Read: **12.3 minutes**

While keywords are the foundation of any SEO efforts, content remains the most important consideration. Even if you have the most accurately targeted keywords possible and they are used perfectly, if you do not have the right content, your practice will go unnoticed – or it might even fail online. Why is this?

Quality Content is Key

Content forms the core of your site. It provides information for your visitors and also offers a home for your keywords. Your content is very important and if you use unoriginal or poor-quality content, you are dooming your efforts to almost immediate failure. You might be wondering just how you're supposed to create content that ensures your visitors stay on your page and that also helps search engine spiders index each page and rank your site. It's relatively simple, so long as you follow the succeeding rules.

Originality

Always create original, well-written content. You need to make certain that you are using 100% original information on your website. It can be tempting to repurpose other content for use as website content – ezine articles, blog posts, product descriptions, and more can all seem to be excellent options for pulling double duty. However, the problem is duplicate content will actually get you penalized by Google and other search engines. This is particularly true with the Google update dubbed "Panda." Your content must be original to your site. If you do not feel capable of this, then hire a professional writer to do it for you.

Compelling

Your content must be compelling – that is, it must provide real, actionable information for your visitors. It should evoke a response in them, encouraging them to take an action, whether that action is calling to set up an appointment, signing up for your newsletter, emailing for more information on a particular service, or something else entirely. If your content is not compelling, then your conversion ratio will be lower than what you need for success. The job of your content is to inform and compel action in your readers, so if it doesn't, then it is failing.

Informative

Your content must be informative and filled with value. Whether exploring the topic of teeth cleaning, whitening technology or dental diseases, it should offer real information of use to your visitors. Remember, your visitors are seeking specific information when they visit your website. Therefore, you need to make it easy to find and easy to digest. This is a chance to become their superhero – providing answers to their questions and problems (Why is my tooth hurting? How can I cover my chipped tooth?) and showing them that your practice is the one to do the work. If you give your visitors the information they want, they will reward you with a higher conversion ratio.

Not providing information, or providing it piecemeal, can pose significant issues. The attention span of a web surfer is relatively short, which means you have to catch their attention immediately. If you make the information in your content (the information your visitors are looking for) hard to find, then they'll lose patience and leave and that's certainly no good for your practice.

Accurate

Finally, the information that you present to your visitors must be accurate. If you offer inaccurate information, you will alienate your visitors. You must strive for 100% accuracy in all of your content, whether you are describing specific dental procedures, highlighting cost breakdowns, or explaining why patients might want a particular service. If your information is inaccurate, you can expect your visitors to realize this and penalize you with reduced traffic and bad word of mouth.

Optimized

Finally, your content must also be optimized with your chosen keywords. Use your keywords sparingly, but make sure that they are present in your content. Hitting a natural density in your usage is vital. You should average one keyword or keyword phrase for every 100 words of text in your content. As mentioned, if you stuff your content full of keywords, it will not offer your human visitors any benefits.

Consumers have become increasingly savvy and can tell the difference between a page written with readability and transparency in mind versus one written for search engines. If your content is unreadable, they'll leave.

Backlinking

SEO consists of more than original content and the correct keyword implementation. In fact, it goes well beyond these concepts. One of the most important things for your practice within the realm of Search Engine Optimization is backlinking – the process of building valuable links that lead back to your practice's site.

Backlinking is one of the oldest optimization methods that still works, but there are some special considerations to be made here. It's important that you understand how these links affect your page rank with Google, as well as how they work in other ways.

The most obvious benefit of backlinking is that it provides additional links leading to your site – it makes it easier for potential patients to find you online. The benefits do not stop there though. Backlinks also help Google determine where your page stands in the search rankings – though this is a complex subject, there are some simple ways to make sense of the process.

First, any backlinks should be from high-quality, high-ranking websites. The higher the page rank of the site linking to you, the more value Google will place on that link. The more valuable the link, the higher your own page rank will be.

Second, the sites linking to yours should be relevant to your own. That is, they should have something to do with the world of dentistry or a specific subarea of dentistry. You might have inbound links from specialists if you have a general practice. Alternatively, you might be a specialist, in which case you would have inbound links from general practices or specialists working in other areas.

Finally, it is best to use a contextual linking method here. That is, rather than having a link like this:

For information on Bob's dental cleaning, click here

You would want to have a link like this:

Robert's services include dental cleaning, whitening services, **and more.**

Contextual linking boosts the value of the link by informing search engine spiders of what the linked-to page is about. It can be a good way to increase your page rank, as well as ensuring that your site is indexed correctly.

Of course, you need to ensure that you go about creating links the right way. Never pay for a link exchange service or link placement service. These can be "black hat" operations that will get your website blacklisted by Google. Instead, try to build a backlink structure naturally, by making real connections with other professionals in the industry.

The Patient Attraction Podcast

Episode 008: The One About Dental Marketing Vultures

Good afternoon and welcome to this week's edition of the SmartBox Web video podcast. I'm your host, Colin Receveur. On today's episode, we're going to talk about all the bad, scary things on the Internet that you need to stay away from as a dentist. We're going to cover some of the marketing tactics that some of the black hat marketing firms use as well as some of the web design methods and strategies that will absolutely kill your SEO performance and your conversion from turning visitors of your website into phone calls that turn into cash.

So very quickly, the purpose of these podcasts is to educate you, the dentist, on all the aspects of web marketing so you can make an educated decision for yourself on if web marketing is beneficial for your practice and your situation. On today's webinar, I'm going to cover about 10-15 points, as time allows, of things you should not be doing and things to look out for with dental marketing firms and dental companies out there regarding your website. So let's jump right in.

I'll start out with two age-old tactics that black hat guys have been using for years and years. I don't know why they still try to use it to be honest because it's been shot down over and over again. Google actually just released their Penguin update. Yes, I said that correctly – not Panda but Penguin update, which is another update that's designed to cut down on spam link building and keyword cloaking and stuff of a black hat nature.

Keyword Stuffing

Keyword stuffing, one of the two items I'm going to talk about first, is where you go to a website and see words like "New Albany Dentist" plastered over and over and over and over again on the website. What they're trying to do is to trick Google into believing "New Albany Dentist" is a search term that Google wants to display this website for. The reason is obvious why Google doesn't like it: because it's not natural – it's not real. Somebody that's built the website and put that keyword in there 1,000 times is just trying to get up to the top and they're probably not offering any good content or they might have a dental website that's just not in good shape; they're trying to quickly get up to the top to get some ranking and visibility. Google shoots that down every time.

Keyword Cloaking

Sometimes you even get blacklisted, which we'll cover a little bit later in the podcast. Another big one is keyword cloaking; it's very similar to stuffing, but cloaking is where it's invisible. There are ways that you can design a website so that you put 1,000 keywords on the page, but they're invisible to the regular user. The reason that this is done is, again, to try to trick Google when it is looking at your website into ranking them again. So keyword cloaking, old tactic, big no no; it always dies hard.

Flash

Flash. Everybody loves Adobe Flash. Colors and motion and all kinds of cool effects. Flash is the biggest killer most dentists think they really love for dental websites. The reason is threefold:

1. Apple products and the majority of other devices can't read Flash so if you're looking at a website that uses Flash on an iPad, an iPhone, or pretty much any mobile device, your website is worthless.

2. Google can't read Flash; yes, they've made some improvements in recent years, they can read some of it and not the other but why would you build a website that Google can't definitively say they can read so that you can be indexed and seen at the top of Google? You wouldn't! It's just silly – so don't do it.

3. It kills your conversion ratio. What that means is a lot of docs that use Flash, open up their website and it's like this tornado of visual effects and movement and pictures, images and slideshows going back and forth and just insanity. Visitors go there, they look at that and they get lost. They ask, "What am I supposed to click on? I don't even know where I'm supposed to look!" There's all this stuff flying around and all this visual motion.

So there's three very compelling reasons never to use Flash; mobile phones can't read it, Google can't read it and your users, while they may like it, it doesn't help turn them into paying patients.

"Spammy" Tactics: Over-Optimization

Another thing that we see a lot of with black hat SEO companies is when they're doing this optimization for you, they're doing "spammy" stuff where they push out a bunch of articles to thousands and thousands of sites including making spammy comments on different blogs and all this crazy stuff. What you need to know as a dentist is that Google is cutting this all out of the equation. If you saw Matt Cutts, Google's head chief of, I don't even know what his official title is – I don't even think he has an official title – but Matt Cutts is a chief tonto at Google and he posted a video on his blog a few weeks ago that Google was coming out with an over-optimization penalty for websites. What that means is if your website looks like it's over-optimized and it's unnatural that you have so many links coming into it, they're going to penalize you because they know it's artificial.

You have to look at this from Google's perspective; they are all about delivering for their customers, and their customers are the people searching. You've got all of these people that are searching and what are they searching for? Why are they on Google? Well, they're on Google because they want to find a local business or they're looking for an answer to a question or a need or a problem they have. Google's job is to deliver them with a result based on a couple of words they type in that fixes their problem or delivers them the business they want or whatever they are searching for. **Google's job is to deliver it.**

If Google was to deliver results based on manipulation, more or less, (which is basically what over-optimizing your website comes down to, you're manipulating Google into thinking you're better than Google assesses that you are) then Google wouldn't be delivering what's best for their customers – for the people searching. It might be because your website doesn't convert, it might be because there are a lot of people that click that little back button as soon as they look at your website, it could be for a number of reasons why Google doesn't think your website is great. That's part of what this latest Penguin update is about; they found an algorithm or a pattern that now they can identify the spamminess and the over-optimization and now they're going to start penalizing you for it.

No One Can Short-Cut to the Top Anymore

They actually rolled out the Penguin update I think on April 24th, about a week ago. I was out of time or I would have posted this on last week's podcast but here we are, the Panda update, the Penguin update; what Google's telling us here is that the Panda update was all about freshness and great content and the Penguin update is removing over-optimization from the equation. You can't just pay your way to the top

---

of Google's organic search anymore. The message Google is sending is very clear; they want great content, they want fresh content and they want content that their readers like, not over-optimized content that you think they'll like.

That's what dentists need to be looking at going forward is how can I provide my users with a great experience? How can I provide them with great content? Optimization is great but don't overkill it. That's the tall and the short on the Penguin update, the Panda update, over-optimization and all that stuff. Let's get on to the next point.

Social Media is Not a Fix-All Solution

Unfortunately there's no magic wand – there's no hidden secret purple pills you can pop, or the blue pill or the red pill or whatever pill is the magic pill – I don't remember. When it comes to social media, I see a lot of docs out there, I actually talked to a doctor this morning based out of Montana; he called in for the first time and was interested in finding new patients. After talking to him for a few minutes, he told me that for the last six months he had spent $2,000 a month on Facebook. Facebook Advertising, Facebook updates; doing all this social media and this Twitter stuff and I really felt bad for the guy. I wished I could have gone back and helped him before he spent $13,000. He literally told me he got nothing for it – not a single patient, not a single prophy even sold. That's the results that we see quite commonly with social media.

You see, these big companies do social media as a key feature of their marketing. We do social media, working with several consultants in the industry: Summit, Big Case Marketing and there are some other guys that we do social media with but only as one small feature of the big picture. We see social media working if you have a national audience like Quiznos or Qdoba, for example. If you don't have this recurring following like most local dentists, local contractors, local plumbers, etc, it's just not worth your time.

I've got a friend that's a dentist up in New York and he has personally been doing his own social media for the last eight months. He posts videos, articles and makes updates a couple of times a day; he is on fire with social media – doing everything he can. I hadn't checked in on him for a while and I went to his Facebook Page the other day and after doing this hardcore for eight months, he had only 34 followers on his Facebook Page. **Only 34 followers for untold hours of his time for eight months.**

All these social media gurus are going to tell you well, you've got to bet on what's coming, you've got to put in and then you'll get back. I'm telling you, I've seen guys that have done this for eight months, a year, two years with local businesses; there's a local contractor in our area, a guy I know, who has been doing social media. He posts videos of these construction projects he does and he does meticulous work, excellent work, very good attention to detail, very good at what he does. He's been in business for a long time, 20-25 years, and he's done all this Facebooking for, I don't know, he says he's been on there for maybe a year, maybe a year and a half. I went to his Facebook page the other day and he had 102 followers. It's just insane the energy and the money that people put into all these buzzwords – they buy into the hype.

Web Marketing Doesn't Have to be Complicated

Everybody's trying to sell you something. The marketing vultures I call them; they're all trying to sell you something and they'll all take your money but the reality is, and it's unfortunate, that guys spend all this money and all this time and energy and they get nothing out of it. **The reality is web marketing isn't complicated; you just have to put yourself with the right message in front of the right audience.** The reason Facebook doesn't work for local businesses – the primary reason that no dentist is ever going to find new patients on Facebook – is inherent in the way Facebook works. For somebody to find you on Facebook or Twitter, they have to know your name and know your business. If you are going to be able to market to them – to drip to them – they're going to have to Follow you, Like you or Friend you.

Take Joe Plumber who's got a toothache and he wants to find a dentist that can fix his toothache. Is Joe Plumber going to go to Facebook, search for your name and when he finds your name click to Friend you or Follow you or Like you even though he's never met you before in his life? I don't see that happening – it doesn't happen. **The only people that are going to Friend or Follow or Like you on Facebook or Twitter or LinkedIn are your existing patients.** Yes, you can get some referral stuff going on if you have your existing patients check into your office and post reviews to Facebook and all this stuff, but even then, you're trying to hit a needle in a haystack.

Google is Where It's At!

Now let's say your patient that's coming out of your dental chair posts a review on Facebook and at that exact moment, one of their friends has a dental need and has to be looking at Facebook. It's still a potshot, whereas if you focus on getting your reviews in Google, now you have people that are searching on Google – they have a need, they have that toothache, where do they search? 75% of people go to Google when they have a problem they need resolved. **97% of people go to the Internet when they have a problem that they need resolved or they need a local business.** By and large, they're coming to Google, they're searching for their problem and when Google delivers that result, if you put your reviews in Google, all your good, raving reviews are popping up right in front of them.

That prospect has gone to Google and they've searched for "New Albany Dentist Porcelain Crown," let's say this is an educated prospect and they already know they need a crown. They search for "New Albany Dentist Porcelain Crown" and Dr. Ron Receveur pops up. Dr. Ron Receveur has 27 reviews raving about how great he is and how he uses sedation and he's very gentle and he's got all the greatest tricks. Now you've motivated this cold lead into a warm prospect that may take the initiative to call your office.

Now let's assume that you've spent all of this time invested into getting these reviews and you put them in Demandforce or you put them on Facebook or you put them on Yelp or any of these other places. So now somebody goes to Google and searches and what do they see? Maybe that Demandforce page is optimized well enough that it will show up. Maybe that Yelp page is optimized well enough that it'll show up. Maybe that Craigslist – no, the other list, the female list name, Angie's List – maybe that Angie's List page that you have some reviews on is optimized well enough to show up, but that's a lot of maybes.

If you're going to play the game with the big dogs – with Google, the big gorilla in the room – you've got to play by the rules. So where do you have the best chance of showing up and the best chance of getting your reviews seen? That's a no-brainer. Inside Google; directly inject your reviews into your Google Local Places page. You need to be claiming that stuff – you need to be putting reviews in there, you need to be optimizing it; it's an ongoing thing, just like your website.

Search Network Advertising Vs. Content Network Advertising

We got off on a big long tangent there but I'm going to try to regroup and circle back to social media and why it's such a money pit, an energy pit and a time pit for dentists and local businesses in general. We've tried it, we've seen it tried, from running Facebook Ads to doing optimization and status updates and seven times a day putting new information on your wall and drip, drip, drip, drip; it just doesn't work.

The Facebook paid ads that they offer, a lot of people say, "Well, I do Google AdWords and I do okay." Now when you do Google AdWords, are you advertising on the content network, or are you advertising on the search network because there's a huge different. Here's the primary difference; when you're doing Google AdWords on the search network, your ad is being shown – is being displayed – next to people that are searching. Okay, that's pretty simple. Now have you ever been on Google, reading your email maybe, and you see that little bar at the top where it's got some kind of advertisement? And it's kind of creepy because you're reading an email that your aunt just sent you about how her cat died last week and Google ad pops up with a little advertisement talking about pet burial services. It's like they read your mind, and they kind of do, but I'm not getting off on that tangent today. That is the content network. Completely separate from the search network; you can actually split them in Google when you are setting up your AdWords account. You can split those two up so you're only advertising on one or the other. Most dentists really want to be on the search network.

The content network of AdWords is just like Facebook Ads, it's just a waste and here's why: those people aren't looking for information. They don't have a problem that they need fixed. When you're running ads on Facebook or Google's content network and somebody clicks on your advertisement, usually what's going through their mind is, "Oh, that looks cool, I'll check that out," and that's usually the end of it. If you talk to any reputable pay-per-click marketer on AdWords, they'll tell you when you're doing AdWords, you need to split up your marketing to the search and the content networks. Your search network you might want to bid $0.50 or $1 or $2 for a click and your content network: a nickel a click, a dime a click. **The content network is worth so much less per click because the value just isn't there.** It isn't somebody that has a problem, it's somebody that goes, "That's cool, I think I'll check that out."

AdWords content network is synonymous with what Facebook is doing. You're browsing around Facebook, you put on your Facebook that you like The Voice or you like The Bachelorette or The Bachelor or whatever it is. Facebook reads that and coincidentally, The Bachelor is running an advertisement on Facebook so Facebook shows The Bachelor's advertisement to everybody that has selected The Bachelor as one of their Likes. That's the same kind of thing; there's not a problem there, it's not a call to action, it's just a billboard on the side of the road. It's just another message that gets lost in the 4,000 messages a day that we now get hit with. 4,000 messages a day – it's unbelievable. That's what you're competing against. That's why Facebook just doesn't work for new patient generation. It's just by design; it's not that it's bad, it's just not what it was designed for.

Is Your Website Up to Par?

Moving on past this social media discussion we've had, I see a lot of dental websites that have no call to action whatsoever. They've got some pretty graphics and they talk about how great they are. A lot of them never address their patients' problems – they only talk about the solutions and how great they are. And second, many never have a call to action. I've looked at dental websites before that I've had to click two or three times to even find a phone number to call the office. Your information has to be readily available: right on the front page, because people have digital attention deficit disorder. I told you a few minutes ago, 4,000 messages a day that we're getting hit with – it's no wonder there's a generation of kids that have attention deficit disorder! We're getting swamped with so many things trying to lure us in we don't have time to give anything attention.

I did an analysis this morning for two clients, one based out of Chicago, one based out of Tennessee. The client of ours based up near Chicago, actually up in Northwest Indiana, 25.7% of all of their web traffic came from a mobile device with 1,200 people on their website last month alone. He actually sent me an email so I just posted some results; we've been working with him for 30 days – check out the results button at the top, Dr. Randy Schmidt. I remember looking at those mobile search numbers a year ago and we were looking at like 3, 4, 5, 6%. 2012 is the year of mobile search. 2011 was local, 2010 was video, 2009 – I don't even remember what 2009 was, it was so long ago. You've got to cater to the mobile audience.

The doc down in Tennessee: 28% of all his visitors – he had 770 visitors last month on his website – 28% of those came from a mobile device. You have to have your information readily available; people want to search, they want to pop open their mobile phone, they want to do a quick search and they want your information, Bam! Right there, available, ready to roll.

The Have to Haves

You have to have a mobile website. I sound like I'm lecturing but looking at these two clients, each of them 25.7% of 1,200 is what, 350 people – 300 and something prospects? 27% of 770 is another 200-ish – 190? 350 prospects of yours a month are coming to your website on a mobile device and they can't read your website – what do you think they're doing? They're clicking back. Right now, they're going back to Google and they're searching again, and they're going to keep looking until they find a website they can read that answers their questions. That's where this world is going. We all want information right now, at our fingertips at any time day or night plus, we all have digital attention deficit disorder so we want it delivered with no problems and no hassles. Technology has advanced so much and it's so available to everybody these days that people just expect it. Five years ago if you had said "mobile website" to somebody, they would have looked at you as if you had three heads coming out of your shoulders. Nowadays, we include mobile websites with every package we do – it's just part of doing business. You have to have it, you have to have a website – there are a couple of "have to haves" if you want people to find your website and you want them to call you and you want to be successful at marketing online.

There are no hidden tricks or magic wands or purple pills or red pills. Marketing on the web isn't complicated. It's not full of all these buzzwords, it's not something new that you have to dump tens of thousands of dollars into every six months. You just have to get a good base and you have to pour a solid foundation. You have to have a solid website, you have to have your local listing on Google Places claimed and optimized and then you build from there. You have to have some video and you have to have a way that people can contact you risk-free.

Be the Go-To Dentist!

People want more information about you and you want to keep your name in front of people, so it's a match made in heaven. Offer them some more information, in exchange for their email address and now you can send them an email or a text message or a postcard in the mail or a letter in a month or two months or six months and drip on them over and over again, keeping your name in front of them. Eventually, they're going to have a need. They're going to break a tooth off or their daughter or son is going to jump on a trampoline and knock a tooth out or something is going to happen and they're going to have a need and they're going to think, "You know, this dentist, he's been sending me all this great information – all this educational stuff. He's not pushy, he's sent me his free report, he had a webinar talking about how he could help me, he's done all this stuff for me. He's a pretty good guy. I think I'm going to go see him now – I think I'm going to call him now that I have a need."

That's what you want! You want to be that go-to dentist. You've educated your community, you've built your name within the community and when people have a need, they call **YOU**.

I tell you what, if you want to learn more about how to properly structure your website, to capture the new patients you want, to generate new patients, to generate phone calls, we've got a new free report out, **The Dental Website Audit**; we're getting ready to launch version three next week. It's a free 33-page report right now – it's going to be about 40 pages on the next version, but if you download it today, send me an email and I'll send you a copy of version three as soon as it's out. It's a free download on our website – it's a PDF, just click and it downloads. If you'd like a hard copy, we can mail you a hard copy too.

All you've got to do is plug your information in; the place to get it is www.DentalWebAudit.com. Take a look at that if you're looking to take your website to the next level. If you don't know where to turn, it'll give you a lot of clarity, it'll show you exactly what you need to do to be successful with your dental website to attract the types of patients that YOU want.

That's all for today. Colin Receveur here saying keep moving forward.

Chapter 6

Follow-up and Tracking: Maximizing Your ROI

Word Count: **3882**
Approximate Time to Read: **8.6 minutes**

"Patients have to have seven positive interactions with you before they actually buy or do business. So, that means they see your billboard, they see your Twitter, they see your website, and so on seven different times before considering your practice."

~ *Woody Oakes*

"Another important aspect of dental marketing, which is, I think, more and more crucial, is to be able to track where the new patients come from. Regardless of what advertising and marketing methodologies you use, it's important to track them so you know that the money you're spending is being well spent and what kind of return on investment you're getting. One of the great products that Colin has is a way to track those by assigning different phone numbers to each one of those, and then providing analytical data on a very timely basis so you can decide if you want to continue with a certain marketing effort – is it paying off, is it doing well, or do you need to take that money and put it in another place?"

~ *Michael P. Abernathy, D.D.S.*

"The ability to know where the calls are coming from: being able to see exactly, which campaign is being successful – I know where the marketing dollars are going. It's nice to have that report. And daily, when the call comes in, I get an email about it and I can listen to it if I want. And we can monitor what is successful and what is not so we can fine-tune and tweak and be as successful as possible."

~ *Robert H, Klein, D.D.S.*

While social media marketing and Search Engine Optimization will play an essential role in driving your success, you need to know how to track that success. It is vital you know your exact ROI on all your marketing efforts whether online or offline. How do you do this? There are some handy tools and processes that can help. This chapter will highlight the best options out there.

Drip Marketing Tools for Success

We dug into drip marketing quite a bit in an earlier section, but let's take a look at how this concept applies to followup and tracking to ensure you're able to maximize the ROI on time and effort spent marketing online and building your networks.

There are numerous tools that can be used to help you follow-up with potential patients. For instance, in the realm of social media marketing, HootSuite (http://www.HootSuite.com) is an excellent tool. This was mentioned in conjunction with Twitter usage previously, but it has greater capabilities than that. In fact, HootSuite can actually help you spread your message throughout all your social networking accounts including Facebook, Twitter, your specific business Facebook page (as opposed to a personal account), LinkedIn, Ping.fm, WordPress, MySpace, and Foursquare.

HootSuite also offers the ability to track the results of your social media marketing efforts with detailed statistics and metrics; page views, visits, pages read per visit, and quite a bit of other information is available here. This program is free to use on a rather limited basis, but chances are good your practice will benefit from the paid membership. The paid membership allows you to access all the features, but it also allows you to have more than one person working on your account.

Another option for your drip marketing needs is Infusionsoft (http://www.InfusionsoftForDentists.com). This program doesn't work quite the same way as HootSuite though. This is an automated followup program that focuses more on email marketing and customer relationship management (CRM) than social media marketing. However, Infusionsoft offers some pretty significant advantages that make it an ideal inclusion in any fully-fleshed marketing plan. What does the program offer?

First, Infusionsoft is considerably different from other such options. It offers intelligent automation that helps you grow relationships with prospects rather than driving them away by inundating them with emails from autoresponders. The system uses autoresponders but they can be automatically started or stopped depending on the actions taken by a prospect. Not only does that ensure you are not sending duplicate emails to an individual, it also saves you a tremendous amount of time and effort.

Another benefit of Infusionsoft is that it's web-based, meaning you do not have to install anything in order to use the software, saving you time and space on your hard drive. You can also access it from any computer with an Internet connection, which means you can provide follow-up services to current patients and leads even if you are at home, traveling, or on vacation. In a nutshell, Infusionsoft allows you to keep in touch with those who visit your website, those who sign up for more information via an opt-in or double opt-in system, and your current patients. It also enables powerful customer relationship management, allowing you to track potential sales, create quotes instantly, and more.

Tracking ROI

Tracking the return on your investment is a must. Programs like Infusionsoft and HootSuite cost money, but you need to track the return on your investment of time and effort put in with social media marketing, as well as traditional marketing methods. Interacting with others on Twitter, Facebook, and LinkedIn, as well as posting updates to your blog can take an enormous amount of time. It is vital to track your results throughout all your online and offline efforts.

Every marketing medium you utilize has an effect on your bottom line. If you don't know for certain that each medium is providing a high return on your investment, you're really doing little more than throwing your money away. A comprehensive marketing strategy will leverage several mediums including print ads, direct mail, radio spots, social media marketing, Search Engine Optimization, and more. Tracking the results of each medium can be difficult, but phone call tracking can help ensure you have the information you need to make solid, informed decisions based on real information about your ROI from each medium.

What Is Phone Call Tracking

Phone call tracking might sound a little confusing if you have never used it before. However, it's actually relatively simple. At its heart, its nothing more than a system used to help you identify exactly how well each of your marketing mediums is performing. You'll be able to determine if you really are generating leads from your Facebook presence or from that costly radio spot as well as the exact cost per lead generated through each marketing method you use. This information is invaluable, particularly in troubled economic times and in highly competitive industries.

Of course, the service does come at a cost. However, you can offset those costs with the savings you generate by eliminating low-performing marketing mediums. The information you gain from using phone call tracking will help you tailor each medium for maximum ROI or eliminate those advertising mediums that are underperforming by a substantial amount.

How Does Phone Tracking Work?

You will find a number of phone tracking services available – each one having its own unique quirks that sets it apart from others. However, they all tend to operate in a similar fashion. Each call that comes into your practice has its origination tracked. This is done by assigning specific, unique numbers for each advertising medium and utilizing advanced analytic methods. When the lead calls the number, the information is recorded and the call is forwarded to your practice's phones where the call will be answered. In addition, the service will actually record the communication between the caller and the person answering the phone. Having recorded calls to fall back on will help you identify areas where you can improve on customers service, as well as having a reliable record if a dispute were to arise.

You will receive detailed analytical information about the origination of each phone call in the form of graphs and charts. These will provide you with a visual means of gauging your ROI from each marketing medium – you will be able to tell exactly how many people called in from a PPC ad, how many leads were generated by your Facebook ads, and how many called based on each of your other marketing methods. With the information provided, you will be able to determine exactly, which mediums are performing best, which ones are costing you money and how you can best alter your marketing strategy to maximize your ROI.

The Patient Attraction Podcast

Episode 002: The One About Why Just Doing Ads Isn't Enough

Welcome to the 2nd video podcast. I'm your host, Colin Receveur. In this episode, I'm going to show you why "just doing ads" simply isn't enough.

What today's podcast is going to show you is the four critical elements that your web marketing MUST have to be successful this year and beyond. And as a free gift to those who stay till the end of the podcast, there will be a special link to get a free copy of my latest book.

Now, this book contains the secrets on the 2nd, 3rd, and 4th elements that only we use with our best clients to keep their websites producing month after month. Most other "marketing gurus" out there are still on just the first of the four steps for their clients, and to be honest, the dentists are being left high and dry when it comes to actually attracting new patients and putting dollars in the bank.

I'm heading into the video studio today. We had tornadoes sweep the Louisville area yesterday, high-winds and tons of power outages. We had to leave the office mid-day so I'm hoping nothing got shocked or surged when power came back on, so this episode is going to be short and sweet.

I'm going to dive into more details on these four elements in just a minute …

Why Listen to Me?

If you haven't listened in before, I'm Colin Receveur, speaker, author, invited columnist for the Profitable Dentist, DentalTown, and founder of SmartBox Web Marketing where we, simply put, get dentists more qualified patients in the niches they have advanced clinical training. The purpose of these podcasts is to educate you about dental marketing so you can make an informed decision about what's best for you and your practice in this new dental economy. But enough about me. Here's what we're going to cover …

Four Critical Elements that You MUST Have to Succeed Online

1. **Visibility** – AKA The First Date – The tools and buzzwords we know as SEO, PPC, AdWords, local search and mobile optimization are just that – tools. Lots of guys spend tens of thousands on only this, never get results, and are confused to what's going on. This is only the first step ...

2. **Pre-Qualification** – No, this isn't pre-qualification for financing. This makes sure your patients are educated and informed about how you can help them. Without pre-qualification, you'll get a flood of phone calls that expect insurance to cover. I'm going to show you how to pre-qualify all your patients so you don't waste your time with phone calls and consults that go nowhere.

3. **Follow-up** – If you're not following up with your prospects at least 10 times, your large cases are going elsewhere, plain and simple. Just as you wouldn't buy a car or house on the first pass, your patients aren't accepting treatment either. I'm going to show you how to automate all your follow-up so you can keep in touch with your prospects for two years after they visit your website.

4. **Tracking** – The best laid plans are a waste if you don't know, without any doubt, what you got for it. I'm going to show you how we track your exact return on marketing investment from web visitor to phone call, consultation, case presentation, case acceptance and $$$ collected and in your pocket. It's really a lot simpler than you'd believe but most guys don't have the system or technology in place.

Now onto the good stuff. Starting with #1 ...

1. **The First Date – Visibility for your practice** – The first step of any web marketing campaign is your prospects must be able to find you on the web, no matter if they search on Google, Facebook, local search, or on their mobile phone! The alphabet soup of "buzzwords" you've heard (SEO, SEM, PPC, SMO, etc.) are simply the tools used to achieve a top ranking visibility. Many dentists when they are paying a marketing firm to handle their marketing, this first step is the only one that gets done!

I'm not going to dive into the specifics of each "tool" here, that's the topic of another podcast in itself, but you must be doing organic SEO, you must be doing PPC, you must be doing video optimization, local search is a critical aspect, online reviews, social networks (especially Facebook, Twitter, YouTube and LinkedIn); each tool is one you definitely want in your war chest, working for you.

With the Internet in a constant state of flux and Google never letting us in on the new rules of how their game is played, you have to make sure you have a dominant online presence that covers ALL FACETS. No longer is it okay to just have your website at the top of Google. You must now dominate the entire first page of results.

2. **Pre-Qualification** – Once you've attracted a prospect's attention, now you have to hold onto it long enough to compel them into action. But before they call, you first need to pre-qualify them for the types of dentistry you want to perform. If not, you'll waste your and your staff's time fielding lots of phone calls and consults for patients that never move forward with case acceptance.

Don't just talk about what you offer – the rule is to talk 80% about them and 20% about you. Address THEIR problems and you'll become their hero. When you educate your prospects, they will respect you and look to you as their expert, as well as become better consumers of the dentistry you offer.

If your website looks like and carries the same message as your competitor down the road, why would a prospective patient choose you? Your message must be unique and different – a USP (Unique Selling Proposition). Put your USP under your competitors name. If it sounds okay, you're not unique enough. How do you do this? Through KILLER content and GREAT video. No longer is it okay to have a dental website without powerful video. No longer is it okay to just drive masses of hits and clicks to your dental website without converting them into patients. If your phone isn't ringing, it's a complete waste of time and money.

3. **Follow-Up** – You might "get found" online, but 85-90% of your website visitors are NOT ready to immediately call you. By offering to send them valuable information in exchange for their contact info, you can answer all of their questions and become their "hero" all while keeping your name in front of them until they are ready to buy.

You can do this via email blasts, autoresponder emails, newsletters, social networks, snail mail postcards, flowers, gifts, faxes, voice broadcasts … all kinds of ways. Much of this can be automated so you and your staff are free to do dentistry.

So how do you get started? With your advertising lure. Like fishing, you have to have a good lure or worm to get the fish onto your hook. Your ebook, free special report, case study, white paper or your printed book can be your advertising lure. Once they opt-in, you can contact them automatically once every couple weeks and keep your name in front of them with info, education, offers, etc.

The same goes for Facebook and social networking: offer your prospects a gift or coupon or prize in exchange for "Liking" or "Following" you. Most dentists using social networks just post updates and get nothing from it. It's not the tool that's broke, it's how you use it that doesn't work.

4. **Tracking your ROI** – All your time and effort is wasted if you can't figure out exactly what works and what doesn't. With our Zetetics™ Phone Tracking system, we can tell you down to the penny, which marketing works and, which doesn't so you don't waste your marketing dollars.

   How do we do this? We assign a unique phone number to every piece of marketing you have. These phone numbers ring through to your front office, but we can track everything as well as record the call. Our system allows you to know exactly how many calls came from each piece of advertising, as well as further track who scheduled consultations, accepted treatment, and how much money you produced/collected.

   When you buy stocks, bonds, or invest, you know your cost basis and your profit or loss. When you market, it isn't any different. Don't settle – know exactly what you're getting.

The Four Take-Aways From this Episode

1. **Visibility** – The web is in a constant state of flux – spread your eggs into many baskets and play with ALL your tools to get your name found EVERYWHERE. No longer is just a single ranking good enough, you need to DOMINATE the web with multiple positions.

2. **Pre-Qualification** – Your website and video must have a compelling

message, but it must also weed out the unqualified tire kickers. You simply don't have enough time to talk to everyone. Target the niches that are more profitable and attract the patients with money in their pockets.

3. **Automated Follow-up** – The best visibility and website in the world won't sell the large cases, and it's insanely cost prohibitive to assign a staff member to manage all your follow-up. Now you know how to automate your follow-up and put it on auto pilot to keep your name in front of your patients.

4. **Tracking** – Those forms at your front desk are incredibly inaccurate. Use phone tracking to know exactly what produces and probably more importantly, what doesn't. You wouldn't expect your stock broker to give you estimates – why would you spend tens of thousands on your marketing and settle?

Get a copy of my book shipped to you

As promised, there's a link that should show up at the bottom of this video. When you can request a free copy of my latest book: ***How to Stay in Front of Your Patients Until They are Ready to Buy – The Dentist's Guide to Social Media and Drip Marketing.***

www.WhyPatientsDontBuy.com

This 100+ page book is packed completely full of valuable information, real case studies, and examples of drip marketing campaigns we've ran with our best clients. And best of all, it's available for only $1 to everyone that listened in today. Simply go to the URL above and we'll ship a hard printed copy to you.

With the Internet in a constant state of flux and Google never letting us in on the new rules of how their game is played, you have to make sure you have a dominant online presence that covers ALL FACETS. Your prospects might find your video, your website, your social media page, your mobile website – the dentists who embrace this fundamental shift in how information is delivered, embrace the technology, and most importantly, answer the real questions their patients are asking – those will be the ones that take the lion's share of the new patients.

So that's it for today, hope you have a great week and see you again soon!

Chapter 7

Online Marketing Methods

Word Count: **4868**
Approximate Time to Read: **10.8 minutes**

Vital Tips to Maximize Value

Before we launch into the ins and outs of the various online marketing methods you need to harness, a few words need to be said about maximizing the value of those methods and your efforts.

- **Never forget the 80/20 rule.** 80% of your results come from 20% of your time invested. On the other hand, 20% of your results will consume 80% of your time.

- **Market with the 60/40 rule.** When you walk into Subway for lunch, do you want to read about the history of their business, who founded them, or how great their subs are? No, you're hungry and you want to eat! The same is true for your patients. Instead of greeting them with your bio, credentials, pictures of your office and waiting room, simply answer the question they are asking.

  Your marketing's message should be 60% about them FIRST, then 40% with how you can help them solve their dental problem. If you give them the solution to their problem, communicating in a language they can understand (not "doc talk"), then you have a much better chance of earning their business.

- **Rome wasn't built in a day** and your marketing campaign won't be either. Don't try to implement everything we discuss in this book in a week. Develop a plan of action, and steadily implement the ideas we outline.

- **Design and implement your first drip campaign within 7 days.** There is no better way to learn the process than just doing it. Find a list of at least 50 prospects and build a drip marketing campaign to nurture them into patients.

- **Make a commitment to marketing.** Even with technology making it easier and less expensive to reach your target audience, too many practices only advertise when sales are down – costing them tens of thousands of dollars in lost opportunities when the sales were up. Develop a consistent marketing strategy you can keep going in good times and bad.

- **Drip marketing is not the "silver bullet."** People buy from people they like. Focus your marketing efforts on ways to elevate your status in your prospects' eyes. Differentiate yourself. Drip marketing will complement your efforts doing both.

- **Don't just read, consume and digest.** Whether you're a note-taker, highlighter, page corner-folder, note-scribbler-in-the-white-space, or you just have a photographic memory, this information is worthless if you don't **TAKE ACTION**. You can't take action without remembering what you read here.

"The first time you share tea with a Balti, you are a stranger. The second time you take tea, you are an honored guest. The third time you share a cup of tea, you become family … "

Three Cups of Tea *by Greg Mortenson and David Oliver Relin*

Just like how the three cups of tea in the story above can easily illustrate how people get to know one another, they can also illustrate a basic business concept too: drip marketing.

The process of becoming familiar, and also trusted, is the goal of high-quality marketing. You introduce yourself in an official and appealing manner and if you do well, you are more than welcome to "visit" or communicate again. After a while, you are a familiar "friend" whose communications are appreciated, trusted, and respected.

Marketing can emulate those sips or drips of tea shared between strangers. You can have that first encounter with new friends, but then you can begin sharing more frequent interactions until you are totally familiar with one another. The key is to keep repeatedly "sharing your tea" in order to allow your newfound acquaintances to develop a real taste for it. It is then that you will have provided them with an adequate set of expectations and a strong level of trust, and they will move forward in your professional relationship.

In other words, if you keep dripping good information and offers for your dental services and products in front of prospective patients (and even with existing patients), you are going to create a relationship based on trust and value. This will result in the "conversion" from prospect to paying patient.

But does this tactic always work?

The National Sales Executive Association (NSEA) found that it can take up to twelve times of contact or communication before a consumer decides to do business with a particular individual or group. This can seem a bit overwhelming to someone who is unfamiliar with drip marketing, but if you are reading this, you've taken a giant step in the right direction toward turning more prospects into paying patients.

It is likely that you've done the SEO, created the social networks, added tons of video content to your site, and have articles and blogs frequently updated and submitted to the appropriate directories. Now what? How do you go about touching your prospective four or MORE times?

If you've done all of the things mentioned above, you have also probably developed a very detailed marketing plan, but what we're talking about are the weeks or months after you have successfully implemented it.

If you are actually following a powerful plan for marketing, you will have a constant schedule of activity booked well in advance, but you will also have all kinds of additional ideas in mind too. This section is about all of those additional activities and ideas that anyone striving to successfully market their dental practice must use. What are they? In the next pages we will introduce you to:

- Drip marketing
- The most effective follow-up tactics
- Social media marketing
- Automation and autoresponders
- Advertising "lures"

While it is quite likely that you will have put to use a basic "marketing guide" for a dental professional, and even used specialized guides such as those focused on videos, this section is going to really help you complete the process of directing traffic to your office and making conversions. How?

We will help you to do the activities identified above through some relatively simple ways. When finished with this section, you will:

- Use autoresponders to keep continually "dripping" information to prospects in a multitude of ways.

- Use social media to create a true "following" or online community to, which you are DIRECTLY speaking/marketing.
- Use Infusionsoft, or another autoresponder, to completely automate all of your postal and/or direct mailing pieces.
- Have a good collection of "advertising lures" that will get patients to respond every time.

We should note right away that there will be a heavy reliance on social media. This is because it costs almost nothing and generates a huge ROI (Return On Investment) when done properly. You will need to view social media as an extension of the drip marketing tactics you will master here, and you will quickly understand just how effective the social networks can be at keeping your name in front of your prospects.

Why does that matter? After all, if you have created a system for directing traffic to the site, why do you have to keep your practice's name in front of people you have already contacted? The shortest answer to that question is this: why flood the market with one surge of materials when you can keep a persistent drizzle of high-quality materials flowing to potential dental patients? We'll answer that in the first section on Drip Marketing.

After that, we'll explore in-depth the steps that are necessary to really master your social and drip marketing campaign. This means we'll look at the best ways to:

- Develop a follow-up sequence that incorporates
- Autoresponders
- Free offers and bonuses
- Optimize methods for social networking
- Establish opt-in pages
- Create a series of automated messages
- Track the effects of every marketing effort, down to the penny

If you are a dentist who has already laid the proverbial groundwork for marketing by the creation of a website, SEO campaigns, video library, and other materials, you can get started right away!

If you haven't done a lot of marketing, made a website, or even learned about the ways in which marketing for a dental practice work, you can still gain a tremendous amount of useful information from reading the following sections. In fact, you can rely on all of these tactics as your primary efforts simply because they will help you find new patients through direct communication and free service social networks.

If you are ready to learn all about the most comprehensive marketing tactics, let's begin!

The Patient Attraction Podcast

Hello and welcome to this week's episode of the SmartBox Web video podcast. I'm your host, Colin Receveur and on today's episode, we're going to talk about the psychology of your dental website. What is your dental website really saying to your dental prospects and your dental patients?

But first, got a little housekeeping: I've got some important announcements to make. I just found out this week that I'm going to be a dad at the end of this year, so I'm pretty stoked about that. My wife and I have been married for coming up on two years now so I'm pretty excited – pretty excited. So that's some good news!

I'm actually heading to the airport right now heading up to the Jersey area to do a Premium Package video shoot for a very savvy dentist that we've worked with for several years. He's doing a lot with sleep apnea, doing a lot with dental implants, has a CAT scanner in his office – very, very cool stuff. I'm going to have about 20 minutes here, maybe 25 minutes depending on traffic before I get to the airport so this will be a pretty quick podcast. We're going to touch on the psychology of your website: what your website really says, pitfalls to avoid on your website as well as in the latter part of the podcast where we're going to touch a little bit on referrals: how to get referrals, what's going on in your patients' minds when they're giving referrals and how to exploit that to your advantage to get more referrals.

The "We We" Problem

The first thing that I guess really prompted this podcast on this specific topic was we've been doing a lot of these Swift Kick! video critiques. If you haven't seen them yet, click on the Video button under Media at the top of our website to view our most recent Swift Kick! videos.

What I've been seeing is a lot of the "we we" problem. I've blogged about it a couple of times before, but the "we we" problem is essentially where your website just has I and We all over it: I am so great, we are so great, we do such great work, we do better work than the guy down the road. You have to differentiate yourself! You have to show that you are better than the guy down the road, but flat out coming out and just saying "we're the best guy in Dallas, Texas, or Chicago, Illinois," is just not getting the job done. It's one thing if your patients say it, it's completely another if you say it yourself. It comes off as kind of self-absorbed, kind of arrogant; a lot of bad things come out when you try to say that you're the best.

The secret to differentiating yourself and letting your patients know you're better is what I hinted to a second ago; if your patients say it, it's okay because it's coming from an unbiased third party that you were able to help. That carries a lot of trust and that carries a lot of weight with it and if you get your patients to say it, it's very believable. If you say it yourself, well I can sit here and say that we're the best dental web company on the face of the earth, but that doesn't really matter to dentists. A dentist comes to our website, they look at the work we've done, they look at the video stuff we're doing, the marketing automation to stay in front of your patients, the phone tracking and that's what sells them; that is our differentiating factor. You have to come up with a way to differentiate yourself in a way that your patients can understand that isn't you just touting yourself with a subjective adjective; best, better, great, gentle – whatever it is.

You Have to Position Yourself

Your patients are searching right now: every county of the country, every state, every city; patients are searching for answers to their problems **right now.** They're looking for answers to their missing teeth. They're looking for solutions to their sore dentures. They're looking for a way to fix their snoring at night or they're waking up tired in the morning and they think they have sleep apnea and they want to fix that. Or, many dentists are getting into Botox and that's a huge market right now that's, especially in the dental field, pretty untapped. There are guys searching out there for ways to look younger, the NewGenics stuff/the Botox. I hear dentists say a lot, "Well, why would I advertise for that? Who's searching for that?" Well, there are a lot of people searching. If you can position yourself as the answer to the question they're asking, you're going to be able to be that source of information and you're going to be that go-to guy. They're going to see a couple of your videos, see your website, and as they read more and more about you, learn more and more about you, you continue to answer their questions and give them great information. You're going to be their hero; you're going to be their go-to guy – their expert.

I've kind of harped on this in other podcasts as well but **the currency of the future is information**. I was at a dental conference last year and one of the keynote presenters got up on stage and talked about how you don't want to put too much information on your dental website. You want to make them call you and you want to put just enough out there so they know what you do and they know you do a good job, but you don't want to give them all the answers because you want them to call your office. I just wholeheartedly, completely, 100% disagree with that approach. You need to be putting everything on your website, all kinds of information, giving them all the answers upfront because:

It makes you the expert. You look like you are a god among dentists. No disrespect intended to our Lord but you look like the man. You've got all the answers, you've got the biggest website filled with information, much of it you yourself are explaining. One of my big pet peeves is dental websites that have stock video on them: you click on it and it's from other dentists or it's from these companies that just cookie-cutter it and they put your name and text right above it. It's these educational videos where they show the titanium post going into your jaw, they show the locator and they show this technical stuff. Your patients don't want to know that! They don't want to know anything more about that than you want to know how the plumbing works in your house. All you want to know is when you flush the toilet, the stinky stuff goes away and **that's all your patients want to know is that when they bite down, they're going to be able to chew; when they go to sleep, they're going to be rested; when they go to the dentist, they're not going to be in pain.** They don't care how it works, and if they do care how it works, there's Wikipedia, there's all kinds of references out there that will gladly provide plenty of technical documentation and reference for them to see. Your website should be about you. You should be delivering information, showing how you can help them, showing them how you alleviate their fears and then let your patients take over.

I had a dentist from Colorado call me recently and asked me what the role of patient testimonials are on a website. I said well, they're kind of multi-role. The first is the obvious; they set you up as the expert. They show your patients that you do good work, that you have satisfied above and beyond people's expectations in the past and they give you credibility.

The second role that patient testimonials play that many people don't realize, is patient testimonials attract the types of people that their testimonial resonates with. If you do a bunch of patient testimonials and all the testimonials are that Dr. Smith worked with my insurance, he was very good, it didn't cost me any money over and above my insurance, he maximized it, yadda, yadda, yadda, then you're going to attract the types of patients that want that kind of care, all kinds of insurance, that level, that type of care. If your patient testimonials talk about how you do great implant work and you were very gentle and that yes, while the investment was considerable, it's the best money that they ever spent, then you're going to attract a little bit higher socio-economic class of people that have a little bit of money to spend and appreciate a higher level of service.

Make sure when you're shooting the testimonials, you recognize that your testimonials really can do a lot of your demographic targeting, a lot of your heavy-lifting from a marketing standpoint for you. When you're selecting who to do your testimonials and what kind of work they had done and all this, keep that in mind.

But back to the psychology of your website. If you're going to enter the conversation that's going on in people's minds – people that are searching for missing teeth; loose, sore dentures; sleep apnea, can't sleep, not rested – you have to enter that conversation that's already in place. I think we've already established that. To enter that conversation, you really have to see your patients' problems through their eyes. Another pet peeve of mine is when you go to a dentist's website and all they have on their website is a menu list – a buffet I call them – a buffet of services that they offer. They expect the patient to be able to relate that buffett list to their needs. Your patients don't want to know that you do dental implants; they want to know that you can help them chew again. Your patients don't want to know that you do cleanings and whitenings; they want to know that they can smile with confidence. Same for sleep apnea: they don't want to know that you can make them a sleep appliance; they want to know that you can help them to wake up in the morning and feel rested. We all know the heart implications, the total body health implications of sleep apnea – it's huge! They want to know that they're going to be healthy and well.

Look at it from your patients' eyes. All the "we we" stuff: we do appliances and we do this and we do implants and I do that and we're the best – you're not resonating your prospects. I'm sure a lot of it is true, but **you have to resonate with your prospects.** You have to speak the same language that they're speaking if you want to attract them. What I hear a lot is, "Colin, I've been doing this marketing and I have all this 'we we' stuff and it attracts patients and I've been doing this for years and it works." Well, it's like playing darts. You can play darts and you can score points on a lot of parts on the dartboard, but if you want to specifically target the types, the socio-economic classes, the demographics that you want. If you want to specifically target boomers that have some money to spend and want to chew again with the help of dental implants, then you've got to speak directly to that audience! You have to profile that audience and figure out exactly what they want.

One of my mentors talks about the target profile and how you take one customer – one patient – out of all of your patients – out of your thousands of patients – you take one of them and you sit down with them and you talk and you go back and forth and you ask questions. You find out what his real problem, his real pain was, and then you build all of your marketing around this one person. While it's kind of an extreme approach, building all of your marketing and all of your message around a single person, it does raise a lot of eyebrows in the sense that you now have a very good idea of what it takes to attract that guy. If that guy is the type of guy that you really want to bring in, well now you've got a winner.

You Need to be Focused on Your Patients' Needs

That's what it comes down to. Focus on answering your patients' problems. They're searching, and if you can provide **that** answer, you can be **that** guy. Another example: we've got a dentist on the East Coast that we've been working with a couple of years now and we have him in really good shape. He's got a great website, a ton of video (all kinds of video), first page rankings, all kinds of stuff. He called up and he wants to put a little blurb on his website that he is a patient advocate and I said, "Well, why do you want to put that you're a patient advocate?" He said, "Well, duh Colin, I work for the patient. I don't just try to sell them what will make me the most money; I'm a real patient advocate." So I said, "Okay, I'm sure patients appreciate that but if you just put on the top of your website, 'I'm a patient advocate,' that doesn't really carry a lot of weight."

People are savvy. Patients, customers – they're savvy these days. That's one reason why the written testimonial online has fallen so far by the wayside; patients know that people just make that stuff up: go get a picture from any number of websites, write something up, type it up, put a name on it and paste it on your website. This isn't 2000 anymore or 2005. That's one reason video is so powerful because the written testimonial just doesn't carry any weight anymore. And not just the written testimonial but simply putting one sentence at the top of your website that says, "I'm a patient advocate and in this day and age, this is extremely important," just flat out doesn't carry any weight. It's just jargon. It's just a buzzword.

If you flip that and you put at the top of your website a quote from a patient that says, "Dr. Phillips is a true patient advocate," now you're getting somewhere! Now you've got an endorsement from a patient who felt like he was being oversold at another dentist and went to this dentist and that dentist but you, Dr. Phillips, were the patient advocate who told him the truth. Dr. Phillips said he didn't need implants; a simple one-unit crown can work and save you a couple thousand bucks. Now you've got an endorsement from a patient that says you're a patient advocate. Now you've got hopefully, a video testimonial from that patient who says you're a true patient advocate.

You have to structure your website in a way that enters the conversation that your patients are already engaged in.

Dentists who don't understand the Internet or haven't really 100% bought into the fact that this Internet stuff is going to be around for the long haul don't realize the dominant force going forward that people find information on is these reviews sites: Yelp and Angie's List and Google Places. They think simply if I don't set one up, I don't have to do it; it's kind of like the blind eye. The truth is your patients are doing it. You're getting reviews online whether you embrace it or not. If you embrace it, you can use them. If you get a negative review, you can try to mitigate it. There are a lot of ways that a negative review can be made out to be very positive but you have to embrace it – you have to know that you're even getting the review first. The same thing with video and with the web: you have to embrace it, you don't even really have to understand it, you just have to take advantage of the tools that are at your disposal.

Referrals

People give referrals because they're happy with what you did. But more importantly, they give referrals because they want to feel good about giving referrals. Think about the last time you ate somewhere: you ate at a good restaurant and you told a friend about it. You said to your friend, "This is the best place, they have the best spicy tuna hand rolls and the best sushi ever. Incredible!" Why are you telling that person that? You're telling that person because you're excited – because we all have a natural inclination when we have a good experience or we are really happy with something that we want to tell other people about it. People that give testimonials and give referrals, they're doing that because they are extremely happy with you.

I've seen it described before with three faces: you've got the sad face, you've got the okay face and then you've got the excited face – the big excited face. The sad face obviously, you're probably getting a negative review. The okay face, you didn't wow them, you didn't excite them, you're probably not getting a good review over that. But the excited face – the big smiley face, that's the kind of patients you want. Those are the kind that are going to pay, that are going to stay and are going to refer. If you can build your tribe with people with big smiling faces, you're going to do alright.

Keep that in mind when you're asking a patient for a referral. They do it because they want acknowledgement, because they want to feel good. You've helped them to feel great now they want to give back and they want to do something that they feel great about too so they're going to give you a referral. When you get a referral, immediately acknowledge it: send them a gift in the mail, a gift card, flowers, anything, but acknowledge the referral because that's why they're giving it; they want to be thanked. Just like they're thanking you for the great work that you did, you should thank them when they do something good for you. That's how word of mouth works.

When somebody comes in from a referral, take care of them. Do good things for them because the referral that is in your office is already pre-sold, they're in your office because of a good recommendation. You don't have to sell them; they're not a patient that found you online and you have to prove to them you're going to do a good job They already know you're going to do a good job because they got a referral from their friend. Keep that in mind.

Just to quickly recap, I'm pulling into the airport here, the important things from today's podcast are: **make sure you are entering the conversation, you are getting inside your patient's head and**

speaking their language. Speak to their problems and speak with answers and give them a lot of answers, give them all kinds of great information because that's how you're going to win them over.

And the second point to take away is **with referrals, make sure you acknowledge them, make sure you thank them.** Those referrals are just gold in your chest. We chatted earlier about the Swift Kick! video critiques; if you are interested in getting one for your practice, contact us by going to http://www.smartboxwebmarketing.com/contact-us/ and we'll be happy to put one together for you. We'll show you everything you're doing right or possibly doing wrong.

That's all for today. Colin Receveur here saying keep moving forward.

Chapter 8
What is Drip Marketing?

Word Count: **6254**
Approximate Time to Read: **13.9 minutes**

At any given moment, 9% to 18% of your target audience is thinking about the need for your dental services or is **considering recommending** a dentist like you to someone they know. Though most practices do a pretty good job of following up with the immediate buyers of their services, statistically speaking, the vast majority (97%+) of dental practices do a TERRIBLE job or DON'T MAKE ANY EFFORT AT ALL of keeping in contact with those who only casually consider coming into their practice. These casual buyers represent the future patients of your practice.

The reality of sales and marketing is if your practice and your name isn't on the tip of their tongue at the moment they are ready to buy, that patient will be going to your competitor. It's as simple as that. **This is why drip marketing is so effective.** Let's take a look at some statistical information in order to understand exactly WHY you must integrate drip marketing into every aspect of your marketing plan – from social networks to email marketing.

The National Sales Executive Association released the following statistics:

- 2% of sales are made on the 1st contact
- 3% of sales are made on the 2nd contact
- 5% of sales are made on the 3rd contact
- 10% of sales are made on the 4th contact
- 80% of sales are made on the 5th-12th contact

But it doesn't end there.

Glenn Fallavollita, CEO of Drip Marketing, Inc., published a study in 2010 showing that medium to high-value sales take 15 to 30 "cups of tea" (telephone conversations, face-to-face meeting, voicemails, letters, emails, and so on) before a cold prospect will be converted into a paying patient. Yes, this does indeed mean that, as a dental professional, **90%+**

of your potential prospect-to-patient conversions will come only after many "cups of tea" with them.

Understanding and Using the Numbers

Why does it take SO long for a potential patient to decide whether or not to utilize your professional services?

One of the strongest answers to that question is simply "trust."

A 2009 book by Dr. Frank Luntz indicated that **consumers are "less happy, less confident, and less trusting than any other generation since the Great Depression."**

Clearly, this means that anyone selling goods and/or services is going to have to take this absence of trust into serious consideration. This is especially true in the face of the basic facts, i.e., it **takes at least four contacts between you and a potential patient to even get a response!** It is also something a bit more challenging for dental professionals because people do hesitate to contact dental offices (mostly due to fear) and many worry about the costs associated with the work.

The trick then is to find the ways to get your dental practice in front of the potential patient at least four times, but in a way that establishes trust, builds a good relationship, and creates a system of follow-up that uses multiple points of contact.

Low Key, Non-Pressurized Trust-Building Approach

What are those points of contact? They are the "drops" that you can keep "dripping" in front of them during all of your drip marketing. You will be able to do this without causing irritation or losing their interest and without "flooding" them with too many offers. Are you already seeing the visuals these descriptive terms are seeking to create?

How to Stay In Front of Your Patients Until They are Ready to Buy

Envision a flood of rushing water ... it inundates everything, passes through, and is gone. Now picture the gentle dripping of a peaceful rain shower ... it slowly saturates everything and does not overwhelm. There is the difference between standard "blitz" marketing and the more contemporary and useful "drip" marketing.

If you use those "number of contact" figures from the list above, you know you have to contact potential patients at least five times but you also know that some generic or standardized approaches may not get the results you want. This is due primarily to the fact that these tactics fail to establish the mandatory trust, and they don't communicate on a personal or modern level.

Building Trust through Communication

The first method we will use to establish a trusting relationship between potential patients and yourself is a giveaway. No, you will not offer free services, but you will give them useful information entirely free of charge. We most often recommend what is known as an "eBook" (though newsletters are a good option too), which is a professionally written "electronic book." This is automatically delivered to a person who registers their email address or full contact details with your site.

Now, before you panic and think that you have to sit down and write a book in order to get new patients, don't worry, you can hire someone to write it for you. We write and print books and reports for many of our clients.

Why Would Giving Away a Book Establish Trust?

First, it gives a visitor a lot of handy information. Let's say that you are now qualified to do dental implants and have started conducting a drip marketing campaign around this specialty. You would have an eBook created about the subject and would then give it away to anyone who visited the site and provided contact information.

The visitor gets the eBook emailed to them automatically (through your autoresponder software, which we deal with a bit later) and gets to read about the many benefits of such dental work. Second, and most importantly, by accepting the book, they have also "opted in" or have given you permission to communicate with them in the future.

Here's the important thing about that: you can now integrate their interest in this procedure into your drip marketing campaign. This means the visitor will now get emails and other forms of communication from you asking about their interest in the work. Perhaps you send out a welcome letter, begin posting updates and information on social networks, send coupons for discounted exams, etc.

Regardless of the steps you select, you will establish a good basis of trust because the potential client sees that you are willing to give away valuable details and that you are <u>following up</u> with them in a direct way (but still non-threatening). By offering "lures" in the form of the giveaways, you can also create a system by, which you will allow your visitors to learn more about you through reliable website content and your strong presence on social networking sites. When someone registers through your new site, you can set it up to ask them if they want your newsletter.

You can give them a chance to become a "friend" on Facebook or a "follower" on Twitter, and you can give them a chance to sign up for your blog or even your YouTube channel. Any of these options opens a channel through, which to drip information.

All of these options will also keep you in their "field of view" and will help them to see the kind of expertise and quality that you provide. It doesn't flood them with information at one time but instead keeps up a steady pattering of details that reminds them of your professionalism and expertise.

The HOW of Drip Marketing

In order to succeed with drip marketing efforts, you must understand that it is something that requires a good amount of planning, organization, action, and follow through. You also have to create methods for tracking everything that you do as well. Don't worry, we'll cover all of this and we'll also show you the best tools to use to ensure success.

The Opportunities Available

To begin, it is important to remember that you have two opportunities when using this sort of marketing:

1. To close the deal with an immediate prospect or buyer.
2. To create an opportunity with a future buyer.

The great thing is your drip marketing does not have to change for the two different groups. This is because the entire program has been designed to have universal appeal to all of your existing patients and to your prospects as well.

How Is This Possible?

Let's rely on that earlier example of new dental implant services; you create a drip marketing plan designed to inform all of your patients, past patients, prospects, and referrals of this new service. When you do the initial step – let's say an email blast and a direct mailing – you may get a handful of immediate sales. That would mean that your drip marketing closed the deal right away, but it would continue working in the future by communicating with those who didn't act right away.

This is the reason that drip marketing is far more flexible and appealing than standard marketing. It keeps you and your services in eyesight of the potential customer, but not in an overwhelming, pressure-filled, or irritating way. It also creates a method whereby you are persistently marketing services and positioning yourself as an expert or the local "go-to" person for some particular dental procedure or product.

Expertise and Customer Perception

How is expertise tied into drip marketing? It all has to do with the flow of information and the image that it paints of you and your dental practice. For example, you will have used five key elements in the drip marketing program:

1. High-quality content that is relevant to the target audience
2. Well-timed communication or "drips"
3. A good mix of campaigns that include emailing, blogging, social media contacts, direct mailing, meetings, and more
4. Evidence-based lures and tools that convey details about your product or service (i.e., eBooks).
5. A strong plan for follow-up

This approach is to ensure that at no time will any of your contacts feel as if they are being overwhelmed with the pressure to act now. Instead, they will be periodically reminded that you are an expert in your field of dental work and/or products, you make a lot of information available to anyone who inquires, and you do not need to pester anyone with calls or constant mailing pieces looking for business.

Can you begin to see the similarities between this process and the **"three cups of tea"** proverb mentioned earlier? The first time you communicate with them, you are a stranger; the second time, you are a recognized individual; the third time, you are a "familiar" with whom there is comfort and security. After the fourth time, there is no alteration in their perception, it is simply a matter of showing them that you have recognized their dental wants and needs and have a good menu of solutions available.

Establishing Trust and Familiarity

How is all of that possible through marketing? Let's use a good example of a drip marketing campaign for dental implants again. The dentist begins the process with a well-worded and appealing email blast that lets the entire database of patients, past patients, and prospects know these services are now available in their office and are also extremely beneficial to those who need them.

A week later, they post a video to their blog about the benefits of these implants and use their social media networks to direct people to this video. They will have selected language that is totally devoid of "sales speak" and instead, designed to give them authority and expertise – i.e., the video might be titled "The Dental Facelift," "How Dental Implants Support Your Face in the Aging Process," etc. A week after that, they post an update to their social networks about their new free book about implants, which is available to those who visit the homepage of the website.

What Does All Of This Do?

1. It establishes this dentist as an expert or the "go-to" person in their industry.
2. It also keeps them in touch with the entire targeted market over a long period of time, but without the use of a lot of sales language or pressure.
3. It continually drips new sources of information on those in the database.
4. In the minds of the recipients, it cements the dental professional as a reliable resource.
5. It is also a process that can go on indefinitely thanks to the availability of automated campaigns and autoresponders.

This last issue is something not to be overlooked because it might take you dozens and dozens of communications before

you effectively make the sale, and if you are doing the appropriate amount of tracking, you can ensure that you have a good ROI on your efforts.

Naturally, this sort of thing cannot just spring to life. It requires you to organize your contacts in a way that creates specific target audiences, as well as develop plans for individual campaigns. This brings us to the five steps necessary for building a strong drip marketing system.

The Patient Attraction Podcast

Episode 012: The One About Designing Your Dental Website's Sales Funnel

Good morning and welcome to another episode of Fast Thoughts on Dental Marketing. I'm your host, Colin Receveur. On today's episode we're going to be examining how to set up a multi-step sales process with your dental website. The reason behind this is if you're looking to attract the types of patients and cases that you want including the larger cases – specific types of procedure cases, you have to elevate your expertise and your image to that of above the next guy down the road. Let's face it, you can have the best hands and do the best clinical dentistry but if you don't relay that accurately to your patients or your prospects, if you don't set yourself up to be the guy that is the go to guy in the community that can do those types of procedures, the community at large is never going to know or want to come to you for those cosmetic procedures or implant procedures or sleep apnea procedures or whatever your niche is.

The purpose of these podcasts is to educate you on what's available with dental marketing so that you can make an educated decision on if it's good for your practice. On today's episode, we're going to be examining how people raise their hands with your marketing, how you can reach out and touch them more, how you can educate your prospects before they ever call or come into your office and how to advance people to the next stage in the sales cycle. You don't want to be that 19-year-old dude that goes for the kill after the first direct mail postcard.

Let's jump right in. I'm going to start with what is usually the first entry point of any web marketing campaign and that's the opt-in form. The opt-in form can take on many shapes and sizes. You could offer a white paper you've written, a free report on how to have the smile you want in less than an hour, how to breathe better, sleep better and live the life you want if you're doing sleep apnea, the nine critical secrets of dental implants, or how to chew better and eat the foods you love.

You can tailor a report that acts as the proverbial carrot dangling in front of your prospects. When they see your free report or they see you're offering a series of emails or they see that you're offering a free webinar or you're offering some sort of informational media – whether it be a report or an email or a webinar or a tele-seminar, some kind of informational media that's going to educate them – in order to get access to this information, they enter their email address. So they plug in johnny@gmail.com and that goes to our system or your system whether you're using AWeber or ConstantContact or iContact. We use Infusionsoft; we make Infusionsoft available to all of our dentist clients because it's such a pertinent part of the process.

So they opt in, they get your free report automatically delivered to them and now they're in the system. Now that you have their email address, you can send them more offers but you don't necessarily want to go right in for the kill. If you're going for the bread and butter general type patients, the barrier of entry is very low: typically you can go for the kill on the first or second marketing piece. You can offer them a $59 first exam and X-ray consultation, get them in the door, find they have a couple of cavities or find they need a root canal or whatever it is, take them to the back, do the procedures right there and you have them right back out the door and you've turned a $59 case into $900. File their insurance and you're done.

If you're looking for elective type cases – cosmetic, implants, sleep apnea to some degree – you're going to have to educate the prospects a little bit more before they decide to pull the trigger. As case size increases, the level of trust required to close that case also increases. If you want to get them to raise their hand, you're going to have to educate them a little bit. Don't tell them how a dental implant works – your patients don't want to know clinically how you place an implant or how you select the size or how you are the best at molding teeth – they want to know what's going to look beautiful and they want to know you're going to do a good job. A few patient testimonials along with some before and after pictures are more than enough to alleviate the concerns of how it's going to look.

The primary fears that patients have when moving forward with larger cases is how much does it cost, will it hurt and how long will it last. A lot of dental websites I go to, they have these educational videos from a big dental company that has a little widget they put on all the websites nowadays for $50 a month. Every time I see that I'm amazed again and again that dentists think patients really want to see how an implant screws into your jaw. That would be like me or you wanting to see how a plumber plumbs under your house or watch a mechanic put on your head gasket or watch a video on how UPS gets your packages from A to B, how they load the packages on the plane and how they fly them to the next destination. None of us care about the process!

We all think our business is extremely interesting. I would love to tell all the nitty gritties of how we do Search Engine Optimization and how we set up the systems we do and how we build and code websites so that we get the results that we do and all this stuff. The truth is, dentists don't care about how a website is coded or how you do SEO. What they care about is new patients coming through the door – is the time and effort we're spending on our website going to generate new patients? That's the only question most dentists want to know.

Of course, there are a few that go yeah, I really like this web marketing stuff and I want to know more about it. Everybody has interests in multiple variables but by and large, 95% of your patients – of your paying patients – are not going to care about how you select the implant or how you put it in the jaw or any of the technical stuff that you as a dentist are very interested in.

I had a meeting with Woody Oakes the other day. I was shooting some videos for him and during the video shoot, one of the things Woody said was most dentists spend more time selecting their handpiece than they do choosing their spouse. I chuckled because that really made sense to me – that really hit home. A lot of dentists spend so much time on the clinical side with continuing education but they never focus on marketing their practice and actually getting new patients in the door. In their defense, this is 2012 – this is July 14th, 2012, and we had the '90s, we had the 2000s, both of them were just absolutely booming – the best 20 years we've had in the past century. Only in the past few years have things changed to where you can't just put your shingle out and expect a steady flow of new patients to come in the door anymore.

When you're marketing to these prospects, don't go for the kill on the first postcard. If you're trying to capture dental implant patients, set yourself up to be that go-to guy and offer them a lot of information. I remember I was sitting – I'll use Woody as an example again – I was sitting in one of Woody's seminars – this was April, 2010, Woody's "Excellence in Dentistry" seminar down in Destin, and one of the speakers got up on stage and said, "You don't want to put too much information on your dental website." It just blew me away that somebody would say that – that somebody would say that you don't want to inform your patients, you don't want to educate them, you don't want to give them all of the information they need to make a decision! You most certainly do! You want to give them everything but you do want to make sure you give

---

them the right kind of information. Your patients don't want clinical, they don't want to know how it works because frankly, you showing them how a dental implant works or how you choose an abutment or what handpiece you have or any of that, none of that answers their concerns.

You've got to get inside your patient's head. Your patients have these concerns that they're thinking about – they have these questions in their head and they might not be asking them. But the questions are going around in their head like your luggage at the airport. If you don't get your luggage off the carousel – off the luggage claim at the airport, it's just going to keep going around and around and around again. You've got to get your luggage off to leave the airport. If you want your patients to move forward with case acceptance, you have to get those bags off the carousel.

Is this guy going to do a good job? That's a question that you cannot answer as a dentist. You can tell them you're going to do a good job, but how much weight does that really carry if you, as the dentist, are the one telling the patient that? I'm sure you say it with a lot of sincerity and conviction, but you're still the person saying it. If I tell you I'm going to build you the best website known to man, you could probably appreciate that but does it have the same weight and carry the same impact as if I have another client say it or as a client saying it about you that you do the best job possible, this dentist is a true patient advocate, he does yadda, yadda, yadda? Of course that's much more powerful! Somebody else saying it about you is much more powerful than you saying it about yourself.

How much does it cost? All your patients want to know how much it is going to cost. Even if you've got the best clinical hands in the world and you do the best work, it doesn't matter – how much does it cost? That's a question that you must be answering on your website if you want to capture these larger elective cases.

Is it going to hurt? Again, you can have the best clinical hands in the world but if you don't address the fears that your patients have, you're never going to move forward. They want to know if it is going to hurt. Is he going to make me feel comfortable while I'm in the dental chair?

All of these concerns you can address in this free report that you offer on your website. Most free reports that we ghostwrite for our clients are 10-20 pages in length – substantial information. We just finished up a 14-page free report for a dentist that's wanting to capture sleep apnea patients. We built him a website just for sleep apnea, we put a free report up on all of the questions that sleep apnea patients want answered: do I need a CPAP machine? Do I need surgery? I have obstructive sleep apnea; can a dental appliance fix that? Your patients are extremely knowledgeable in today's world. This has been a revelation that's come about in the past five years. We've had the Internet for 15 years now – mainstream Internet for 15 years, let's call it 1997. I was a geek, I had Internet in 1993 but most guys didn't get Internet until the mid-late nineties.

We've had Internet for 15 years but up until 2006/2007, we didn't really have widespread broadband access. YouTube didn't come about until 2007. WebMD didn't come about until that same time. Wikipedia didn't exist until that same time. These titans – these giants of information where people can find answers to any questions they want – didn't exist until the last five years. Your patient that used to come into your office and look to you or go to the library or just ask around to get information, now they get online and they Google. One search and they can get on these websites and find all the procedural information that they ever wanted to know. They are this knowledgeable when they come in.

Back to the doctors that put those educational videos on their website showing how an implant drills into your jaw and showing how you prep a crown. It's just madness; it's just not an elegant way to motivate your prospects. Your patients already have all that information at their fingertips. They don't want to know how it works; they've come to your website to see if you're the man or the woman for the job. By telling them how it works again doesn't get them closer to calling you or accepting treatment from you, just plain and simple. If you want to capture the elective cases, the niche cases, not always elective sleep apnea, large cosmetic cases that sometimes insurance might cover part of – all the different niches of dentistry, you have to show the patients that it's not going to hurt, how much it's going to cost and that the work you do is going to last. Showing them educational videos on your website doesn't answer any of those three questions. Frankly, if you've ever watched or seen the statistics on those little educational video things, you'd probably take them off your website today and you'd never put them back. Very few people ever even watch those. We've installed tracking using our new advanced analytics that you've seen on our blog to see exactly where somebody clicks on a page, how much time they spend reading certain areas of your webpage and the numbers on those educational videos. They're just horrible, nobody watches them.

Even the people that do watch them, it's not setting you up as the answer. Your website is an educational tool, but you don't need to educate your prospects on the clinical aspects of dentistry. That's not why they've come to your website. They've come to your website to find a dentist. They've searched for a dentist, they've come to your website because they want to find a dentist, they probably know they need a procedure, they're in pain, they hate their dentures, they know they have sleep apnea, they want cosmetics because they don't like their smile, or whatever their problem may be. They've searched to find a dentist because they have a problem. They've searched for a dentist because they want an answer.

If all you do is offer them the clinical answer of yeah, here's how an implant works: an implant can go into your jaw and it costs $1,200 and there – okay, you've just answered one of the questions that I told you was important: how much does it cost. I wouldn't give away prices, but I would definitely write a very compelling document on how much does it cost without giving away your prices. It sounds silly, but you can answer the question without answering the question.

By showing compassion, that you are concerned for your patients' concerns, that is what's going to win patients. You put videos on your website, you answer the questions they have: what does an implant actually do? How can it be used? What situations is it best in? A lot of dentists won't use minis on the upper. You can give them a lot of information applicable to their situation that's not clinical that will help them make a decision.

You drip this information on them; you've got their email address since they've opted in for your initial report. You drip it to them. Once a month you send them an email. Once a month you send them a postcard in the mail. This is not a massive direct mail campaign that costs thousands and tens of thousands of dollars – these are people that have come to your website, raised their hand that they are interested and **want** more information. If you have 200 people that opt in from your website every month, that means you're sending out 200 postcards a month. What do 200 postcards cost to send out … a few hundred bucks? Printing and postage and everything, a few hundred bucks. Who wouldn't take 200 hot leads for a few hundred bucks a month? The ROI on drip marketing is difficult to track because it is a long sales process and you are doing a lot of nurturing and educating. We've done some crazy stuff like setting a doc up with 50 call-tracking numbers and putting a separate call tracking number in every email. We can prove that it works but of course tracking the ROI is a little bit crazy when you do stuff like that. Generally we just use a single call-tracking number in all of the emails nowadays, which still shows incredible results.

You're keeping your name in front of that prospect until the moment they're ready to buy. They have a pain, they research, they find out you're the guy, they opt in, they get your free report, they like your information, they get your newsletter, they watch your teleseminar, they watch your webinar, maybe they buy your book that we've ghostwritten for you or maybe you've written your own book – we help a lot of docs write their own books. They have all these touch points that you're able to educate and inform them with and then … maybe they decide to live with it or maybe their finances aren't in the right position. Then a few months later, they get their Christmas bonus or they get their tax refund or, God forbid, Aunt Susie dies and they get a little windfall from her estate or her inheritance; now they've got the money to do it.

You drop them an email or a postcard once every two weeks with more information, how you're helping, case studies, other patients you've helped, what those patients had to say. We had a guy that we filmed at a dentist client's office who loved taffy – loved to go to the state fair and get taffy. It was his favorite thing in the world to do. He's had dentures for 31 years, hasn't been able to bite into the taffy and chew it and this doc had done an all-on-4 procedure with immediate loading and instantly this guy was able to go down to the store, buy some taffy and bite into it and he talked about the sensation of eating the foods he loves in his video.

That's the most powerful thing you can do is to reignite the pain of what your prospects are feeling. When your prospects watch a testimonial video like that, the only thing they're thinking about is, "Wow, I love honey crisp apples." Me personally, I love honey crisp apples. I won't buy any other apples; if my wife comes home with anything other than honey crisp apples, I don't eat them. Of course, they're seasonal so I only eat apples for a part of the year.

Everybody has their pain and you have to agitate that pain in order to motivate them to take action, to move to that next step. Don't be that 19-year-old dude that tries to close on the first postcard! If you're going for these larger case sizes whether it's cosmetic or even large bread and butter cases where people have a lot of problems in their mouth and they know it's going to cost a lot of money to fix: sleep apnea, implants, dentures, Botox – any of the niches – motivate and agitate their pain. Motivate them to take that next step. Now you've got more information about them, now you've got their email address and you've given them a free report. The next step is hey, would you like to opt in for our newsletter or we'll send you this free DVD or we'll send you a printed hard copy of our new book if you give us your mailing address. Who's not going to accept a free book or a free DVD if it's offered to them? Especially when it's somebody that they've already opted in to and already got a ton of valuable information from. Now they go for just a little more information and they can get your book delivered to their mailbox for free – no cost. Of course, we're all going to do that. If you knew you were getting something good in your mailbox, you'd give your address out.

You get their mailing address and then you send them that stuff. And then chances are when they put their phone number in, they put in their cell phone. 50%, I think I'm recalling this statistic right, 50% of US households do not have a landline. I'm going to have to look that up and verify that but I remember seeing that number somewhere. 50% of US households do not have a landline. I think there might have been an age demographic on that as well but anyway, a large majority so now you can text to that phone number as well.

You have their address, you have their cell phone, you have their email address: you can text them, you can postcard them, you can email them. You don't want to overdo your welcome; you don't want to hit them more than once every week or ten days. Most times, once a month is very sufficient. In a lot of campaigns, we'll structure them so you send them an email on week two, a postcard on week four, maybe a text message on week six that invites them to a free question-and-answer telephone conversation – basically a party line where you can set up all your patients to call in and answer any questions they have right there over the phone – no risk, no pressure, just a live Q&A session. It's something we've used to great success to bring in leads. **Your marketing should always move them to the next step.** Don't go for the kill, but move them to the next step. Your marketing message needs to be structured so that they're always moving forward toward the goal. When they're ready for the goal, then you can present it to them. After you've hit them with five or six or eight pieces, then offer them the consult or then offer them the $280 or $500 CDP, complete dental physical, or a limited time discount offer to come in and get a procedure done.

If you're trying to drag in the larger cases, people that haven't been to the dentist in 20 or 30 years, they've got thousands and tens of thousands of dollars of problems in their mouth, they're very fearful of the dentist, which probably started this whole vicious cycle of avoiding the dentist – you're not going to drag those types of patients in with a postcard that offers them a discount or a free consultation. That's why they've stayed away in the first place because they have a fear of the dentist or they don't want to be made to feel guilty. Until they have a real intense pain, they're still going to keep avoiding. If you can offer a no risk, low risk way to educate them, show them that you're the right person for their job and inform them about how you're going to help them, how much it'll cost, how it won't hurt and how the work that you do is going to last a lifetime, you'll be the guy that earns their business.

That's all for today's episode. I hope everybody was able to get some gems out of this podcast. If you have more questions or would like more information about what we do to help dentists find more patients – find the types of patients and cases that they want – the first step is to download our Dental Website Audit. It's available at www.SmartBoxWebMarketing.com That's all for today. Colin Receveur here checking out. It's a beautiful day with sunny weather; I'm about to play 18 holes of golf. Keep moving forward.

Chapter 9

The Five Developmental Steps of Drip Marketing

Word Count: **2820**
Approximate Time to Read: **6.3 minutes**

Before you can begin using all of the superb drip marketing tactics, you have to develop or build a good foundation for them. **The very first thing that you need to do is develop an up-to-date database of your current patients, former patients, prospects and referrals.** This is going to help you understand, which groups are the appropriate ones for specific initiatives.

Let's return once again to your drip marketing campaign based around your all-new dental implant capabilities. That information would be of value and interest to a broad number of patients and prospects including those with missing teeth, crowns, bridges, and dentures so you could use your entire database to begin marketing.

On the other hand, if you are going to do drip marketing for only new dentures, you would have to structure your database to identify those patients with dentures and any prospects who would have an interest.

Basically, you will want to design the database in a way that lets you know as much as possible about the individuals in order to make the most of specifically targeted marketing.

This means **the next step is to identify your target audience and their specific needs.** This is going to be relatively easy if you have created a very accurate database. If you are a start-up office or have only a small number of patients, you will find that a basic plan for marketing will begin to generate the names and contact information that you need.

What is a target market? In brief, your target market is the group or groups of consumers who would have an interest in your goods or services because they fill a need or a want of the consumer. As a dental professional, you have skills and knowledge that everyone already needs, so **your goal is to make your target audience want to use your dental office to meet their needs.**

"Okay," you say, "give me an example of a clearly defined target market!"

Actually, that is very easy for dental professionals because they tend to have a local or regional audience. You can say that you want to target potential patients or prospects who need dental implants within a 35-mile radius. THAT is a target market. If you say, "anyone who needs dental implants," you will not be able to market the services as effectively.

This leads to **the third step of creating a defined market strategy.** This can only occur after you have identified the specific needs of the target audience and identified how you will go about communicating with those who want such services. For example, you identify the need for dental implants and then develop the strategy for getting your prospects to choose your office to provide this service. Your strategy includes emails, direct mailings, social network updates, and a video series about implants.

None of these plans can move forward; however, until you have done the fourth step: **creating your budget and very detailed calendar for drip marketing.**

Along with the final step, which is to: **create and incorporate your plans for following up with prospects and patients.**

This is a lot of work, but it is good to remember that drip marketing (and the tools used to do it) tend to eliminate a huge amount of the actual, manual effort required for success. This is because there are a lot of options for automating once the preliminary database work is done and the materials drafted.

For example, if you spend the time breaking down your email and contact database into clearly defined parameters such as:

- Referrals
- Prospects
- Patients/Past Patients
- Patients who have spent over $1500 in the past two years

… you will easily streamline the work of drip marketing and target marketing. If you have also worked to create a strong strategy that relies on the different tools available such as emails, direct mail, social networking, and follow-up communications, you can develop your calendar of "events" that will ensure you are on top of each possible conversion or sale.

In order to really begin to understand all of this, we need to look at the individual tools that can be integrated into the tactics identified above. We'll begin with the one activity known for helping to develop a database of potential patients or to get new interest from former patients – advertising with lures. Before we do this, however, let's take one last moment to address the definitions of the entries contained in your database: referrals, prospects, patients/past patients.

The Names in the Database

The **referrals** are going to include the people who heard about you from others. This could be via word of mouth from a patient or past client, or it could be from some of your marketing efforts for another service. You need to establish a protocol that harvests specific information from anyone who contacts you, whether they use an online form or simply call your dental office, you should be gathering the following:

- Full name
- Mailing address including city, state, and zip
- Email address
- Home and cell number
- "How you heard about us"
- The services or products they are interested in hearing about

When you get such basic information from any inquiry, you will be able to add this person or household to your database and use this information to include them in any of your "drips."

The **prospects** are those who have already contacted you at least one time in the past and who are always to be viewed as potential patients.

The **patients/past patients** are just that; you should view them in the same manner as the prospects in terms of contact and special offers. You should also be sure that your patients and past patients receive the "niceties" such as newsletters and informational materials. You will use this database in the ways already mentioned including direct mailings, social media, emails, and CRM (Customer Relationship Management) software such as supplied by Infusionsoft. Before we begin an in-depth look at those methods, let's focus on that truly potent way to grab the eye of a potential patient – a free gift!

Advertising with Lures

We already mentioned drip marketing helps to establish you as a true authority on dental issues in your patients' and prospects' eyes. Your "drips" are going to constantly communicate your expertise in specific areas. This helps them to begin viewing you as the "go-to" solution for any needs of that kind.

Can You Further Establish Yourself as an Expert?

Through the use of free reports, printed books, white papers, eBooks, videos, and newsletters, you can give away very valuable information that will allow you to "reap" a huge harvest in the future. Remember, as you use these freebies to draw new prospects to your site, you will also be gathering their information. For instance, you should always have a page of blank fields that must be completed before the gift is sent their way. This is the best method for building the database because it allows you to make the informational fields you need to know about the prospect mandatory for the electronic filing of the form for use in your drip marketing. For example, they cannot "submit" the form successfully in order to download the freebie until they give full contact details, an email address, and indicate how they found your site or the landing page for the giveaway.

Also, we cannot overlook the ways in which your social networks can be used to offer up free materials too. Though several following sections are entirely focused on social media, we will mention here that you can use Facebook, Twitter, LinkedIn, Google+, and many other networks for giving away materials that reinforce trust, establish you as an expert, improve your position in search engines, and continually increase the size of your database of prospects and/or patients. For example, you can create a tweet or status update that directs people to your blog with a "Free Book on Dental Implants," etc.

Give Away the Goods and Freebies

So, how is it done? We'll operate on the assumption that you have **already** developed a website for your practice and have also implemented many of the basic marketing tactics. This means you have done a lot of SEO work, created many links and backlinks through blogs and articles, purchased PPC ads, worked with a service like Google AdWords to ensure that your site is performing at optimal levels, created a blog, made a YouTube channel with a library of informational videos, claimed your Google Place page, and developed social networks (or at least made professional pages within each of them).

The Three-Step Opt-In

You are probably also using a three-step opt-in process that takes baby steps toward earning a potential patient's trust. That would be to get a Facebook "like" from them, obtain their first name and email address, and then obtain their mailing address and phone number. We look at this a bit later but it is something to remember when first designing your giveaway sales funnel system.

How Do You Get the Phone Calls? (The Fourth Cup of Tea: Trust)

If you have done most of these things, you are probably getting a good position on the search engine results pages but that doesn't mean that you are getting a lot of **conversions** from prospects to actual patients. This is because the three-step opt-in progression mentioned above is the same as that first and second "cup of tea" we mentioned earlier. Those steps are going to qualify as primary points of contact but they will not always help to establish trust and convert a website visitor or potential customer into an actual patient at your dental office.

One of the best and most assured ways of changing the tone of that conversation, however, is to give the patient something of value and yet, ask for very little in return. For example, as a dental professional, you can easily find a way to create any of the following products.

- **Digital products such as eBooks, infographics, and documents** that are free and shared freely with others. Remember, these are great places for inserting links back to your website or blog.

- **Free reports, useful articles, white papers, and newsletters** are also good giveaways when they are about specific subjects. Again, these are good for inserting links and backlinks within the byline areas of the pages. Newsletters are also a good "invitation" to remain in contact with subscribers and for promoting related services or products.

- **eBooks and/or printed books** have already been mentioned, but you can use these in ways that are much more diverse than other digital products. For example, you can make sample documents that offer only a segment of a book, which works as a teaser. This means that visitors get the book for free just by clicking on a link, but have to follow a special link embedded in a page of the teaser to head directly to your website or blog. It is here they will need to register to get the file download of the whole book. The link to the teaser can be passed around freely because it is only when the reader wants the full book that you will harvest their contact information.

- **Guest posts on blogs and other sites** that offer free "products" within your byline. For example, work with another dental professional (usually not one in direct competition with you) to do blog exchanges. You can each offer copies of free reports or eBooks in the bylines of each other's work, with links that take readers to your site for more information, etc.

- **Subscription-only videos** are also easily made and require the viewer to submit basic contact information in order to "enroll" in your free video course on a particular topic. For example, you might make a series of videos entitled "20 Days to Healthier Teeth and Gums" or "How to Brighten Your Smile at Home," in which you could be selling services and products, enhancing your SEO, and generating conversions from your subscribed viewers.

- **Surveys on your blog or social networking pages** that give participants a free gift. For example, you could give a discounted teeth whitening coupon to anyone who completes the survey. In the page about the survey (whether it is on Facebook, Twitter, or in your blog), you will explain how the information obtained is to be used and published. For example, you could create a five-question survey on a relevant dental subject, compile all of the statistics, convert them into a chart, and publish it to your site. You would then send a message to everyone who participated and include a link to those results. By offering a discount, you are giving away something in exchange for the participants' time and obtaining some vital information about your potential and current patients.

- **Presentations and webinars** that are of value to your potential patients. You can easily take all of the text from one of your blogs or articles and turn it into a slideshow full of infographics and clips that promote the benefits of one or more of your services. You can market this free presentation on your blog, social networking sites, video channel pages, or in the "News" section of your website. Visitors can click the link, give their contact information, and receive the presentation as a download. They get the ability to use the materials, share them with others, and learn of the benefits of your expertise in exchange for providing their contact information.

- **Traditional gifts** that include exceptional prizes and opportunities. You can easily run contests and promotions on any of your social networks, blogs, or website pages. For example, people love electronics, gift baskets, and free services. You could use this sort of traditional giveaway to promote one particular area of your practice or to alert patients, past patients, and prospects of some new opportunities.

Any of these items will work wonders for attracting a somewhat steady stream of visits to your website, blog, social networks, etc. The best thing is they will also begin positioning your dental practice as a go-to solution that is trustworthy and professional. This will come automatically when you effectively use all the tools of marketing and advertising such as social networks, emails, etc.

While you may be wondering just who is going to manage all of this sending of eBooks, gifts, etc., you need to know that you can actually have all of this done automatically. This will be fully explained in the next chapter on leveraging autoresponders but it helps to know there really are comprehensive solutions that can track and facilitate your free offers.

What if you don't want to pay for software or services that do this for you? The problem with the manual approach is you will have to create extremely strict protocols and schedules and then find a way to stick with them. Don't forget: time is money! The time it would take someone to follow through with your schedule of responders will not outweigh the cost of autoresponder software, with a lot fewer headaches!

Here's How the Free-Gift Scenario Works:

1. Choose your giveaway product (this means drafting an eBook or purchasing a gift) and choose, which of your online locations to promote it: email, direct mailing, blog posting, etc.

2. Track the requests for that freebie by manually obtaining all of the submitted information from email replies, direct mail responders, blog communications, and any other way your prospects are receiving your freebie.

3. Send out the digital file or the physical product promised. Create a system that tracks this process and prompts you to do the follow-up, as necessary.

4. The follow-up could be as simple as an email asking if they have received their gift and what they thought about it, or it could be some sort of sales follow through such as a call asking if they would like to have a consultation with you about the procedure or dental product being promoted.

5. Finally, monitor the ROI on your efforts. This may seem costly to do for a few prospects, but what you may not realize is most drip marketing campaigns will run for a year or more. Over the course of that time, you will likely have several hundred prospects!

Because you are already a full-time dentist, it is not likely that you will want to take on the full-time job of handling this one area of your drip marketing. This is why we strongly recommend the use of software and services specially designed to make this much easier and far more successful than what you can do on your own (more on this later).

Chapter 10

Leveraging Autoresponders

Word Count: **9121**
Approximate Time to Read: **20.3 minutes**

"Colin has mastered Infusionsoft and is just easy to work with.

"Colin is also managing our monthly email newsletter that goes out. I honestly have struggled for years and years with our CRM software called Infusionsoft and I just never could get past 'go' with it. Colin has taken that over and mastered it so we're doing some ongoing email campaigns now, as well. "

~Maxwell R. Gotcher

"Automatically being able to drip on a dental patient through your website is just awesome.

"The metrics and analytics that they supply to find out where the patients came from – what they want, the types of offers that attract them – being in a marketplace, it's not just in Texas where we are but all over the United States, makes a huge difference because it's different from area to area. When you start getting these cookie-cutter little deals that they charge you just a small fee upfront, you're getting what you pay for – which is absolutely nothing."

~ Michael P. Abernathy, D.D.S.

"The first thing I was most interested in was your ability to do the autoresponders. Other companies couldn't do that. I knew that because I've been in business and marketing. I really wanted to be able to track the patient when they click; I wanted to be able to stay in touch with them, and no one else, to my knowledge, did that.

"First and foremost, you seemed to grasp what was needed and that's staying in touch with the prospect."

~ David Dinsmore, D.D.S.

What Can Autoresponders do for a Dental Drip Marketing Campaign?

It is important to know the terms "follow-up sequence," "autoresponder," and "drip marketing" tend to appear together frequently. The first two terms are virtually the same thing, their purpose translating to nothing more than you, as the dental professional, **presenting your offer(s) to your website, blog, or social networking visitors**. The best feature about them is the communications and offers that you extend are actually with the permission or per the request of the prospect or potential patient!

Let's do a simple illustration of how this works. (This is where that "three-step opt-in process" mentioned earlier will enter the equation.)

1. You work with an autoresponder program or firm that helps to improve your web presence within social networking sites and blogs.

2. They create what is known as an opt-in page for your free offer or for more information about a specific issue. This is not the homepage of the website but is a landing page that is added to the site and reached only by a special link sent via email or posted through social networks.

3. When a visitor views that page and submits their contact information, this will trigger a series of automatic (and completely personalized) messages or communications with the prospective dental patient – with the goal of eventually converting them into an actual patient.

4. A good service will use any array of communication styles their dental patients want. For example, there can be emails, pre-recorded phone messages, direct mailings, postcards, letters, gifts, and more. The point is the sending of these items will be done according to a schedule that is very attentive to "recency." This means that the time spans between the follow-up communications is not too short OR too long. If you flood someone with too many offers or materials, they will simply use the opt-out link in one of the messages to stop receiving your correspondence, but if there is too much time between communications, you run the risk of a prospect forgetting about you altogether.

5. The autoresponder will also create a method of tracking the effectiveness of the message or offers, allowing you to make necessary changes for the highest ROI. This is not as simple or non-essential as it might sound. For example, the tracking technologies available in web and voice communication can indicate the precise email, giveaway, or message that your prospects have responded to, allowing you to track them and the revenue those patients have given to you down to the penny, giving you a very clear indicator of your ROI on each drip marketing campaign.

6. These systems use something known as CRM to monitor when a patient is going to be removed from the database altogether (if they opt-out of receiving messages), changed from a prospect to a patient, or moved up in terms of the frequency of their communications. For instance, some of the best tracking software knows when a patient follows up on an offer and then increases the amount of communication, but can also recognize when none of the offers have been accepted and decreases the level of communication.

We are going to look at social media in a later segment, but for now, it is important to understand that although **you will want to do a huge amount of your drip marketing through your social media**, you probably will not want to fully automate this. Managing social networks is a big issue and something that you can find professional support with, but one thing you don't want to do is depersonalize a social network by having an autoresponder reply to every new friend, follower, connection, etc.

For example, let's say that you did use an autoresponder to follow-up with every new follower on Twitter. Even if you drafted a very personalized and "human" sounding response, your Twitter timeline or feed would reflect that same message over and over again. This is not a good image to project. Instead, you could make plans to direct message (DM) or @ mention them, retweet them, or simply follow them.

Autoresponders are meant to instantly begin the process of establishing trust and demonstrating that you are looking to provide prospects or patients with a solution to their dental needs. This means you have to keep everything as personalized and "real time" as possible if you hope to win out over the competition.

Differentiating Yourself from Your Competition

Let's just consider some simple facts about marketing:

- Marketing is intended to understand what is important to the TARGET AUDIENCE. In other words, THEIR needs, wants, and desires, and NOT YOURS.

- Your marketing should create the anticipation that your business will EXCEED the expectations of potential patients, but will also exceed the expectations of the dental industry in general.

- Your marketing plans should send out messages AROUND THE CLOCK. The messages should stand out against the other marketing campaigns for your area without breaking the bank.

How Does This Tie into Autoresponders?

If the modern dental patient can be looking for better, more affordable, and faster solutions to their needs, and can do so on a 24-hour basis thanks to the Internet, you want your marketing plans to be out there pulling in as many of them as possible. Just as they are looking for answers in real time, your autoresponder is going to reply to them in that same way, creating the connection (in their opinion) that you are a realistic solution to their needs.

For example, a potential patient hears about dental implants and begins doing an online search on their mobile device to learn more. Their preferred search engine provides your information in the first page of results because you have done all that you can to improve your ranking. They browse around your site and request further information on dental implants (which you have cleverly developed a strong drip marketing campaign around). They submit their request for information, get an immediate email reply that the materials are on the way, and also get the link to their free eBook immediately as well. This means they have ALL of the answers they need as soon as they visit your site AND the answers have been phrased to position your dental office as the best solution.

Choosing Enhanced Responses

It is important to remember automation is not all about canned or stock messages that come only in the moments after a prospect or patient acts on one of your offers, communications, messages, etc. Consider that one of your marketing goals is to EXCEED EXPECTATIONS. This means autoresponses should also include:

- Specially timed messages that can include birthday greetings, reminders of upcoming events, release dates for new eBooks or freebies, etc. All of these direct messages should be designed to deepen relationships.

- Triggered messages – you can opt to use motion sensor technologies that trigger an automated response whenever your patients interact with your site or pages in a certain way. For example, if they visit your page on Smile Makeovers, you can have automated messages sent about complementary services such as teeth whitening, etc.

- Offline options that include things other than emails. For example, you can follow-up a request for more information about dental implants with the mailing of a substantial brochure or printed eBook about them. This sort of relationship building is often known for having one of the highest response rates.

- Workflow functions that keep things under control such as updating databases based on an individual patient's behaviors. For instance, a prospect that converts to a paying patient has to be transitioned from one category to another. There are automated programs that can do these tasks based on recognizable patterns in autoresponses. (This is often called CRM, and is well worth the investment simply because it is an optimal approach to managing patients and your drip marketing efforts. We discuss this a bit more in the section on Infusionsoft.)

Now you have a good idea of what you can use autoresponders to handle and why you really must integrate them into your drip marketing plans. Simply put, they are the core of a drip marketing campaign because they can allow you to respond instantly, keep prospects "warm" and active, and establish a deeper personal relationship between your dental practice and your patients or potential patients. They are capable of being fully tracked, meaning you will understand your ROI and get a clear view of precisely what your dental patients need and want.

Email Campaigns

Using email campaigns seems like the proverbial no-brainer. This is especially the case when you have taken the time to organize and shape your database, but this is the point in time when things usually fall apart.

Why? You cannot just type up a quick email about your newest services or products and send it out to everyone who has been good enough to supply you with their address, nor can you use some sort of template email to send out a blast to your database either.

For one, you have privacy to consider – not everyone wants to receive unsolicited emails offering your dental services or products, and you have to consider how you will go about concealing all of the different email addresses.

Also, you won't have an effective way of ensuring that the emails were delivered or of tracking, which emails your prospects and/or patients have responded to. Additionally, most standard email services do not supply commercial patients, or even personal email accounts, with tools that measure "click throughs," email opens, and more.

Naturally, not all of your emailing activities will be the direct approach or solicitation types. There will also be the need for emailing options that fall under the autoresponder category. Thus, we can come to the conclusion that not only will email marketing need to be designed to accommodate a bit of "general" communication, but also to function as a two-way channel for communication.

Because of this, **it is important to ensure you have access to the following tools for email marketing:**

- Email blasts or broadcasts
- Full email autoresponse service
- "Drag and Drop" email developers or builders
- Spam checking or scoring
- Web forms and form building tools
- Direct mail, voice, and fax options
- Reporting

Not a lot of software packages or services offer an all-in-one solution, but we will review Infusionsoft, which can help to streamline your email, and also consider a few other services and opportunities for comprehensive email marketing. We recommend this sort of solution to those who have already cleaned up their databases and who have started creating materials to post on their website or to use as lures.

If you put it into the "three cups of tea" context, an email can operate on each level: the first meeting of strangers, the second meeting of acquaintances, and the third meeting of friends with the goal being to ensure that the relationship is developing in this way at each step. This happens when you understand the different kinds of emails and what they need to contain. It also happens when you know how to go about most effectively utilizing email options.

Different Kinds of Email

You need to understand that the autoresponders are all about the creation of trust and the establishment of your customer service policies. Not only can they help by sending out very targeted **response emails** to follow-up on any opt-ins or inquiries, act as a virtual representative, and pass on a very specific message, but they can also be totally personalized. **This is one of the essential facets of any type of email campaign: you must incorporate what you have learned about the individual prospect/patient and their needs and wishes (as the target market).**

The email response and the email communication offers and information will all have the same look and language, even though their purposes are not always the same. Because of this, you have to constantly build the same sort of language into emails and autoresponses. For example, you want all communications to be very clean and professional, but you also have to choose phrasing and wording that cultivates a personal relationship. By doing this, you will be able to interact with a very wide variety of prospects and patients who need your services, reinforce the positive features of your brand, and yet, allow all of your patients and prospects to feel that they have made a very well-informed decision.

How? The basic ingredients of a potent email include the following details obtained from your online forms and links:

- Name provided in the online forms

- Information that is customized based on details provided in the online form
- Cross selling information based on details from the online form (i.e., inquiries about smile makeovers can have a line about teeth whitening).
- Opt-out link that lets them instantly end communication based on their online form submission
- Links to relevant information, social networks (including buttons to "Follow Us on Twitter," Facebook, etc.), and blogs

Incorporating this information into your emails will give you the maximum amount of control over the message and provides for good tracking. It also gives you the peace of mind that each email is providing small drops of information, building your relationship with clients and prospects within your drip marketing.

Fitting Emails into Your Plans

You now understand what emails should contain, and you also understand that they can be a primary point of contact or a response to a contact initiated by the prospect or patient. How then, do they fit into drip marketing plans?

Essentially, email is **one of the tools** necessary for drip marketing and YOU get to decide WHEN and HOW it is used. This takes us back to the need for a marketing calendar and a comprehensive plan for drip marketing a specific service or product. Remember, you are always going to have a target market; you will know exactly what that market needs and will attempt to demonstrate how your dental practice is the best solution for that need. This simply means you must **use emails to communicate the information your prospects and patients require** while using language and features that continually emphasize that you are an optimal choice.

The Need for Tracking

How do you know if your emails are working? This is going to be done via a range of tools. You can start with software and services that track the responses to links sent in emails. For example, when you work with software to develop an email campaign, that software can be prompted to track when a link is used, who used it, and how often they actually click links in your emails. This software will then promote that email address to a category indicating their interest. The software can also work in the other direction and track how infrequently someone clicks on the links, thereby recognizing when a contact is not responsive.

You can also use Google Analytics to track email campaigns through a process called "link tagging," which involves the manipulation of the links in your emails. When a prospect or patient opens the manipulated link from your email, Google Analytics takes the details from the special URL and creates a digital cookie. The cookie is then stored to their computer where Google Analytics will be able to then associate actions taken on your website by that particular person and relay that person's activity back to you.

One last thing to consider is the need for spam checking. This is a method of measuring how easily your emails may be blocked, rejected, or filtered out by spam software in your recipients' email systems. Because spam is such a problem, a lot of email providers have implemented radical filters that scan incoming emails in order to identify specific triggers or terms. For example, the filters may look at the way the email is formatted, assess its language and phrasing, and even review the writing style. If it considers the email to be spam or overt solicitation, the filter may toss it into the recipient's spam folder where they may fail to get your message. Fortunately, there are software options that will review any email that you create and give it a grade or check for its spam factor. This is something to take into serious consideration when choosing any automation software or drip marketing services.

It may sound confusing, but link tracking is something many business sites do in order to conduct basic tracking on their emails and customer management. Because it is time consuming and a bit complicated, we once again recommend the use of software that does all of this without a lot of additional steps or processes; Bit.ly and Google Shortlink (goo.gl) are both great to use for this.

Tying Up Emailing

Your dental practice needs to rely on email campaigns to drip market products and services to prospects and patients. You will want to deliver these messages to the target market at the right time in order to be effective. This means you need to personalize the messages based on what you know about the target market and also approach this market in a professional and appropriate manner.

Using emails is one of the most direct forms of communication because so many people now view it as their primary point of contact. We don't hand out mailing addresses as often as we do email addresses. When your patients and prospects give you their email address, they expect to have at least one email from you.

This also means a dental professional will have to create a schedule for sending out email blasts or broadcasts, and will also have to design independent programs of response and interaction with individual target audiences. Consider making drip marketing campaigns for specific products and services like smile makeovers, cleanings, dental implants, etc. Then use software to manage each email feature for the individual campaigns. This will allow optimal two-way dialogue and tends to generate the best results.

Of course, this does not mean that people no longer expect physical mailings from their dental providers in addition to electronic communications. This is one of the final components of drip marketing and the next topic we cover.

Let's Not Forget Snail Mail

Good old-fashioned snail mail should never be forgotten. It is one way to provide your prospects with tangible proof of your professionalism, interest in providing them with service, and your expertise. It is done best on a fully-automated basis. For example, a snail mailing could include books, DVDs, sugarless candy, gift cards, toothbrushes, coupon books, printed materials, postcards, newsletters, or letters, among other materials. The trick is to know how to get the materials in the hands of the prospect or patient in a timely manner. It is also necessary to understand the appropriate time to do broadcast mailings too.

This means there are two kinds of mailings that drip marketing requires:

- The contact mailing that sets the stage such as postcards announcing new services, promotions, etc. These are mailings done directly to the target market.

- Specific or per-request mailings. These are mailings that might be the result of an online request for more information or when a customer accepts a lure such as a free book, prize, etc. These are done directly to the individual prospect or patient.

Who handles these mailings? Generally, you as the dental professional will play a role in deciding upon the content and text, but it is advisable to have the printing, processing, and mailing done through a fulfillment house or printing service. By doing your fulfillments this way, the mailings will be completely automated and taken off of your to-do list. Infusionsoft can manage this for you, hands free.

Here's an illustration: you become fully certified to do dental implants and decide to market this new service to all of your patients and past patients as well as to your list of prospective patients. You work with a drip marketing firm to develop a campaign for the dental implants. This campaign includes two physical mailings of post cards that are timed to 12-week intervals. These will correspond with an email campaign, blog posts, and social networking alerts too.

For instance, your calendar may look like this:

- **Week 1 (The 3-Step Opt-In Phase)** – Create the landing page for your new service on your website. Embed a link to a coupon for a free consultation or simply create a redirect to your online appointment page. Once the landing page and all of the ground work is completed, you can begin with an email blast to your entire database with information about dental implants and new service offerings. Also, make posts on Twitter and Facebook about the new services with a link to the landing page.

- **Week 2** – Release a video tutorial about the incredible benefits and affordability of dental implants. Your social networks are used to alert prospects and patients of this video.

- **Week 3** – Do a postcard mailing about the service with details about contacting the office for a free consultation to see if dental implants may be a good fit for them.

- **Week 4** – Use this week to assess the results thus far.

- **Week 5** – Submit articles about the benefits of dental implants to article directories and be sure they contain links to your landing page. Also, be sure your blog is focused on this service during the first 12 weeks of this campaign, but only update the blog once or twice during that time.

- **Week 6** – Post a snippet of your video to your Facebook wall or to your blog with an update about the "success" of your new service.
- Proceed with this plan for at least a full 12-week period.

Remember, throughout this time, you will have to follow through with any lures you've used such as eBooks on dental implants, coupon books for other services, etc. A good drip marketing service can ensure that most of these tasks are automated and handled for you, particularly the snail mail components.

By now, you may begin to recognize that marketing your dental practice could easily become a full-time job and in the super-competitive dental markets, it is almost a good idea to find full-time help. Fortunately, you don't have to take on another office staff member or try to divide up the work between your existing employees because there is software and professional services that can meet your needs.

Rock On with Infusionsoft

Touted as the "**#1 all-in-one marketing automation software used by thousands of small businesses to generate leads and grow sales,**" Infusionsoft provides most of the tools you need for your drip marketing campaigns. Infusionsoft has a full array of email marketing tools, CRM opportunities, auto responding capability, and even some e-commerce solutions. We highly recommend the use of Infusionsoft as a complement to your carefully structured drip marketing campaign because it puts many of the essential tools in your hands.

This means dental professionals will want to organize their database, identify their target market, begin making plans for marketing specific services or products, and start collaborating with a web marketing firm to help them determine how best to enhance their website and use "out of the box" solutions like Infusionsoft.

In the Resources section, you will find some great information about web marketing resources and contact details for Infusionsoft's website too. This will steer you toward most of the tools you need to get things started.

Though we have been discussing drip and web marketing in great detail up to this point, we have not yet focused on one of the most potent aspects of it – social networking. Now that you understand all of the other steps and tools available, we can begin to address this essential subject.

The Patient Attraction Podcast

Episode 011: The One About Automating Your Dental Marketing

Hello and welcome to this week's episode of Fast Thoughts on Dental Marketing. I'm your host, Colin Receveur. On today's episode we're going to cover different methods that you can use to automate your dental practice's marketing, follow-up and referral system so that you can free up staff time in your office, avoid the human error of forgetting to follow-up and to really streamline things in your practice.

The major takeaways from this episode – this is going to be a very meat and potatoes episode – I'm going to show you a lot of real ways to jump in, automate your follow-up, automate your referral system, automate your marketing in your dental practice so that you can keep your name in front of your prospects until they're ready to move forward with case acceptance. Like I said, I'm going to be showing you the exact ways that we do it with our clients and make some suggestions on different pieces of software to use and how to implement it including what you can do today in less than 30 minutes to get started.

The reason for these podcasts is to educate dentists on the technology and of course, the availability of patients on the Internet. Finding those new patients, attracting those patients – especially the ones in your niches, whether it is implants, dentures, sleep apnea, Botox, cosmetic dentistry or even just general bread and butter type dentistry. So let's jump right into the podcast.

One of the biggest time sucks of what I see a lot of dentists doing right now is they have a spreadsheet or they have a big dry erase board in their staff lounge or office, and they're keeping track of patients that have come in or have called or you have done consults for. You're keeping track of where they are in what stage of the sales process, what pieces of material you've sent them, what letters you've sent them, if you've made the two-week follow-up phone call, if you've made the four-week follow-up phone call – it's a very complex system. The biggest problem with those systems is they're prone to human error; your staff gets busy, your staff is sick, you have staff turnover, stuff doesn't get done. The system that you once had implemented and your staff was trained on has fallen by the wayside. Now that follow-up, the internal marketing you were doing, the referral system you had going, has plopped and it's dead in the water.

The first thing I'm going to show you is how to automate your follow-up – how to keep your name in front of your patients without taking a minute of your time, all done automatically. A lot of companies have newsletter signups on their website but the problem with newsletters signups is they're not interesting. Oftentimes, the website just says, "Here, sign up for our newsletter! Enter your email address!" The signup rate for those is very, very low and the reason is: they're boring; there is no incentive really for a prospect to sign up.

You might get some existing patients to sign up because they know who you are and they know what you're about, but for a new patient that doesn't know you to sign up for a newsletter is rare. They might get spam, the quality might be low, there's no carrot that you're dangling in front of them to get them to opt in. The method that we often use is writing a free report. We ghostwrite free reports for our clients anywhere from 10 to 25 page range on a variety of topics. We've written them on sedation, sleep apnea, implants, dentures, the miracle of dental implants, **Don't Die with Your Teeth in a Glass, You Don't Have to Live with Your Teeth in Your Pocket, Stop Snoring** – all kinds of different topics. The purpose of the free report is to give your prospects that carrot, that enticement to give you their email address or their postal address. Once they opt in, you have their email address. You instantly send them (automatically – and I'm going to show you how to do that) this free report. But the contact doesn't end there.

Once you have their email address, you can now send them a letter or a postcard or a text message, if they've given you their cell phone number, once every couple of weeks for **years** after they have made contact with you through your website. There are a number of different pieces of software out there that can accomplish this. There's AWeber.com, there's ConstantContact.com, there's MailChimp.com. We use Infusionsoft, which is a very robust system and has very, very complex set of solutions and technology that is much more than any dentist needs, but works best for our business. When we're setting up for our clients, we actually use part of our Infusionsoft application, which allows dentists to benefit from that kind of robustness, that kind of power without having to pay the big fees associated with actually getting their own Infusionsoft app.

When you buy AWeber or ConstantContact or MailChimp or Infusionsoft, you can set up these preconfigured sequences. What you do is you log in and specify okay, when a person opts in right now, I'm going to send them this email that has this attachment, this PDF attachment or this free report. Then on day 25, I'm going to send them this follow-up email, day 45, I'm going to send them another follow-up email, day 65, I'm going to send them another follow-up email. etc. **This is something you can implement on your website in under 30 minutes.** Go and get signed up for an AWeber account; I've worked with AWeber for years, they've always had a great product. ConstantContact.com has a great product as well, I would heartily recommend either of them. Go get signed up. They do all the work for you, there's no coding, there's no HTML. You sign up, you create your new sequence, you click Edit to write your email and you click Save when you're done and then you say, I want to send this out "X" number of days after this person opts in to get my free report. **You can start building a list and start building your tribe through email systems right now!**

Another tactic we use is to give prospects an idea of what you're really giving them. You want it to have value; you're not just giving them information, you're giving them tremendous value in your free report. We will often create what looks like a book on the website, just a little picture of the eBook or the free report that we're giving away, just so that a prospect can visualize it. We've found this to have a big impact on how many people opt in. There are a lot of different places that can do this. We do the graphics work in house. I know I've in the past used a place called KillerCovers.com; they do a tremendous job. They will create your eBook for you. Basically it's a graphical representation of what your book could look like if it went to print. Put that little picture next to the opt in on your website, creating a little place that says, Opt In To Get Our Free Report: *The Nine Secrets of Dental Implants* or *The Miracle of Dental Implants* or *How to Chew Comfortably and Eat the Foods You Love Again*. You have a little picture of the book next to it and right below it you have a box where they can put their email address in. They opt in and then AWeber automatically sends them this free report and starts dripping them with updated information.

One of the big questions we get is what do I say to them? What do I possibly have to send them once a month with more information in it? The answer is: you want to send them something that has value. You want to give them a lot of information because when you're able to educate your patients, you're going to set yourself up as the expert because they are looking to you for your knowledge and your expertise. Once you have set yourself up as the expert, you have now begun the process of dominating your market area. After you have developed some materials: a free report and autoresponders to keep your name in front of people, you'll begin to see quite a development of a mailing list.

One of the marketing gurus that I follow said last week that "people sort their mail over the garbage can." I thought about it for a second and I thought that's true, that's how I sort my mail. I get it out of the mailbox, I walk to the house, I stand next to the garbage can and I sort it. Before I even go into the house I throw away what looks like trash. That approach is the same way people go through their email inbox. People sort their email with the delete button and if you don't have a good rapport built up with people and your subject line isn't compelling, your email doesn't stand a chance of being read meaning no new calls either.

Education-based marketing is tremendously effective at bringing in patients, educating your patients and avoiding the pram that usually happens in the consult room. If the education begins in the consult room, your patient is getting overloaded with information; they're getting flooded with too much to comprehend. You're trying to educate them, you're trying to show them their options, you're trying to sell them and close them in a 30-minute or an hour setting. If you move the education forward, show them their options, show them what's wrong and why it's wrong and how to fix it, then when they come in to your consult, the only thing you're talking about is price, will it hurt and how long will it last; the three primary questions that your patients are asking in their heads about your procedures. Then you're able to hit the emotional points that will trigger the sale. **That's what you should be focused on in the consult: the emotion of what's going on in their life and in their mouth.**

We've been doing a lot of the Swift Kick critiques lately and one thing I've noticed on many, many, many dental websites is a lot of them have video. Now it's often a lot of template video, which is the same thing as having a template website, but oftentimes in addition to being template video, you have video that is strictly educational. Not educationally oriented from a perspective of developing a relationship with your patient or your prospect, educational from a procedural standpoint. In other words almost an informed consent type of education.

The World Wide Web has exploded in the past three or four years. The Internet has really been around for 10 or 15 years but up until 2007/2008, we didn't have YouTube or Wikipedia or WebMD; these behemoths of information on the Internet. These super information sites haven't existed until the past three or four years! Consumers are very aware of this. I saw a statistic yesterday: 72 hours of video are added to YouTube every minute. **72 new hours of video are added to YouTube every minute**! It's just incredible! Consumers can practically self-diagnose themselves; your patients can go online, they can read Wikipedia, they can read WebMD, they can Google search, they can go on YouTube and find videos of whatever they need to find from repairing their car to building a house to fixing their teeth. If your videos on your website are geared toward that same kind of information, you're missing a tremendous opportunity to connect with your patients.

It's not the procedure that your patients are interested in. Showing a patient a video on your website about how a root canal works or how a crown works, how you prep for a crown or how you prep for porcelain veneers does not move you any closer to case acceptance. The reason is the three main questions the patients are asking: will it hurt, how much does it cost and how long will it last. Showing a patient how you prep for a veneer or crown does not answer any of those three questions! It doesn't tell them how much it will cost, it doesn't tell them if you're going to charge them a fair price or not, it doesn't answer the question of will it hurt or will you hurt them, and it doesn't answer the question of will you do it right. Just because you see a video of how to build a house doesn't mean you can go out and build one. Just because you get on YouTube and watch a video of how an engine goes together doesn't mean you can go and become a master mechanic at Ford. Just because you have a video of prepping a crown on your website doesn't mean that the patient has any faith that you're going to do it right and it's going to last.

By only focusing on the procedural aspect of your procedures and your treatments, you're missing a tremendous opportunity to answer those three questions to connect with your prospects at a much deeper level. Your videos should be educational: you should be telling patients that if they've been turned down for dental implants in the past that you have the solutions for them through bone grafting, different implants and a CAT scan you have right in your office. If you've been to a doctor before and he told you that you need a CPAP machine for your sleep apnea, we have the solution for you! You can come in here and we'll make you an oral appliance that is much like a small retainer you wear in your mouth. If you've been to the doctor before and he has tried to tweak and tweak and tweak your partial and it's still uncomfortable and it still rubs and it still hurts, come see us! We have the solutions for you!

Your patients aren't interested in knowing how you do a bone graft or how a different sized implant works. Now there is a small percentage that is going to be extremely detail oriented and is going to want to know those kinds of details; we're talking 5% or less. 95% of your patients don't have any interest in how an implant screws in or how you do a bone graft or how a sleep apnea appliance moves your jaw and depresses your tongue. That's just not what a patient is interested in knowing, and if they do want to know that information, you can simply explain it to them in another video that you make. But **your video marketing should be geared toward connecting with your patients, humanizing yourself, beginning to develop a relationship and develop trust with your patients.** The procedural aspects don't move you any further toward them calling you and accepting your treatment and giving you money!

Develop video on your website that humanizes you and humanizes your staff. Put video on there that provides social proof of patients that have come in and have had work done and are extremely happy. Patients want to know if it's going to hurt. Well who better to answer that question for a patient than your existing patients? Patients want to know if the dentists charges fairly. Who better to answer that question than your existing patients? Put a video camera in front of them and ask them, "How did you feel about the cost involved? How did you feel about the investment?" Patients want to know how long will it last. Well again, you can answer that question yourself but does it carry more weight if you answer it or does it carry more weight if you have a patient answer it for you? You can say all these things about how great you are but when somebody else says it about you, now it really has impact.

Turn a video camera on and put a patient in front of the camera and ask how they feel about the quality of your work. How do they feel about the investment they made in their mouth? Did they have some cynicism coming into this procedure when Dr. Smith said it would be pain free? How was the experience for them? Ask these questions and your patients will light up like a Christmas tree when you do. You can check out some of our other podcasts and other videos on our website. We go into great detail on how to have a successful video shoot and how to do your reverse dental testimonials so I'm not going to dive into that too much here on this podcast. I think podcast 002, maybe 003, we dove into that pretty deep.

You have to enter the conversation that's going on in people's minds. Patients aren't interested in the process of dentistry anymore than most dentists are interested in the process of how an electronically fuel injected motor works in a modern vehicle. Sell your services by educating your patients and your prospects on the type of information they want to know. **The buying decision by and large is emotionally driven; does it hurt? How much does it cost? And how long will it last?** Those are really intangibles – you can't put them in a wheelbarrow and if you can't put them in a wheelbarrow, it's generally emotional.

We often justify our emotional buying decisions with logic, but the buying decision itself is emotional. If you can educate your prospects – if you can inform them of what options are available and then tell them what options are best for them and then leave it all up to them to choose … For example, "Do you want to go with a traditional denture? Your upper palette's going to be covered meaning you won't have any taste or temperature sensors on your upper palate and your lower denture is going to have difficulty chewing some foods. Or do you want to go with an implant supported detachable? Or do you want to go with the permanent fixed?" Show them the different options that are available and what you can do for them including the advantages and disadvantages of each.

More is Less

A well-educated patient can make a choice amongst a couple of options; don't give them ten choices. There was a very interesting book I read a while back, *The Paradox of Choice* by Barry Schwartz – get it on Amazon, it's a very good read on the consumer mind and how, if you give people too many choices, they don't choose. **Offer your patients choices; a well-educated patient can make a decision amongst two or three options.**

How do you educate them? Education is not a one-stop shop. You can't educate the patient over the phone, you can't educate the patient only in the consult room. Education is a process that not only do you have to serve the food to the patient, but that patient has to eat and digest the information. People process information at different speeds. Some people you can dump a boatload of information on and they process it very quickly and they can calculate and make a decision from it. Other people do not process information quickly: you have to give it to them in small portions that they can consume and digest on their own time. By creating automatic follow-up systems – by sending them emails once every couple of weeks, sending them a postcard in the mail once every month or two, sending them a text message – you're going to develop a connection with your patients. You're going to start a relationship with them because all these communications are going to say "Hey Sally," or "Hey Johnny, it's been two weeks since you requested our free report. I just wanted to check in and send you a little bit more information about dental implants."

You're giving them a continuous feed of information that they can process and digest and learn more about the dentistry and the services you offer. The more educated and the more informed your prospect is, the better consumer of dentistry they're going to be. What you'll find is that while a patient is sorting their emails over the delete button, or their postal mail over the trash can, your best return is on the 4th and 5th time you mail out to people. Your best return on an email sequence is going to be the 3rd, 4th, 5th or 6th email that you send out. We've had some email systems we've set up – email sequences that we've seen the best return from the 9th and the 10th email that we send out.

It's all about branding. It's about repetition. People see your name once or twice, they get a free report from you and they're not really interested: they delete it. Maybe the 3rd or 4th email they skim a little bit over and they say oh well, this guy's got some good information, I think I'll listen a little bit more and see what else he has to offer. Fifth or 6th email, now they're realizing that hey, this guy's sending me a lot of stuff, he must have a lot of information. He must be a pretty smart guy to be sending me all this stuff. He's sending me an email once a month, he sent me a handwritten letter in the mail … I'm going to show you some ways that you can automate handwriting your letters, very, very cool technology.

Let's walk through this all from the beginning: your prospect sees your advertisement in the newspaper, they go to your website, they get a free report from you, they get six emails from you and – in my book, ***How to Stay in Front of Your Patients Until They're Ready to Buy,*** I talk about different studies that have been done, specifically by the National Sales Executive Association, which found that with medium sized transactions of around $2,500, 90% of those sales are closed on the 5th to 12th touch that the salesperson has with the prospect. Some dentistry is going to fall under that and some dentistry is going to fall over that threshold but keep in mind I said the 5th to 12th touch. The 5th to 12th time your prospect hears or sees something of yours or gets a letter or an email, after 5 to 12 times of that, 90% of sales are going to close. That's powerful; if you're giving up, if you're only doing a single mode of advertising, if all you have is a newspaper ad that runs once a week and you don't have a website or you have a website but it doesn't have any automatic follow-up, it doesn't have a free report, it doesn't have any video, your prospects might only be getting a bite or two and never calling you. You're missing a huge percentage of sales on the back end.

There's a pretty cool company called SendOutCards.com that we've worked with. What SendOutCards allows you to do is automatically send out postcards and letters to your prospects. Something even cooler is that you can send in a handwriting sample of your handwriting and they will create a font that looks identical to your handwriting. You type on your keyboard what you want the letter to say, and when SendOutCards prints it, it prints exactly in your handwriting – it's incredible. And even cooler than that, we can automate between Infusionsoft and SendOutCards. We have developed a bridge between Infusionsoft and SendOutCards so that we can do that automatically for you. If you want to send out an email week two, a postcard week three, maybe an email week five and then you want to send them another postcard, we can automatically set all that up to send to your prospects without you ever lifting a finger. That is something you can do as well. I don't know if AWeber and ConstantContact have that kind of integration, but I know we have that with Infusionsoft.

I mentioned a little bit earlier in the podcast about an automatic referral system. Well, let me tell you how that works. With Infusionsoft and with SendOutCards and with automated marketing, you can keep up with your prospects. A prospect comes to your website, they opt in for a free report and now you send them emails once a week or once a month for the next year or two. On the other side of that, say you have a prospect that's come in and completed treatment for orthodontics, maybe an implant case, maybe a sleep apnea case, whatever it might be – bread and butter dentistry even. You want to thank that prospect for their patronage. You, of course, want to find out if they have any friends that may need that kind of work too.

We all know birds of a feather flock together. You can use AWeber or ConstantContact or Infusionsoft with SendOutCards to automatically send them emails and postcards once every three months forever thanking them for coming in and getting treatment at your office.

Maybe they've come in and they've had a large implant case done: you can send them gifts in the mail automatically through SendOutCards. Send them letters and say, "We really appreciate your business. If you have any friends that have trouble chewing or don't like their dentures or are embarrassed about their smile, we'd love to help them. We'll give you a $200 gift card and we'll give your friend $200 off if they mention this postcard when they come in." You've literally created an automatic referral system that you can keep your name in front of your closed patients as often as you want. Generally we say once every two to three months is a fair number. It's not too often that it's intrusive or annoying, but it's just enough that you're always there on the tip of their mind. Once every two to three months, you're sending them a postcard or an email – maybe you send them a Starbucks gift card, maybe right after treatment if you have a large case size, you send them a package of Omaha Steaks. The possibilities are endless. Designing your system has endless possibilities. The point is, you want to thank them for their patronage, thank them for their business, their trust in you and find out what friends they have that could use a similar treatment.

You can use these automatic follow-up systems on the front end to grab patients and hang on to them. You can also use them on the back end as an automatic referral system to keep your name in front of your patients until they're ready to buy. That's really the two major takeaways. SendOutCards, AWeber, ConstantContact, Infusionsoft: I strongly suggest you check out these companies and give them a try. If you have any questions, feel free to give us a call. We'd love to help you automate your marketing and free up your staff and get you guys focused on what you really want to be doing with your staff, which is patient care. As a gift for anybody that stayed on until the end of the podcast, I'd like to invite you to get a copy of one of my books I mentioned it earlier in the podcast, ***The Dentist's Guide to Social Media and Drip Marketing, How to Stay in Front of Your Patients Until They're Ready to Buy.***

The URL you can get this at is www.smartboxwebmarketing.com/products/how-to-stay-in-front. You can go there and get a copy of our book and it's going to show you all of the details about what I've talked about here, examples of drip marketing campaigns, everything you need to know about how to ramp up your drip marketing, your follow-up, your automated follow-up, how to create these systems, how to implement them. As I said, they are super simple to create. If you're not a technically oriented person, find a son or a daughter or a grandchild, even a member of your office that is mildly technically inclined, it's not something that requires any kind of coding or HTML or programming or anything like that, it's all very point and click friendly. It'll set all this up for you and you simply click another button and it sends it to your webmaster and your webmaster puts it on your website for you. It's literally that easy.

I would invite you to check that out and make sure you also subscribe to our podcast. There's a little RSS feed up at the top of you can also subscribe to us on iTunes and there's a button up at the top for iTunes as well. Until next week, Colin Receveur here saying keep moving forward.

Chapter 11

The New Yellow Pages – The Death of Printed Directories

Word Count: **2358**
Approximate Time to Read: **5.2 minutes**

Introduction

If you were born in the 1970s or earlier, you were among the last generation to believe that printed directories were the only resources for obtaining contact information. For example, if you needed a phone number, you would normally head to the appropriate phone book. Why do I say "appropriate"? Directories, like phone books, were printed and organized by local areas and listing types. The white pages were given to anyone who paid for a phone and included homes and businesses. The blue pages were for official entities such as government listings. The yellow pages consisted of businesses and organizations and could often serve as a major source of advertising.

The overwhelming majority of advertising and marketing experts have come to realize traditional print directories are on their way toward extinction. This is due to the Internet and how it can easily provide you with all of the contact information and details you need to find a business, service, or product.

When was the last time you used the phone book to find something?

Let's say a potential patient is seeking a local dental office. They are far more likely to go online or use a mobile device to search than they are to start looking for a printed Yellow Pages book. The old-fashioned, printed, Yellow Pages are dying. Even online Yellow Pages and various directories are far less effective than the major search engines. As the title of this section hints, 97% of today's consumers **search online** before making a purchase or contacting a professional [Nielsen]. This means businesses need to focus their marketing and attention on the web.

This section will cover how to get your dental practice found by the overwhelming majority of the consumer market. To start, we will look briefly at the history of the Internet in terms of searches and search engines, and we'll see how Google has managed to become the dominant engine. Then we'll walk you through some simple steps to show you how you can get the best results possible, so you can be found quickly and easily through your patients' preferred format – the Internet and local searches! So, let's get started on your introduction to "The New Yellow Pages!"

You say "Internet," and someone else says "World Wide Web." Most of us think these are the same things ... but they're not!

The Internet is just a collection of servers (massive computers) that houses all the web's contents (video, images, websites, data, etc) and is networked together. Just imagine your wireless network at home or your LAN at your office – the Internet is the exact same concept, just much bigger! But here's the rub: just like a library has a card catalog and librarian, the Internet also needs a method to organize everything so we can find the resources we need. This is where search engines come in...

Searching the Web

The very first way someone could search the Internet was through the use of Archie or GOPHER (DOS format tools). Then Internet web servers began to appear, establishing some of the more modern protocols such as the famous HTML language. HTML converted the developing Internet into a graphical and image – based place, similar to how we recognize it today. This led to the creation of the now famous "web rings" that would allow someone with a particular interest to click from site to site. **I remember these days!** There would be web rings for everyone from flower enthusiasts to football fans, making it easy for web users to follow a series of interconnected blog pages without the need to search out multiple interest pages. This also led to the creation of different portals that helped people create their own sites and pages without knowing the least bit about HTML (Yahoo! and Geocities were two very popular ones).

Basically, the entire Internet was just a chaotic mess of individual websites. There was no indexing done of the data (think of the library's card catalog) and this meant that there was no such thing as a rank or order by popularity or relevance. Search engines hadn't even been invented yet!

By 1994, the first searching tool was created, the WebCrawler, which would allow someone to search an entire page of text for the specific terms. This led to the famous dot-com boom that created everything from Netscape, AltaVista, Yahoo!, and eventually Google. Quickly, Google began dominating the Internet because it created proprietary systems for organizing and ranking search engine results – beginning with PageRank. From that point, things have been changing quite radically.

The Post-Directory Period

By the time Google began emerging as the world's leader in search engines, the directory system was almost done. The search engines now store and retain information about the individual web pages. All of this information is plugged into an algorithm that assesses titles, headings, and meta tags. This information is then referenced when a web user conducts a search, creating a list of relevant results to give back to the person searching. **This is where a lot of people become confused because they don't understand exactly how the engines determine the best order to list the results.** Popularity, relevance, authority of the site, and hundreds of other factors go into Google's equation for determining this order!

Google controls around 70% of ALL searches. Their algorithm is able to take the many different facets of a website and convert them into a relatively accurate assessment of its relevance to keywords being searched for. Of course, when seeking to get a good ranking in the search engines, you have to understand your position doesn't just depend upon the content on your website. What is seen by a web user on your website only accounts for about 20% of all that SEO entails. Offsite SEO includes things like articles, blogs, links, videos, images, social networks, media files, and more. The BEST SEO includes just the right proportions of each item.

Now that you know how the web basically works – through web spiders crawling through many different pages looking for text, tags, and measurable data then indexing this data to give search engine results – you can begin applying it to optimize local listings for your dental practice.

The Patient Attraction Podcast

Episode 006: The One All About "SoLoMo"

Welcome to this week's episode of the SmartBox Video Podcast. I'm your host, Colin Receveur. In today's episode we're going to talk about SoLoMo: Social, Local, Mobile and why it is the future of dental marketing online.

We have a brand new product we're launching next week and for everyone who stays on until the end of this podcast, you'll be able to get a sneak peak at what we're doing and be able to "cut in line" to get first dibs at it. So, just stay on until the end for more details.

Why listen to me?

If you haven't listened in before, I'm Colin Receveur, head chief at SmartBox Web Marketing where we, simply put, get dentists more qualified patients in the niches they want to promote. Today, we're going to be talking about the latest buzzword that's sweeping the internet: SoLoMo. Goofy word – it's actually three words stuck together: Social, Local, Mobile.

Here's the three topics what we're going to cover in today's episode:

1. **The final nail in the coffin** – See why SoLoMo will drive the YP to extinction.

2. **The evolution of "Hyperlocal" Into "SoLoMo"** and the big changes taking place that you need to know

3. **How SoLoMo is going to change all the rules** for dental marketing

Let's do some quick coverage on the background of hyperlocal. Hyperlocal first came about when users searching for local information on Google were able to be connected with businesses, services, and deals in their area. Hyperlocal was like Web 1.0 and SoLoMo is like Web 2.5, if there is such a thing. So imagine hyperlocal, but on steroids.

Take GPS being on practically every phone, social media integrated into every facet of our lives, and over a BILLION people in the world using their mobile phone as their primary source of internet access this year and mush these three together and get a perfect storm nicknamed SoLoMo.

You know, it's pretty amazing what's transpired in the past five years. You take Google, which launched in the late '90s, went public five years later and now has ten billion in profit and employs 30 thousand people. YouTube, founded in February 2005 and bought by Google in 2006 for just under 2 billion, is now the #2 site in the world, 2nd to Google. Twitter and Facebook all launched in the past decade, billions upon billions in revenue and almost a billion active monthly users. These companies, individually are making more money than companies like McDonalds and GE that have been around for 75 and 120 years!

Traditional marketing, the old school stuff like the Yellow Pages and newspapers, has always dominated local markets. But now, local space is extending far into cyberspace with many more players tapping in. With the YellowPages dying off more and more every year, I expect to see it near extinction within 12-18 months. We've been using our phone tracking to monitor the results and effectiveness of YP since 2004 with various clients and without exception, every year the results have gotten worse and worse.

But back on point. Groupon, Yelp, Foursquare and even retailers such as Starbucks have embraced geolocation and social media elements in their business models and their apps. Groupon and Yelp being mobile and local, but Foursquare holds an interesting niche because they've managed to build a business that sits practically smack dab in the middle of all three tactics. Very cool app.

Facebook and Google have also jumped into the SoLoMo game, allowing your patients to check-in at your practice, which shows up in their newsfeed to all their friends and they can leave reviews and see special deals you're running.

One of the next revolutions in mobile marketing is going to be "geo-fencing," which is a way to actively market to a mobile user in your area. With geo-fencing, you'll be able to **automatically** email or text message a friend of yours on Facebook or a patient who has liked or followed you when they get near your office. You can offer them special deals, or just remind them that you're there. **This is truly going to bridge the gap between brick and mortar and the online world.**

Consumers these days want highly personalized experiences – you know, despite what you read in the news, personalized advertising is very good for the vendor and the consumer. So imagine this: your 80-

year old mother who lives in a patio home is browsing Amazon.com and the ads she keeps being shown are for chainsaws and shot glasses.

Now maybe I'm off base here but I know my mother doesn't have much interest in either of those items but imagine this: instead of indiscriminately showing her ads, Amazon looks at what she previously searched for and viewed, and then displays an ad for new crocheting needles or a quilt or christmas sweaters. Now you have a consumer who's seeing things they are interested in and you have vendors willing to spend more advertising because they are selling more. Everyone is happy.

Your location will soon be as important of a metric to the personalization of your online experience as anything else.

This SoLoMo revolution is not coming – it's already here. Like video, it changes the perspective on how to engage your audience. Your prospects want to see quality content, whether it be through a mobile app, socially, on your website, emails, etc. Gone are the days of "just running an ad" and having patients walk in your front door. Your prospects are flooded with over 3000 marketing messages a day and if you aren't differentiating yourself, you're simply blending in with the background noise.

So as I said in the beginning, we're rolling out a new product next week. Our Swift Kick! Marketing Series, which is a SuperPackage of eight of my books, three dvds and a twelve month subscription to our monthly Gold Elite Newsletter. It's not even been made public yet – you guys are the first ones to hear about it other than a few select clients we've sent it to for early feedback. http://link.smartboxweb.com/swift

With our Swift Kick! series, we're also rolling out a new guarantee: the lawnmower guarantee.

You know, a lot of warranties and guarantees you see all have exclusions, terms and conditions, all that legalese non-sense. Our warranty is very simple. If after buying our products, if you feel like they are garbage, you can run over them with your lawn mower then send back what's left. We'll give you a complete refund. I think if you have confidence that your product is the best, you should offer a completely zero-risk way for your prospects to sample you. So that's what we did.

Back to the Swift Kick!, it has everything you need and when I say everything, I mean everything. From theory to technical implementation, we're giving you the tools, methods, and secrets required to successfully and profitably market your dental practice in this new economic age. This is the most comprehensive and toughest web marketing training series you will ever find.

Whether you're a do-it-yourself marketing dentist who wants to know the ins and outs, a dentist who just wants to do dentistry but wants to be sure your marketing firm isn't taking advantage of you, or you're unhappy with your current marketing and want to learn more about how to ramp up your practice, this SuperPackage has the information you need. http://link.smartboxweb.com/swift

That's all for today. Don't forget about the link to learn more about our Swift Kick! See you guys next week and keep moving forward.

Chapter 12

Establish Yourself on Local Search

Word Count: **1805**
Approximate Time to Read: **4.0 minutes**

Get Started with Google Maps

We suggest you use Google Maps to find the physical address of your office. You may see it just pops up as a location or you might see it shows your address as your actual business. Google is a tremendous aggregator of data. The information it has obtained has tagged your address or phone number as belonging to your dental office and created the listing. You may be really surprised to see there are photographs and reviews available for your office too! These are all reasons to quickly claim your Google Place page and to begin directing a regular stream of attention to it. You start by simply heading to google.com/local/add and signing in with your existing or creating a google account.

Your Google Place Page

You will have to have a Google account in order to begin making your page but Google makes this ridiculously simple to do. As you make your way into Google Places, be prepared because entering your address may show there is already a Google Places page for you!

This is going to be for only one of two reasons:

1. Google has already created a page from aggregated data, OR

2. Someone else has claimed the page!

If it is #1, you can proceed to the page to verify the listing as yours, which requires you go through a process with Google. You reach the verification process only after entering all of the details we are about to cover in the next section.

If your listing already exists, you can still:

● Edit the information in the listing

- Suspend it to stop it from appearing on Google
- Add your business as a new listing if you realize the business you're trying to verify isn't yours

Most of the time, no one has fraudulently claimed your Place page and you can continue to go through the verification and optimization steps. This means you have to ensure all of the data is correct and fill out all the sections.

Creating Your Profile

This is one of the primary tips for success with local listings. Take advantage of every opportunity to supply text, images, categories (keywords) and video too!

Your Place page will have:

- basic information
- how to contact you
- hours of operation
- payment options
- categories (keywords)
- photos and videos
- additional details

Basic Information

On the right side of the page where you enter your info, Google will show you a map. As you type in the details, it will actually take you directly to the map that matches the data. Use this to ensure everything looks as it should and you are presenting not only the Places image you want, but also the Maps image too. As you add details to your listing/page, you will see them instantly appear in this section.

Fill out everything to best optimize your page, and be sure you check the information against other online directories at such places as Yelp, Yahoo!, SuperPages, and more. This is to ensure that the aggregators are all using the same data and that a potential patient is not being misled by one search engine with flawed information. (You can also visit the Universal Business Listing website to see if all of the directories and sites on the Internet contain accurate data for your business. There are some fees associated with this service, but it can be quite useful and save some time.)

Categories

Tucked discreetly into the basic information area is the remarkably powerful and important categories section. Google Places views categories as the way to categorize your dental practice (obviously) or to classify it by the use of recognizable and relevant terms. It will usually suggest categories that seem to be a good match. You are obliged to accept one of their options but you can also enter your own if you feel that is best. You can optimize results by adding up to five customized terms. For example, the site gives you a list of drop down terms from, which you must choose at least one; the rest are up to you. Those remaining four categories should include your keywords used for SEO (Search Engine Optimization) purposes.

For instance, your dental office generates the drop-down category of "dentists," and you elect to have that placed as one of the categories. You can also use "emergency dentistry," "cosmetic dentistry," "oral surgeon," "periodontist," and many more. Make sure; however, these categories are accurate and describe your practice correctly. It is okay if they are very specific, but never include geographical keywords in your categories. Google's policies view any geographic terms as a violation and can delist or block your Places page for such an infraction of the rules.

Hours of Operation

It is not surprising to know that all potential clients appreciate if you let them know when you are open! You can choose a single set of hours for each day, or choose two sets of hours (for if your office is closed for lunch).

Payment Options

Potential clients also appreciate knowing the types of payments options available before contacting your office.

Photos and Videos

Once you get into the photos and videos, you have to be ready to use every opportunity available, but also remember to update some of these items on a regular basis too. Having an opportunity to load up to five videos (through an existing YouTube account) is just like having **free advertising options**. You can make videos about new services, introduce yourself as owner and highlight your staff, showcase products, even include videos of any TV commercials you have made.

The photos give the same option, and we suggest you ALWAYS use all 10 available spots. Failing to upload 10 images means you're not taking advantage of the free advertising space Google gives you! In addition to these issues, keeping material up to date will help with the Google+ social network as well. This is an entity that responds to updates instantly. For example, Hotspot, Buzz, Places, and Profiles are all integrated into Google+; any changes made to your Places page will automatically appear across the integrated sites. When you update information often and stay relevant in terms of your industry, aggregators will gather and disperse this new data on a constant basis.

We suggest you also build links into your Places page using videos and images on your website or through articles and blog comments. This way, you are directing people to a page full of relevant data and not paying one penny to do so!

Additional Details

Use this to the fullest extent possible! It gives you up to ten blank boxes into, which you can type anything you feel would benefit your patients to know. For instance, you can add:

- Facebook URLs
- Brand names of services you provide
- "Twilight" or "Sleep" dentistry
- Senior Discounts
- Better Business Bureau approved
- Other services

It is very important to take advantage of this opportunity simply because it allows you to tell your clients anything you cannot tell them elsewhere in the Places page!

Problems and Solutions

Merging Multiple Listings

It is not unusual for a dentist to find their Places pages or local listings appear in multiples. This may be due to more than one dental professional working in the office and Google (or another aggregator) has created a separate listing. It might also be due to a simple difference in name, title, or mailing address that the aggregators have picked up. There is also a common occurrence with those who are using a call tracking number to test the results of their online marketing – which has led to the creation of yet another duplicate listing.

Can I merge all of them? Yes, in most cases you can. Google is a giant indexing machine. If you have listings at professional dental websites for each of the dentists in your office, the search engines will keep generating individual Place pages, so you may want to occasionally check for new listings. A good "work around" for this situation is to follow one of Google's recommendations on their site: take the time to identify, which of your listings has the most benefits to your business. For instance, if you are the owner of a dental office but one of the other dentists seems to have a lot of positive feedback and citations, choose this as the one to upgrade and merge to.

Does that mean you will lose out on the feedback/reviews on other pages? Sadly, yes. It is best; however, to retain the one that seems to be powering your online efforts. Once you verify and merge your listings, all new reviews will appear under your single, unified Google Places page.

Phone Tracking Numbers

Let's briefly look at tracking numbers – these are a fantastic marketing tools!

In this modern era of online marketing, you can use a call tracking number to find the exact return on your advertising investment – even when they are not web related. We have developed a call tracking solution, known as Zetetics, that helps you to assess all of your marketing efforts in order to determine, which one gives you the best ROI. The issue we sometimes see is that some tracking numbers can lead to problems with Place pages, because they end up creating duplicate listings. This is a conflict that is easily resolved through a merge that also uses that tracking number as the primary page number.

Alternately, the basic information page does allow more than a single phone number to be connected to the Places page claimed and simply entering your tracking number into one of the fields could work too, although not the best solution.

How to File Reconsideration Requests

Let's say you check in on your Google Places page once or twice each week. One day, you go to the site to discover your #1 ranking listing is suddenly at the very bottom of the list . . . or not even appearing at all! This means you have done something (consciously or without any awareness) that is outside of Google's policies. They have either deleted your page or deactivated it indefinitely. You should review their Webmaster Guidelines to see if you have inadvertently broken rules. Once you resolve whatever you believe the problem may have been, you may have to visit their Reconsideration page to begin making amends or fixing the problem; the page is very user friendly. It is vitally important that you get on the issue immediately.

You now understand the importance of claiming and detailing your Google Place page. The best thing about all this? It's FREE! This process from start to finish can take up to two months if Google has to review your listing for any reason so don't wait another day – log on and get your practice seen in local searches!

Chapter 13

Online Reviews

Word Count: **690**
Approximate Time to Read: **1.5 minutes**

We are going to allot reviews their own section because they are an issue of incredible significance! If you explore Google Places, you'll see there are many options for leaving reviews. A Google Places page is great for this because it will immediately display the reviews made directly to the site by Google users AND it will aggregate reviews you get on other sites too.

Recently Google has added the ability to respond to reviews left on your Place page by Google users. However, because Places aggregates reviews from outside sources, you will not be able to respond to any of the reviews that show up on your page but were made on other sites. For these, you need to go to those sites and respond to the reviews there. When the information is posted directly through Google, however, you can respond directly on your Place Page, which we recommend you do.

Because of the limitations outside review sites may impose, we **strongly recommend** getting your patients to leave you reviews directly in Google Places. One prime example of why "taking the easy way" for getting reviews isn't the right way to be doing things was recently put into the spotlight. DemandForce, a company that helps dentists collect reviews from their patients, was banned from Google. This means all the reviews Google was displaying on your Places page with the help of DemandForce were deleted! A lot of time, money, and energy down the drain …

Managing Reviews

This is where we want to remind you about public perception. Though you are asking all patients for a review of your work, you do need to accept that you won't always get a glowing report. Don't let this stop you from asking, however, because the modern world of "sharing" through social networks and many websites makes feedback an important issue.

How to Get Reviews

Though a patient may take the initiative and find your page to leave a comment, we would encourage you to follow-up on any dental appointment with an email that has an embedded link. Ask the patient directly for some feedback and give them a direct link to reach the appropriate page. We often buy a domain name, such as "www. ReviewDrRon.com" and set it to forward directly to your Google Places review page. This way, it's super easy for your patients to remember the URL and get to the right place. Any patients leaving a review will have to create a Google account so don't be afraid to offer some sort of incentive to get your patients to do this – it is well worth the effort.

What is your take on a business with nine positive reviews and one negative review? If you're like most people, you're glad to do business with them! We are more than willing to overlook a single negative comment when we see a lot of favorable responses from dental patients. For this reason, **ALWAYS, ALWAYS, ALWAYS be asking your patients to leave you reviews.** That way, if some day you do get a negative one, it will be "flooded out" by all the positives you have accumulated. The one thing to remember is to avoid entering into a public argument or dialog with that one negative review. Do respond in a dignified way, thanking them or apologizing for their dissatisfaction, but do not engage in a fight! Encourage them to contact you directly and you will resolve the problem to THEIR satisfaction!

Remember, your Places page is not just a geographical or Yellow Pages alternative, but a potent marketing tool. The reviews are a major element of the page and will only enhance your reputation, if used wisely.

The Impact of Reviews

Google does not disclose exactly how much the reviews through Google and aggregators influence the local search rankings but we can say for sure that they do play a major role. A rich and dynamic Google Places page is going to strengthen your online and professional reputation. This means you really should spend time optimizing your page, accumulating reviews, AND directing your patients to this page as much as possible.

Chapter 14
Making Sense of Social Media

Word Count: **4203**
Approximate Time to Read: **9.3 minutes**

Facebook, Twitter, LinkedIn, Google+, YouTube, and dozens of other sites fall under the category of social networks. For instance, YouTube is considered a social network because of its ability to allow people to interact and share information and opinions.

This might lead you to ask, "What EXACTLY is social networking?"

The simplest answer is it's the intentional grouping of individuals into specific groups or circles such as "family," "friends," etc. Though this can happen in the "real world," it is something most often found online in the form of electronic networks in which people very selectively choose their "connections." Let me say this another way: **social media is the new "word of mouth."**

We'll use YouTube again as an example: people subscribe for free to the service and then become fans of specific channels. In this way, they begin to develop networks based on their preferences in music, video, etc. Details about networking are useful to the dental professional considering drip marketing because it means they can reach a fairly targeted audience easily, quickly, and affordably by using the pre-existing social networks. Naturally, the trick is becoming integrated or interactive with specific groups and networks that contain people you can connect with on dentistry. This can be accomplished in many ways, including:

- Harvesting information from prospects or patients when they respond to a "lure."

- Incorporating "Like" or "Follow" links on website and blog pages.

- Using pre-existing contact lists to begin soliciting for Friends and Followers on the social networking sites.

- Using pre-existing contacts to develop a LinkedIn network.

- Before you jump into social networking, however, we recommend you learn about it, how it has evolved, what your prospects and patients might use it for, and how you can apply it to your drip marketing campaigns.

Why You Need Tons of Social Networking

Your drip marketing campaign may rely quite heavily on your social networks in order to help you manage your image, strengthen your reputation, and post news, updates, and information about your practice, but you have to look a bit farther. Remember your basic marketing plans that involve:

- SEO
- Articles and blogs
- Website creation
- Video libraries
- Working to create links and backlinks
- The identification of keywords and the use of PPC ads

These can be affected by your social networking efforts at any given time, and you need to be able to keep things organized, targeted, and integrated. Remember when we mentioned you would learn how to drip information to prospects in a multitude of ways and you would rely on social media to create a true following or online community to, which you are DIRECTLY speaking/marketing? Because you are working so hard to cultivate a trusting and deeper relationship through drip marketing, you need to be sure your marketing efforts are never contradictory, in conflict with one another, or that they somehow confuse your followers.

For example, let's say you decide to improve your SEO through the use of video syndication. This would mean your videos are released through channels such as TubeMogul or Traffic Geyser. This creates backlinks and allows your videos to appear on the main search results for Google.

Though this will help SEO results and put your videos in front of many different prospects, if your syndication is poorly timed, it could end up flooding a prospect with information instead of dripping it gently. To your patients, this could mean they get a Facebook status update about a video, an email about the new video through their preferred syndication site, and get details from one or more of the video sharing sites, all at the same time. This is something that must be avoided and requires the use of a detailed master schedule to guarantee it never occurs.

As a dental professional, you are not going to be able to dedicate the amount of time and thought necessary for such wide ranging and complex planning. This is why we recommend the use of software and professional assistance for your drip marketing efforts, including those done through social media. You will always retain complete control over the message, design, and timing of your communications when working with web marketing consultants. These professionals simply assist your practice with making use of all the available tools in the most optimal ways.

You may say it's easy to create a Facebook Business Page, how hard could it be to figure out the rest of it? But do you know how to avoid failing with the use of social media? Do you know how to go about using it and relay the messages you need to express in the most optimal way?

In the next few sections, we will look at the proverbial "dos" and "don'ts" of the four most popular social networking sites in order to demonstrate how they are best used in terms of drip marketing.

Few things have changed the modern world more than social networking. Social networks (and social media in general) have altered the way people communicate, how we interact, and even how we think of businesses. Social media is everywhere – it's impossible to make it through a single day without at least hearing about one of these networks. However, harnessing the power of social media is a bit harder than you might think. There's a lot to understand here, but this chapter will walk you through social networking and how it applies to your dental practice.

What Are Social Networks?

If you haven't at least heard of the more popular social networks, you've been living under a rock. Social networks have been hugely popular for a number of years, though they did not truly go mainstream until the rise of MySpace in the mid-2000s. Today, there are a number of popular networks out there, but they all serve a similar purpose.

In essence, social networks exist to connect people with their friends, family, coworkers, and others. In the simplest possible example, you sign up for an account, create a profile, and then add others as "connections," "followers," or "friends" depending on which network you're using. Once you're connected to another person, you receive notification of their posted updates, you are able to message and interact with them, and quite a bit more. Some of the more advanced social networks have games, groups, applications, and tons of other ways to interact, share, and connect.

The connection is really what social networks are about. They are platforms for sharing, and they're not just for personal use. Businesses large and small are finding the benefits of social networking. A quick stop on your Facebook account will show you just how many major corporations have a presence here, as well as how many local businesses are using these networks to connect with their customers on an intrinsic personal level.

For businesses like your dental practice, the personal connection is really the greatest benefit. Using social media to connect with your patients and prospective patients allows you to give your office a "personal face." It allows you to stand out in their minds as more than just another faceless business. That's essential in the modern world, as competition has skyrocketed and people's attention spans have shortened.

To sum up, social networks are powerful tools. They allow you to reach an immense number of people in your local area, as well as on a regional, national, or even global level, if you want.

Return on Time Invested

Will the work be worth it? Studies of all kinds have determined that modern consumers go online for information and to find local services. This means dental professionals NOT using social networks are missing out on a huge portion of their potential patients.

Also consider good old-fashioned "word of mouth," which is still a dominant factor in how people make up their minds about services and products. **If we don't stand around our friends' or neighbors' yards exchanging opinions anymore, it is because we are doing so in a virtual way on the Internet**. This kind of word of mouth will direct patients and prospects to your office and will take place inside social networks.

Still not sure it is the right thing for you? Consider some of the following statistics available from the Smartbox Web Marketing firm:

- A survey by the National Research Corporation discovered that one in five Americans use social media resources to find health information and advice.

- One in two people state they trust the website of a health provider, and one in four indicated they are likely to choose their health care based upon opinions stated on social media sites. (There is proof of word of mouth in action!)

- One survey found that 50% of the respondents would be interested in changing their doctor for one that can offer them more access to online services – almost 20% of American patients can't reach their doctor in an efficient way to obtain medical information or make an appointment.

- In the study mentioned above, 81% of the respondents said they would be comfortable with online medical registration and would share their medical history if they could use a secure online service.

- A study from Doubleclick found a growing number of consumers rely upon reviews and recommendations from friends before selecting a local vendor (another bit of evidence that word of mouth is alive and well). This implies a dental professional will want to get messages to targeted groups via Facebook, Twitter, and YouTube in order to reach those most likely to recommend their services to others.

- A different study by Intuit Health found Americans expect their physicians to be easily accessible online.

- Currently, around 85% of Americans use the Internet to research everything regarding their health, according to a Pew Internet Project survey.

Here we see people are trusting a combination of social media information and online information, and they anticipate access to a medical professional through the Internet as well. This means if you are to meet one of the three primary goals of all marketing – to exceed customer expectations – you absolutely must appear on the social networking sites.

Remember, your social networking activities are designed to convert patients, cross sell related services and products, and generate leads or prospects through the use of lures. You can then use those lures to get contact information and permission to begin drip marketing to your new contacts. Of course, this means you must conduct social network marketing in the best way possible.

The Right Way to Network

Even as the social networks have grown in numbers and size, they have also changed quite radically. For example, mobile applications now have liberated people from their desktop or laptop computers and allow social networking to take place in "real time" and from almost anywhere.

As little as five years ago, a person on Facebook would update their status to reflect a mood or thought, but not to "tag" their current location. Today; however, someone can use their mobile device to open a browser or open the Facebook app, log into Facebook, and insert a geo-tag that lets everyone know where they are, what they are doing, and who they are with. Almost any of those details can be converted into links that take the reader of the status update to a new browser page with more information.

This means social networking is not something of interest only to college students or teens who want to stay in touch, but is actually a potent tool for communicating directly and on a personal level with patients.

Popular Social Networks Today

Social networks today truly are "a dime a dozen." There are far more out there than you could ever possibly use. Most of them are not good choices for you. It really pays to know, which ones to focus your efforts for the best return on investment. While there are hundreds of different networks, you really only need to focus on the top four.

Facebook

Facebook is the undisputed leader in the world of social networking. Currently, Facebook boasts more than 500 million active users – that's not including the inactive accounts. About 250 million of those users log into the network on a daily basis. What does that mean for you? Simply put, it means it's the perfect place to develop a presence for your dental office and is also one of the best ways to do a huge amount of targeted drip marketing.

Facebook is not only the largest and most popular social network, but it offers the most tools for business users. Creating a business page here is simple and easy and can also be connected to your personal page, if

---

you so choose. From your business page, you can share updates, news, changes, and other happenings. You can also share videos through your "wall," communicate with others, and track your business' performance through the network's analytic tools. You'll also find that Facebook has an ad system built in. This works very similarly to systems like Google AdWords, but tends to be more affordable.

Twitter

Almost as well-known as Facebook, Twitter functions a bit differently by using limited text updates as the primary means of communication. At its heart, Twitter is a microblogging platform. You can also use this for drip marketing. Of special interest to dental professionals is the majority of Twitter users tend to be over 40, make higher incomes, and have more disposable income than any other social site on the web.

Once you sign up and create an account, you are able to follow people (they'll usually follow you in return). You send out short messages of 140 characters, called "tweets" to your followers. You can also share videos, pictures, and websites through your tweets. The real beauty of Twitter is you can actually start conversations with your followers in real-time. You can also integrate Twitter in your online marketing quite easily: you can highlight specials, new services offered, discounts, and more through your tweets.

LinkedIn

This professional networking site is a good way to reach fellow professionals, find answers to almost any professional question, and get information without a lot of sales speak or commercial hype. LinkedIn operates in a similar way to Facebook, but it has a very different focus. This social network is designed for professionals who are looking for better networking with others in their vertical market, or even outside of their vertical market. While you might not find many direct patients through LinkedIn, it can be a great way to grow your network and draw in new patients indirectly.

In addition, it can be an excellent way to build new relationships with those in related professions – specialty dental services, dental surgery, orthodontics, and the like. The network offers groups you can join to help connect you with more people, as well as to build your reputation as an expert. It also offers a number of other powerful tools designed specifically for business users (as opposed to the consumer focus of Facebook).

Google+

Though still "in the works" in terms of businesses and organizations, Google+ is certainly one of the up-and-coming social networking functions. Not only is this a very controlled social organization, but Google has plans for integrating things like Google AdWords and Analytics with this innovative tool.

You will use these four sites to create a following of prospects and patients to drip market all your blog posts, videos, new landing pages, and more onto. This is going to be done through status updates, tweets, and the like, but it does take planning and organization to do well.

We should also note YouTube and Google as potent tools for social media drip marketing. When you develop a following on your YouTube channel, you begin to have higher and higher position in the YouTube search engine. When you tag the videos properly, you also get a very high ranking in the Google search engine results. This means ANYONE who "Googles" for your dental services is going to see your video in the first page of search engine results, which is going to be a very effective way to get new patients through social media.

Social Networks Vs. Social Bookmarking

For those new to the whole social media scene, there might be some confusion over social networks and social bookmarking sites. While they have a few similarities, these are very different animals. Social networks are more in-depth and focus on providing a specific experience to users.

Social bookmarking sites (Reddit, StumbleUpon, and the like) focus on sharing news, website links, and other items of interest between users. While they are built for somewhat similar purposes, social bookmarking sites are not quite as important for your practice. They can be useful, but they can also be difficult to use. It's best to focus on the three social networks listed above to start, at least until you have your social media strategy fully planned.

Your Practice and Social Networking

By this point, you probably have several ideas of how you can use social networking to benefit your practice. Social networks can be immensely valuable tools, allowing you to connect and share with others in your area and thereby, boost your profitability. However, there are things that might not have occurred to you yet.

Creating a Personal Appearance

The first thing you need to understand is social networking is all about connecting on a personal level. Your business must make use of these networks in the same way you would, personally. That is, you have to take the time to interact with others through your posts and updates. For instance, if you update your Facebook page regularly with event notifications, specials, and related news, those who read those updates will comment on them. It is vital that you take the time to reply to those individuals. Doing so offers two distinct benefits: first, it helps give your practice a personal face and second, it shows you are truly there to interact with others and really care about what your patients think. You show that your practice is about your patients, rather than about profit.

Creating a personal face with social networks is actually pretty simple. There are a number of methods to help you develop your social network presence. Here are some of the best things to do with Facebook:

- Post special discount rates for services offered.
- Post Facebook-only discounts or specials for your followers as a reward for their loyalty.
- Post news about your practice such as changes in staffing, changes in services, new products offered, etc.
- Post news about events you will be attending (conferences and the like).
- Post videos of procedures.
- Post videos of company events (company picnics, holiday gatherings, and more).
- Post pictures of "star" patients such as children with the cleanest teeth or something similar, but make sure you have permission to post those pictures before you do so.
- Post before and after pictures of procedures such as laser whitening (with permission, of course).

These are only a few of the ways that you can use Facebook to promote your business, give it a personal face, and interact with your patients on Facebook.

You can use LinkedIn in a similar manner but remember, this network is designed for professionals rather than for the average person. Tailor your updates, posts, and interactions for a professional audience, and you will do well.

Special Notes on Twitter

Twitter is an interesting network, with some very practical uses. While you can use it to post pictures with an add-on service like Twitpic, you'll find that it's more useful as a way to make your Twitter followers aware of posts on Facebook, new entries on your blog, or new updates to your website. However, the real value of Twitter, as mentioned before, lies in your ability to start up conversations, to answer questions, and build your reputation as an expert.

The more you interact with others (answering questions, commenting, and sharing directly), the more followers you will gain and the more value you will gain from this network. It's a powerful, valuable tool that can greatly increase traffic to your website or blog, but you'll have to make sure that you use it correctly. You'll find that if you do nothing but post links to your other sites, people will be unwilling to follow you. The key here is to provide value and interaction without being overly self-promoting.

A Word of Caution: Spammer Alert

While social networking and social media can be excellent tools for your practice, you need to exercise great care here. If you take the wrong actions, you can be labeled as a spammer, and recovering from that can be almost impossible.

To avoid the appearance of a spammer (or of a business out for nothing but money), you need to make sure you interact with others in your social networking efforts. Take the time to actually get to know some of your followers on Twitter, for instance. Speak with them, answer their questions, or compare notes with them if they are part of the profession. Not only will this help ensure that you are not labeled as a spammer, but it will also help increase your number of followers on Twitter. Often, potential followers will check your timeline before they decide to follow you. If all they see are promotional tweets, chances are good they are going to opt-out of connecting with you.

The same rule applies to your interactions and use of Facebook and

LinkedIn. You must use these networks the way they were intended – for interaction. If you never comment on the posts of others, never answer questions or respond to comments on your own posts, or simply ignore those who choose to connect with you, you'll never be able to leverage these tools to their full extent (and you might actually find they offer no benefit at all).

Chapter 15

Social Networking: 101

Word Count: **2845**
Approximate Time to Read: **6.3 minutes**

Getting Socialized

What is the right way to get started with social networking? We recommend you do the following:

- Create a Facebook Business Page and begin finding "fans."

- Create a Twitter account and search for "followers" from your contacts or database.

- Create a LinkedIn account and profile and import your contacts.

- Create a Google+ Page and begin building "circles" with your patients and prospects.

- Create a YouTube channel where you can post your ever-increasing library of videos and begin directing visitors to it.

- Integrate any drip marketing software (we suggest Infusionsoft – see Resources section) with your website and your blog.

- Create your blog. This is something we will go over in detail shortly, but you will want your blog to have a similar appearance to your website and be listed in the most appropriate blog directories. You will also have to create a schedule that keeps the blog updated with unique, SEO materials automatically.

In addition to this, you have to ensure that your website and blog have the appropriate links or icons that allow visitors, patients, and prospects to begin following or "liking" your pages with a single click of their mouse. You also have to consider how to optimize the pages for mobile browsing. Remember, websites don't usually work well with mobile devices but as millions of sites have already found, by making a version of their site mobile devices are automatically directed to, they have increased their practice's accessibility and customer satisfaction. Be sure your content is mobile optimized too.

Before you begin to panic at the size of this to-do list, you should know you can always work with professionals who can support your efforts and help automate as much of this as possible. (See the Resources section for details.) This may be the smartest approach because you are going to do a lot more through your social networking than just contact your potential patients or prospects.

Not Failing at Facebook

HOW – let's repeat that – HOW can you fail at Facebook? It is one of the simplest venues to use … or is it? Let's look at the top mistakes a dental professional might make when setting up their account and using it for drip marketing. In this way, we can learn how to actually succeed in meeting drip marketing goals!

1. **Make a Good Impression** – When you build your dental practice's Facebook page, be sure you present first-time visitors with a nice and welcoming "face." This means you must maximize the use of the profile picture space. Don't rely on stock art or a logo – that's not social! This requires pictures of YOU and other dentists in your practice appear at the top of the page. You have 180 by 540 pixels available, which means you can insert images and office contact information, if desired.

2. **Setup Your Custom Username** – Anyone who creates their own Facebook page has the chance to claim their individual "username." This means you can direct people immediately to your page by giving them a unique URL. For instance, would you rather have people see they can visit www.facebook.com/apps/application. php?id=12332145665 or would you prefer to direct them to www. facebook.com/YourDentalOfficeName?

3. **Create Extra Pages** – While allowing people to see pages without being a Friend is a wise decision, taking every visitor directly to your Wall is not. Instead, you should take advantage of the ability to add pages to your Facebook site and direct people to those pages where they encounter special offers or information.

Adding pages allows you to retain ultimate control over the looks of your profile. You can remove unwanted pages like "Friend Activity" and replace them with things like "Benefits of Dental Implants," "Videos," etc. In these pages, you can create opt-ins that will ask for information about the visitor and help you increase the number of Fans and database prospects.

Unfortunately, the process of adding pages is done through the use of the Facebook Developers area and is not altogether simple. Because it is also something that has to be coordinated with the blog, website, and other materials, it is best done with professional support and assistance. Once the pages are created; however, you can then direct people (using the appropriate embedded links) to these pages and drip market accordingly.

4. **Keep Special Pages Special** – Though your Wall might be public, you absolutely must not make the special pages easy to access with a single click. Instead, you should require a visitor to simply hit the "Like" button in order to read the information or view the video.

Why? Let's use a single illustration of the power of this tactic. A Facebook Friend gets a message you have a new report on Dental Implants available. They follow the link and are sent to a special page in your Facebook profile. If the information was just sitting there, it would have taken the visitor straight to the page, but if you ask that person to "Like" the report before being able to view it, it means their action is going to appear on their News Feed.

For instance, all of their friends (whether it is ten or ten thousand) will suddenly see that "John Smith likes Benefits of Dental Implants" (which will appear as a blue hyperlink in the news feed). This will also bring other interested parties who click that "Like" button and distribute the news accordingly. This is a beautiful way to use modern word of mouth!

5. **Getting information from those who Like your stuff** – When creating an additional page in Facebook, you can insert an opt-in that gets the details you need for your database. Remember, you tend to need some sort of special lure to get that information so the person who "Likes" a page in order to see it will have to get something like a newsletter, eBook, or white paper report offered to them in exchange for contact information. This person will then get the pre-established number of contacts or communications (say one per month for the next year) for the drip marketing campaign they just opted-in to. This will ensure they are never flooded but also that they don't forget your practice either.

6. **Integrate updates** – If you create a new blog, it should appear on your Facebook Friends' News Feed, as a status in Twitter, be made available through LinkedIn, and show up in your Google+. The same can be said about your tweets appearing in the other social

media ventures from your Facebook News Feed to your Google+ status. When your updates are as well-integrated as this, it means all your contacts are going to see at least one of the posts.

Integrating Facebook into All Your Marketing

What else can be done on Facebook in order to drip market? You can use Facebook for:

- Short video posts
- To introduce new staff members or for employee spotlights
- To allow prospects to request your books and free reports
- To promote seasonal services (For example, prom season and wedding season run concurrently and are good times to offer teeth whitening specials or smile makeovers.)
- To direct people to your blog, new articles, online store, etc.
- Creating forums or Q & A opportunities for patients to ask questions and get timely and concise answers (Try to avoid going straight for the sale and actually give them some resources.)
- Enhancing your professional reputation with the sharing of useful articles or stories about other dental professionals

This list could go on farther but for now, it is useful for you to see that you can really enhance the effectiveness of a drip marketing campaign through a socialized site like Facebook.

Tweeting Tweets on Twitter

If Facebook is so comprehensive, why bother with Twitter or other social networking sites? It has to do with demographics.

The average Twitter user is 35 years and older.

This is someone who will have disposable income, concerns about general as well as dental health, and an interest in using technology to find answers and even a bargain or discount. Twitter can deliver precisely what this demographic is hoping to find. For example, you can integrate regular or frequent tweets into your drip marketing plans, but you want to avoid any sales speak. Yes, a lot of businesses make specials or offers known through tweets, but why do that when you are trying to establish trust and develop deeper bonds? Instead, make your tweets valuable to those in your network. For example, "Loving my spinach salad @ restaurant name and link. So good for my teeth and bones!" This catches the eye of your followers who will consider the restaurant (naturally) but also remember their dentist tweeted them about something OTHER than dental work, offers, etc.

You could also keep track of trending topics and do relevant tweets about those too. For instance, if calcium supplements are in the news, create a post related to them. This is of use to your patients and followers, and many will retweet if the information is valuable enough.

This retweeting is going to get you a few more followers, persistently enhancing the size of the network and effectiveness of your social networking campaigns. Remember; however, you do not have to follow everyone who begins following you. Try to keep your list of people you follow as relevant as possible. Be sure anyone on the list is going to be interested in what you are sending, and will be likely to tweet or retweet what you discuss.

Don't forget to be a good Twitter follower and make a point of retweeting and/or mentioning the interesting information some of your patients or prospects send out too. Also, if someone retweets YOU, make sure you thank them or @mention them. This is going to deepen the relationship between you and make it far more likely you will be the recipient of good word of mouth.

Twitter's Unique Structure

Why all of the back and forth? Twitter uses a timeline structure that shows the nature of the communications. You need to be sure your timeline is a good mix of the four primary message formats for the site. For example, there are:

- Plain text tweets
- Tweets that contain links to other websites
- Tweets that link to your website
- Tweets that link to a landing page based within your website

You want a lot of activity from potential patients heading to your website and landing pages, but you do not want the Twitter timeline to consist only of blatant marketing activity. Instead, you need to interact, socialize, and develop relationships that help to increase the number of people likely to encounter your information. This can only happen when you use Twitter to the fullest degree, as explained above. Here's what it might look like:

1. You tweet about a great calcium-rich energy bar a patient recommended.

2. You tweet a link to the homepage for that energy bar and thank the patient.

3. You tweet a link to an article on your website about the importance of calcium.

4. You tweet a link to a landing page on your site for discounted dental checkups. This landing page has the opt-in system that captures the data you want for the database, but the following and retweeting of these links is going to also bring you some new prospects as well.

Link to Your Prospects with LinkedIn

LinkedIn is a much more direct networking tool. It will use your list of contacts and seek them out in the LinkedIn network. For example, let's say that you have a Gmail account; the LinkedIn engine will detect this and show you a list of people "not already" in your network. If you choose to connect with someone from that list, it will send an email indicating your interest in connecting. They will be given the choice of adding you or not, and the same applies to your profile. For example, it shows others you belong to LinkedIn but only if there seems to be a logical connection, i.e., a dental surgeon friend has you as a LinkedIn connection and one of their fellow dental surgeon acquaintances sees you on a list of potential connections.

Once people are connected through the network, they get weekly updates showing all the recent activities on the network. For example, you see all the new connections made by your existing network, any social networking posts, etc.

LinkedIn is a good way to get recommendations from your patients and to connect with other dental professionals. Just as others see you have welcomed someone into your Facebook network, they see the same on LinkedIn, encouraging cross-connections.

Consider too just how valuable it is that your LinkedIn connections can supply you with other professionals to refer your patients to if you cannot perform the procedures they want or need, and vice versa, they refer patients to you.

Of course, the primary way you can use LinkedIn as a form of drip marketing is by answering questions posed on the network on a regular basis. This tags you and begins reinforcing your reputation as an expert. You can then link these posts to your other social networking sites, i.e., "For some answers about the problems associated with gum disease, visit 'link to LinkedIn response.'" This is just another way of adding more depth to your social "image" and also establishing stronger connections with peers and patients who are glad to give good references. Consider this interesting commentary on LinkedIn that appeared in a 2007 blog post (http://blog.guykawasaki.com/2007/01/ten_ways_to_use.html):

- All 500 of the **Fortune** 500 are represented in LinkedIn. In fact, 499 of them are represented by director-level and above employees.

This same blog goes on to note most people use this website in order to get a job or make a sale. This is because it is direct, improves visibility and Google page ranking, enhances SERPs (Search Engine Page Results), and gives access to that fantastic "LinkedIn Answers" feature. It is this feature that a dentist working on his drip marketing campaign can really take advantage of. It allows you to send out questions to the network, get professional responses, and continually keep open forums in the eyes of your entire network. This feeds, or drips, information to people on a continual basis, but is not information that will be viewed as marketing or "sales speak" because it is something occurring between dentists and related professionals.

For example, if you have developed a drip marketing campaign for dental veneers and want to send out a message to all of your potential patients about how they are effective and durable, you would simply post a question about veneers and get some professional feedback – letting them do the convincing. You would then create links to this forum and allow your patients to see the evidence for themselves.

The New Google+

Google+ is a system that uses defined "Circles" to decide the level of communication that is received. For instance there are Circles for friends, family, acquaintances, and colleagues PLUS you can also create your own custom circles. This means you can create a circle for patients, referring doctors, college buddies, or any other group, as you see fit. You can then use the subsequent features such as Hangouts, Huddles, and Sparks as ways to gather people in your Circles together and call attention to something – whether an event, person, or product.

How are all of the names pulled into the system?

The Google+ application has been designed to recognize your existing contacts from your e-mail system. For example, if you have Gmail or Hotmail for your personal and/or professional email connections, the Google+ application sees this and automatically lists them on the main page. You simply "drag and drop" that person into an appropriate circle. You can have the same contact in multiple circles at the same time, which is why this is shaping up to becoming an ideal business and marketing tool.

These same controls are due to be incorporated into the business component of Google+, and we strongly suggest any dental practice offer itself as a test partner in order to get in on the proverbial ground floor of this tool for strong communication on a local, regional, national, and even global level.

You can plan on using it as a direct tool for communicating with patients about services and products BUT you can also rely on things like Hangouts, which opens a Chat option for up to ten people at a time. **This means you could create a Hangout as a form of live webinar** or for others to communicate about one of your services.

The Sparks feature lets you tag things that are of interest to you on the web and then share them with friends. You probably already understand how this works in terms of drip marketing: you write a blog, add the link of your blog to your "feed" of Sparks, and send out a notice to all of your patients (friends/acquaintances/etc.).

Chapter 16

Blogs ... Yes, Blogs are Social Networks

Word Count: **2611**
Approximate Time to Read: **5.8 minutes**

Blogs are the tool that can really "wrap things up." For instance, you can do all kinds of drip marketing through your social networks and website efforts, and you may inspire someone to dig a bit deeper. When they do, they will tend to discover things like your Facebook page, Google+ account, LinkedIn profile, and your blog. Unlike the social networks; however, the blog is free, unrestricted, and its contents can really validate everything a prospect or visitor has seen up to that point.

Once you have them at the blog, you can filter everything they see through your particular "lens," which is why they have so quickly become one of the primary marketing tools of choice.

What Your Blog Can Do

- Provide news updates
- Deliver folksy or conversational stories about dentistry or oral health
- Give you a personality
- Promote specials or new services
- Answer questions that patients frequently ask (which could lead to an entire series of blog posts)
- Explore unusual or specific techniques available for dental solutions
- Create the image of you as the expert

Because search engine algorithms change so often, it is always important to create blog content that is fresh, relevant, and timely. This ensures the keywords used or the materials embedded in the blog (such as infographics, videos, links, etc.) are read properly too. This will happen automatically if you have incorporated blogs into your drip marketing plans!

Your blog will complement your social networking and website materials. It is **another point of reference or method of directing attention to your practice.**

If you look at the sample 12-week plan mentioned in the section on snail mail, you can see blog posts figure prominently. They are not the strongest facet of social networking, but they must not be overlooked. You can make high-quality content available that can be freely reposted anywhere and, which automatically includes your byline and link. This ensures anyone who likes what they read and wants to share it with others will also be drip marketing the information as they direct prospects back to you! It is also a remarkably effective way to conduct top-notch SEO as well.

Remember, millions of people are using social media each day and a large number of them may be searching for answers that are available in one of your blog posts or articles. You need to be sure they find it and when they do, they are guided back to your website, landing pages, or social network sites. This ensures they become a part of your database OR they find reliable information they share with others, which also results in more prospective patients.

Your blog is going to establish you as a knowledgeable expert due to the content you choose to include. This is one of the goals of drip marketing because it means your audience can trust you. This is reinforced by the SEO benefits gained through the use of a well-written blog. For instance, if someone in your local area types in a specific question about a dental issue and you have covered it in blog posts, social networking forums, and on your website, they will get a "stacked" result. This means there will be more than a single link with your URL, automatically positioning you as a reliable professional and expert. Not bad for writing an in-depth article or creating a single presentation!

You must also be sure any new blog updates appear on Facebook's News Feed, Twitter, Google+'s Stream, and LinkedIn, if relevant. In this way, you are ensuring total integration, a core principle of successful drip marketing.

Blogging for Your Practice

When blogging was created a relatively long time ago, it marked the shift of the Internet to a user-centric, sharing-minded focus, making it one of the most important evolutions of the Internet. There is conflicting information out there about blogging though. If you have noticed headlines proclaiming the "death of the blog," you might be wondering why this topic is included at all. Let's put those myths to rest.

Is Blogging Dead?

The answer to this is a resounding "no." Blogging is very much alive today. So what has prompted so many to announce that blogging is on the way out? That's a bit complicated, but understanding the situation will help you see the value of blogging for your practice.

In the Beginning ...

... there was no such thing as a blog. If you wanted to have a presence online, you were relegated to developing your own website. Blogging changed that, offering a way for the everyday person to have a web presence, to share with others, and to start building a reputation. Blogging took the place of personal websites.

Blogs became immensely popular right off the bat, being used by everyone from affiliate marketers to the average person simply wanting to share information, pictures, and stories with their friends and family. Quite a few blog platforms popped up, many of which are still around. Two of the largest still play a major role in the online environment today (more on those later in the chapter).

For a long time, blogs remained the primary way for people to share information with the rest of the online world, but then came social media sites like MySpace and Facebook. More and more people began to gravitate toward these sites as they offered many of the benefits found with having a personal blog, but also integrated others that were unavailable previously. As more people started using, sharing, and interacting within the bounds of social networks, people took notice of the shift and proclaimed that blogging was dying out yet this is very far from the truth. Blogging is still very much alive. For proof, you need only look at some of the most popular sites on the Internet – many of them are actually blogs. You'll find personal blogs, company blogs, entrepreneur's blogs, adventure blogs, and more. Blogging is far from dead; it is still thriving, making it essential you put it to use for your practice.

Why You Need Blogging

Why should you bother with blogging? What could you possibly stand to gain here? To understand the real value of a blog, it's important to separate websites from blogs, based on their usage.

Your Website: Your website is the public face of your practice. Here, you will list the services you offer, provide a bit of information about your practice, discuss your staff, and more; it's all very business oriented. Your website is vital, certainly, but it cannot do all you need to accomplish online.

Your Blog: While your website is your practice's public face, your blog is its personal face. This is where you "let your hair down" and really talk to your readers. Blogging is an excellent way to interact with your patients, with other professionals, and even develop your standing as a leader in the industry (though that's certainly not a requirement).

We should also discuss a few other characteristics of a good blog. You'll find blogs are a lot like social media both in their casualness and in the way they encourage interactivity. That interactivity is the primary reason you want a blog, and here's why.

Why Interactivity Matters

It once was considered acceptable for businesses to be impersonal. It was the norm for almost all companies to be little more than faceless commercial presences. That is no longer true. The modern world has shifted, almost back in time, actually.

Before the rise of large national chains and international conglomerates, small businesses had a real presence in the community. They had a personal face; those who frequented the business usually knew the owner by name and likely knew all the staff as well. Today's business environment calls for a similar personal connectedness. Increasingly, consumers, customers, patients, and clients demand they "know" the companies with whom they do business. Having a blog allows you to do that and more.

Even if your content is top-notch, if you do not interact with those who visit your blog, you will remain a faceless, impersonal business. Obviously, this will not be true for your current patients, but potential patients want to know more about you and your practice. The best way to do that is by having an active blog.

Choosing Your Platform

As mentioned, there are a number of blogging platforms out there you can use. However, the two most popular (and most useful) are Blogger and WordPress. Which is right for you though? They both have some pros and cons that need to be understood before you leap into the world of blogging. You also need to decide where you will host your blog: on your site or elsewhere.

A Bit about Blogger

Blogger is now owned by Google, which means you can create your blog under your Google account and integrate it with all your other Google tools and systems such as Google Places. There are some other benefits to using Blogger as well. First, Blogger is free to use. WordPress has a free version, but there is also a version designed to be used with a paid hosting plan. Blogger stands alone, with no need for any hosting other than what Google supplies. It's also very easy to customize your design and layout. Simplicity is the rule here; however, there are a few drawbacks to using this platform.

If you like the look and feel of WordPress themes, you might not find yourself loving Blogger. Blogger does have more themes available than the free version of WordPress and the themes are a bit more personal without the need for in-depth customization. However, Blogger can be a bit too simple though; some of the analytic tools you might want to use can be hard to access (or not available).

A Bit about WordPress

As mentioned, WordPress is one of the largest and most popular blogging platforms out there. It's also a good way to design an entire website. Technically, both WordPress.com and WordPress.org are free; however, that's not the full situation. To determine, which one you want to use, you'll need to know a bit more.

WordPress.org: This is the original WordPress setup. With this platform, you have access to the widest range of templates and themes, but you will have to have your own hosting plan and domain name, both of which come at an additional cost. You can also edit and customize themes and templates to meet your needs.

WordPress.com: WordPress.com is totally free; it's hosted by

Automattic so you have no costs for hosting or paying for a domain name. However, you do not have access to the same number of themes and templates as you do with the .org version and you cannot customize any of the themes beyond the built-in layout and design options other than custom header images and logos.

Making this decision can be hard to do, particularly if you are new to the realm of blogging. WordPress tends to be the most frequently used simply because of its immense versatility, as well as its ability to be hosted with another web host. Another mark in favor of WordPress is the immense number of high-quality themes available with the .org version.

Blogging Tips for Dental Practices

Most tips about blogging can be applied across the board, regardless of what type of business you represent; however, there are some special considerations for dental practices hoping to leverage the power of blogging. This section will detail some valuable tips for all bloggers, as well as specific considerations for your practice.

Update Frequency: One of the most frequently misunderstood aspects of blogging is the frequency with which you update your content. Many people feel updating once per month is sufficient. The reality here is much different. Ideally, you need to update your blog once per week, at minimum. The best update frequency is between one and three updates per week. The reason for this is that frequent updates encourage search engine spiders to index your blog more often. The more often this happens, the better your search rankings will be. The more often you rank for specific keywords, the higher your overall page rank will be. It's very difficult to rank for a particular keyword with only a handful of posts containing that keyword, so make sure you update as often as possible.

Update Length: The length of your updates is really up to you. However, you should bear in mind that Google likes longer updates more than short ones, particularly with one of the latest changes to their algorithms (the Panda update). In an ideal world, your blog updates should be about 500 words long as a minimum, with longer updates being preferred. This is not a "hard and fast" rule but more of a general tip. Obviously, not all blog updates are going to be 800 words long. You might even find it difficult to make 500 word posts regularly. What is important is you make an effort to keep the majority of your posts 500 words long or longer so you benefit the most from search engines.

Update Originality: When creating updates, it can be tempting to source news stories and articles relevant to your topic. Innovations in the dental industry occur on a regular basis and you are going to find these articles potentially useful. However, it is vital that you realize Google penalizes for duplicate content. If you are not worried about search engine rankings, then you're free to post what you like. On the other hand, if you want to maximize your page rank, you need to ensure all posts are original, relevant, and optimized with your targeted keywords.

Topics, Topics, Topics: This is where you really need to separate yourself from other bloggers. The tips listed above apply to everyone; however, as a dental office, you are going to need to ensure you post on the right topics. Ideally, your topics will be those of interest to your patients and potential patients. Obviously, posting about your services and the technologies you use every day in your practice are all good topics for blog posts. Posting about these help your patients and prospective patients understand the processes involved in procedures they might need or want. However, there are many other topics here you should consider.

For instance, how-to lists are incredibly popular with both real readers and search engine spiders. This means you can post how-to information on almost anything from keeping your teeth white to preventing plaque buildup, removing stains at home, identifying the signs of gum disease, and countless others. These types of posts are excellent because they offer added value to your readers – they give them something that they need, with nothing asked in exchange. That is one of the most important concepts in the modern online environment: consumers expect more "bang for their buck" and have also come to expect businesses to offer them value beyond the scope of their in-house services.

Another excellent post option is to post videos; remember the video library discussed earlier? This is a good way to make them pull double or even triple duty. When you use videos as blog posts, you can avoid being penalized for duplicate content (Google doesn't penalize for duplicate video content) and still provide added value to your patients. Almost any type of video can be used here, but make sure you do more than just embed the file in your page, you need to take the time to write a bit about it – why you're posting that particular video, what your patients can gain from watching it, and other important information.

Chapter 17
Paid Marketing Considerations

Word Count: **5727**
Approximate Time to Read: **12.7 minutes**

"Now, before I could recommend Colin to any of our doctors, I had to put him to the test personally, so I put him to work doing Pay-Per-Click marketing, as well as Search Engine Optimization, for my personal private practice as well as our consulting business. Needless to say, the market in Seattle is very competitive and needless to say, the national market for consulting is highly competitive. The reality is, he was put to the test, so what's the result?

*"Well, **we dropped our spending by 50 percent in our Pay-Per-Click ads with better results** and in both my private practice as well as the consulting business – not one, not two, but ten top key phrases, all first page in Google results. It really doesn't get any better than that. Like it or not, 35 percent of large elective cases show up or don't show up via your practice website, and all the things you're doing online. For regular dentistry, the majority of those searching for 'just a dentist' are doing that research online."*

~ James McAnally, D.D.S.

Obviously, the entire point of having an online presence is to increase your practice's profitability. In order to do that, you need to know a bit more about the various online marketing methods open to you, as well as how they work. There are other powerful tools that you need to use, only some of which rely on social networking to operate.

PPC Campaigns

PPC, or Pay-Per-Click, campaigns have been around for several years. They offer you the means of having your paid ads appear beside organic search results when a consumer searches for that keyword or phrase. These used to be excellent ways to boost traffic to your website or blog. They are still relatively good at generating traffic, but they can be very expensive campaigns to operate. The more competition there is for your targeted keywords, the more you will have to pay for every single person who clicks your ad, whether they convert to a customer through your website or not. Obviously, for very high-competition keywords, these are not the ideal solution.

There are a couple of other considerations here, as well. For instance, consumers have become pretty savvy about telling a real search result from a "sponsored result," which is how your ads will appear. With that being said, they can still drive traffic your way and might represent a decent marketing option.

Facebook Ads

As mentioned in the previous section, Facebook has their own PPC ad system that can be used within the network. You can custom create your own ads, targeting your specified keywords and even include images if you want. You'll pay for every person who clicks the ad, so make sure that you target lower-priced keywords for the best affordability.

The Facebook ad system is highly beneficial, as it also allows you to target your specific audience on the network by demographic information, geographic information, and other criteria, ensuring that only those users who will benefit you the most see your advertisement (helping cut your costs further). You can create a Facebook ad right through your business page on the network and can also track your advertising performance over time. This allows you to make fine adjustments to increase your results or decrease your costs.

Google Places (Local Search)

Local search is playing a dramatic role in increasing website traffic. It makes a lot of sense – your patients will be looking for services you offer in their area, rather than on a global scale. Google Places is an excellent way to help ensure your prospects are able to find you, as well as a good way to stand out from other offices in the area.

One of the most innovative things about Google Places is it pulls up your office listing with a map of the local area. This allows prospective patients to determine exactly where you are located in town. The search includes a picture of your office (if you so choose) as well as information about your practice such as how long you've been practicing, the services and treatments you offer, and other important information for patients.

There are few better ways to get noticed today over Google Places. It's a far better option than using Google AdWords, particularly for local searches (which is where you want to rank). Finally, you can also gain access to important information through the program such as search metrics, keyword usage, and other valuable data so you can base further marketing decisions on solid information.

Best of all, there's no charge to list your business with Google Places – free advertising is hard to beat!

Google Boost Ads

Google Boost ads work hand-in-hand with Google Places, allowing you to advertise your business on maps and through mobile Google searches, as well. The Boost program is a Pay-Per-Click advertising option, but you'll pay far less for these ads than you would through other PPC programs. This is because you are only competing against businesses in your local area targeting the same keywords, rather than going up against big national companies. Boost ads also give you the ability to drive traffic to either your website or to your Google Places page (which is free to create).

Google Maps

Google Maps is a powerful tool, and one of the most frequently used map systems by consumers out there. You can also market your practice using Google Maps though you will have to enroll with Google Business Solutions to do so. You can do this directly through http://www.Google.com/services. Just click the "Get Started" button and you can enroll.

Advertising with Google Maps will put your business on the map – literally – when a consumer searches their local area (via Google Places). The map system has been integrated with Google Places so a single account will work for both programs.

Article Marketing

If you are seeking a low-cost, high-impact way of marketing, then there are few things as beneficial as article marketing. This form of marketing has been around for a long time, but it's effectiveness remains. How does it work?

In the simplest possible example, you write an informative article on a specific topic related to the services you offer. The article should be optimized with keywords but they should be used naturally, not stuffed into the content. At the bottom of the article, you will include what's called an "author bio box." This is really just a couple of sentences about you, but you also include one or two links from your article to destinations of your choice.

Once you have written the article, you must submit it to an article directory. Here, the article will be housed forever, helping to boost your reputation as well as driving traffic to your website. In addition, articles from directories are frequently used as ezine content and in other ways across the Internet. Each time this happens, you gain an additional link back to your website or blog, boosting your traffic even more.

There are a couple of important notes about article marketing though, particularly in light of the Google Panda update. In order to be effective, articles now need to be 500 words or more in length, and they need to be completely original. Also, do not give in to the temptation to use your article on your own site at the same time it's being housed on the directory. This creates duplicate content and Google will punish you for it.

The Patient Attraction Podcast

Episode 010: The One About Marketing In All The Wrong Places

Hello and welcome to this week's Fast Thoughts on Dental Marketing. I'm your host, Colin Receveur. It's a beautiful sunny day here in Floyds Knobs, Indiana, just outside of Louisville, Kentucky where my wife and I live. I've got some exciting topics, some exciting takeaways for you guys today. I'm going to be giving you seven items – seven areas where dentists are spending their money wrong. I've put a lot of thought into this; I've actually had the notes working on it for about two months now, trying to get the notes together for this podcast and thinking about what I want to say and, which items really carry the most weight. So I'm really excited to jump in and talk about it.

The purpose for these podcasts is to educate dentists and specialist: orthodontists, implantologists, periodontists, everybody in the dental profession that is looking for a way to expand their marketing to find the new patients they want. By educating you, you can decide for yourself if you feel that web marketing is a good fit for your practice and your specific situation.

The seven takeaways, it's actually going to be eight but one of them I've already talked about a whole lot: the Yellow Pages. It seems like every week I get a phone call from another dentist that has been spending thousands and thousands of dollars in the Yellow Pages, and their new patient flow is down, their collection numbers are down and they don't know what's wrong. My answer is track it – let's split test it; we'll put a call tracking number in the Yellow Pages and they can find out exactly what it's bringing them, or in 100% of the cases so far, what it's not bringing them.

The seven actual takeaways that are going to be talked about in this episode are:

1. Social media - should you be doing it or not?
2. Spending all of your money on marketing in one place - is that important or should you be spreading your eggs around?
3. Template websites - are template websites worth the money you save or should you be going with a custom website?
4. What about boilerplate content - should you be taking the time to

write your own content or is any content sufficient just so that your patient understands?

5. SEO and AdWords - spending marketing dollars on old websites. If you have a website that's a few years old, can you optimize it, spend marketing money on it and get good results with it?

6. Staff labor - are you having your staff spend a lot of time updating your social media, send out letters and packets, completing fulfillments and sending out emails and text messages to remind your patients of appointments? Or is there a way to automate all of that?

7. The importance of knowing your ROI.

Any marketing dollars you spend are spent in the wrong place if you don't know exactly what you're getting for your money – if you're not tracking your marketing down to the penny. If you buy a piece of real estate or a building or a stock or a bond, you immediately know your cost basis and you know your profit or loss. Your marketing should be no different. If you're not tracking your marketing in very simple terms, cost basis, profit and loss, you don't really know what you're getting for your marketing. Sure, maybe you got 30 phone calls or 40 phone calls. Yes, maybe you know that some of those phone calls came from a website, or maybe you have some phone tracking in place and you ran this newspaper ad and you had some calls come in and they say they found you in the newspaper, but with as inexpensive as the tracking is these days, if you can't just look at a report that tells you everything you need to know, you're definitely leaving money on the table, if not spending too much of your own time trying to deduce what these numbers are or figure them out. There are systems out there, our Zetetics system for instance, that we've designed specifically for dentists to be able to easily and quickly get those numbers right to the bottom dollar.

1. Social Media

Let's jump right in. I'm going to start with social media. Is social media somewhere that dentists should be spending their marketing dollars? There are different ways that you can market with social media; you can do Pay-Per-Click ads with Facebook, connecting to your Facebook business page and there are many services out there that will offer to keep your Facebook Page updated several times a day or several times a week to entice your visitors and give them offers and information.

My opinion on it is it's really a waste of time. Aside from Dr. Zuckerberg – who if you don't know who Mark Zuckerberg is, he is founder of Facebook's father – dentists that are successfully using social media are few and far between – just extremely rare. We have several clients who are doing some social media that have hired outside companies to work with their social media and run Pay-Per-Click ads. We've run a lot of Pay-Per-Click ads for our clients testing it, trying to find out a way to monetize it, trying to find a way to build a following and what we found after several 12 and 24 month studies with Facebook and Twitter is if you're a general practice, you can build a following on Facebook, no question. That demographic of patient – the young, the baby boomers, my generation and the ones in between are certainly Facebook friendly, they're mobile phone friendly and they have the knowledge to Friend you, Like you, and Follow you and you can build a tribe pretty quick.

If you're a dentist that is looking for larger cases: implants, all-on-4s, very fearful patients and an older demographic, Facebook just isn't for you. It's something that a lot of your demographic doesn't use. Right now, the fastest growing segment on Facebook is 55-65 year old women, but just because they're signing up for Facebook doesn't mean they're actually utilizing it. There is certainly a huge generational gap between how a 25 or 35 or even 45 year old uses Facebook, and how a 65 or 75 year old uses Facebook. It's something that the younger generations have grown up with: they know how to utilize it. As time goes on, a lot of the older generation will continue to sign up for Facebook but are they really utilizing it in the same way? The answer is no.

I can name off the top of my head several dentists I know that have been doing Facebook and have been doing daily status updates and doing offers and releasing all this stuff onto their Facebook Page. They have spent hundreds of hours putting little videos together and updates and whatnot and they have a following after two years of 35 people or 65 people. Even those 65 people, if you look at them, they're not the patients that had the larger case size work done! They're the daughters or the children of the people that had the work done.

If you're a family dentist and you're looking for a lot of bread and butter cases, by all means, hop on Facebook and produce a lot of good content. You're not going to build a following if you just release offers. There are all kinds of sites out there that are all about offers and discounts. If you want to build a following on Facebook, talk about yourself, personalize your Facebook Page and your experience. But if you're looking for the big cases, we just haven't seen a lot out of it. It's something that maybe as time goes on and the demographics continue to push upward a little bit getting the older generations on Facebook, we'll see more results with that but for the past couple of years and in the foreseeable future, for specialists in the older demographics, we don't recommend doing Facebook.

2. Should You Put All Your Eggs in One Basket?

We'll jump on to number two: spending all your money in one place. There are a lot of piecemeal companies out there that for $2.97 or $4.97 or $6.97 a month will offer to do your local search optimization for you or they'll offer to do your Pay-Per-Click for you or they'll offer to do your organic link building for you. Some of these companies even charge $1,000 or $2,000 a month to do that. I'm sure they do a great job, but the problem with using piecemeal marketing companies is really kind of twofold:

One is continuity: are you relaying the same message? Are your marketing budgets overlapping? Are you essentially competing against yourself with two different marketing budgets? And the second is one of consumer mindset: if a consumer searches for "Louisville, Kentucky dentist" on Google and you are ranked number one in the SERPS, you are going to get statistically 35% of all of those searches. That's a pretty good chunk of traffic! And of course, if you have a good website on the backend, you're going to convert a good number of those to calls. If you have a lot of good video, you're going to convert even more of those into phone calls and patients.

Let me give you another scenario. Somebody searches for "Louisville, Kentucky dentist" and now they see you number one but your videos are number two. Maybe one of your niche websites is number three. Your Facebook page is number four. Your Twitter page is number five. And your local search page – well it would be a little bit higher to the top but your local search page is number six in there. You dominate the entire "above the fold" page on Google. Now that's something that sure, you're going to get that 35% of clicks if you get to the number one position, but 94% of prospects are going to click on the number one through six results. Statistically, if you're number six or seven or below, you're getting a very, very small piece of the pie.

Yes, there are a number of companies out there that can do piecemeal marketing very well, but if you are not dominating the first page of Google, you're just giving business away to your competition. You should have multiple pieces of real estate on the front page of Google for the keywords people are actually searching for in the local search, in the mobile search, in the organic search, in the natural search listings, in the paid listings, on AdWords Express and on the local search paid listings – which is a newer area that a lot of dentists don't realize even exists out there. You can do local search optimization and you can even pay to promote that listing with Google. Google has monetized everything and for a small fee, they'll let you take advantage of better placement, which is paramount in today's world. It brands your practice, it dominates the whole first page of Google, and not only do you dominate the whole first page, but your competition is nowhere to be found because they're on the second page or lower! It's the only way to go if you want to take the lion's share of new patients.

3. Template or Custom Website?

That being said we'll skip on to number three: template websites. A lot of dentists out there have a template website. Some of them are a few years old. Several years ago (five or six), template websites were okay: Google didn't have the technology to detect template websites. Now if you've heard of the Google Panda and the Google Penguin updates, Google has developed a technology to see if your website looks "cheap," for lack of a better way to put it. There are a lot of companies out there that are selling websites for $50 or $100 a month with no commitments and no set up fees. They throw up a website as fast as they can. Those types of websites that have boilerplate content, that have template websites, have practically been wiped off the map in the last year, definitely in the last couple of months. As you may be aware, April 24th, which was just a few weeks ago, Google released its Penguin update, which was really the final stake in the coffin for template and boilerplate websites. With the Panda update last year, they really drove hard and they killed off a lot of the template and the boilerplate stuff but with the Penguin update here just three or four weeks ago, the template and boilerplate sites are non-existent. They've literally just eradicated them off the Internet.

If you're wondering if you've been hit by it – if you have a website that's a little bit old or if you're not sure where you stand in the search engines, go to Google.com and do some searches for yourself and see if you show up. Make sure you're looking at the organic listings, the local listings, Mobile searches (search on your phone) – search in all the different places that your patients are going to be searching: some of them search on the go, some of them search on iPads, some of them search from their office on their computer. They search for all kinds of different keywords that you should be using on your website so you should know what keywords your patients are actually searching for. Don't assume they're simply searching for "Louisville dentist" or "(your city) dentist" – in many cases that is not true.

4. Boilerplate Content

We're kind of hitting on number four there as well: boilerplate content. Google has the technology now to compare your website to all the different sites across the Internet. If you have duplicated content or you're using a site that does not have custom, unique stuff about you, they have heavily penalized you at this point or will very, very shortly in the future once they roll this out to all the websites. As you can imagine, having several hundred million websites to review and critique, even Google with their massive computers take a little bit of time to do it.

5. SEO and PPC

We'll roll right into our next point of talking about older websites – websites that are a little bit aged – with SEO and PPC. One of the common questions I get is when a new client comes to us and says, "I've got this website … we paid a lot of money to have it created a few years ago. What can we do with it – can we use it? Can we just pay you to do optimization on it and send some traffic to it?" The answer is yes, you can always do optimization on something. You can always do Pay-Per-Click on something. But here's the low-down on that: your website is cheap compared to the cost of the optimization and the Pay-Per-Click in an ongoing fashion. Most dentists out there have spent somewhere from $3-5,000 on a good website. They're spending anywhere from $1,500 to $4,000 a month on monthly optimization so if you're not sure that your website is absolutely killer, why would you spend the money to drive traffic to it?

First off, if your website is a few years old, if you don't have a lot of unique content, a lot of good content, if you don't have a lot of video, if your page isn't structured in a way that is Google friendly by today's standards – not two or three or five years ago's standards – your site is not going to get the same results and the same ranking and the same number of phone calls as a new website will get.

The point I'm trying to make here is – let's say you spent at the low end of a marketing budget – you spent $1,500 a month for six months, so you spent nine, maybe ten grand on optimization or Pay-Per-Click marketing or some kind of ongoing marketing service for your website. Let's assume that because your website was older, you had diminished or zero results from it. You've spent $9-10,000, you're $9-10,000 further in the hole and you have nothing to show for it whereas if you had spent $3-4,000 up front, which means you've spent $12-13,000 now and revamped your website, added video to it – all of this advertising over six months with the monthly fees as they were incurred, produce quantitative results, which would you rather have? $10,000 with nothing to show for it, or $12,000 with lots of results, lots of phone calls, lots of closed cases and dollars back in your pocket.

When you're talking to web marketing guys and they tell you that your website is a little bit old, it's not that you didn't do a good job making it or creating it, it's not that it wasn't a good website three or four years ago or even two or three years ago – it's simply that Google changes the rules so fast. If your website is not constantly kept on top of it and you wait several years, you're out of the game. Just look at the changes Google has made in the last twelve months: releasing Panda and Penguin causing dental websites that were made 18 or 24 months ago to be cut out of the game. It's the evolution. It's certainly going in a good direction because the quality of the websites have greatly improved and that's what Google is after. They want extreme quality. They want lots of content and lots of good video and all this media that people can digest and engage with. Eighteen or 24 months from now, will the same tactics that we use today be producing results? The likely answer is no. It's constantly evolving, it's constantly changing, it's an ongoing cat and mouse game with Google to find out what works and implement those strategies for our dentists to stay on top of it.

To summarize, yes you can do optimization or Pay-Per-Click to an existing website, but it's not money well spent, in my opinion and it's often handled on a case by case basis. It's not necessarily whether your website is over "x" age or "no, we can't work with it" or "yes, we can," it's something that we review and look at. Oftentimes, there are a number of good aspects on a website and we can simply go in and change the ones that aren't current, update the ones that need updating and keep a lot of the existing site that you built. It's all case by case but that is the general strategy that we're looking at. You can spend money on anything, but is it money well spent? Generally no, but it's handled on a case by case basis.

6. Staff Labor

Let's jump in to number six. This one involves staff labor. A lot of offices are doing good follow-up. Some offices aren't, of course with some have no follow-up. Some have a number of good follow-up strategies in place: they're sending out letters, they're sending out text messages.

We were doing a video shoot up in New Jersey last week and the front office staff were actually text confirming all the patients that had appointments the next day from their personal cell phones. I was like "Wow, how much time are you guys spending doing that?"

There are all kinds of systems to automate your appointment reminders, your appointment confirmations as well as your marketing engine. Our Zetetics system, for example, can automatically send out emails, postcards, letters, text messages and can send faxes if by some chance you want to send your patient a fax. We can send out all these different mediums automatically to your patients in a pre-configured way that you don't even have to touch.

If you've got this big Excel spreadsheet or you've got a big dry erase board on your wall and you're trying to keep track of who's called in, who's warm and who's not, who you've presented cases to, who's accepted treatment, who has completed treatment and you want to generate referrals from them, we have the follow-up systems to automate all of that for you. Part of this system includes an automated referral system where we can send out postcards and letters and gifts to patients that have completed treatment for **years** after they come to their practice. Send them a postcard in the mail every few months that says "Hey! We really appreciate your business. If you have any friends that we could help to chew comfortably again and eat the foods they love, we'd love to help them. We'll send you a $200 gift card to the Cheesecake Factory and we'll give your friend $200 off your treatment if you recommend them." **Automate what can be automated**. The follow-up stuff can be automated, phone tracking can be automated so you're not stressing about trying to find out where these calls came from, your referral system can be automated; the technology exists out there right now with Infusionsoft and AWeber and ConstantContact, and all these systems that are doing email automation. There are systems out there, such as ours, that can do more: text messages, emails, letters, postcards, the whole shebang.

Automate it! Free up your staff! I know from personal experience. We switched to Infusionsoft in 2008 and I literally, before we switched to Infusionsoft, we had AWeber and we had ConstantContact and we had some homegrown systems for our marketing and we were using Act for our contact management, our CRM, we had all these different systems that didn't really communicate with each other – it was just a disaster. When we switched to Infusionsoft, it was an investment but it literally freed up an entire staff member who was dedicated to just managing the systems and inputting the data into the different systems. Literally $45,000 a year we saved going to Infusionsoft. Sure, the investment was there. We spent $15 or 20,000 converting to Infusionsoft and getting that rocking and rolling, but now we're saving $45,000 a year on staff labor. I don't have a staff member assigned to doing that all anymore – we've got a very, very streamlined system. Automate it, automate it, automate it! I can't stress it enough.

7. Knowing Your Return on Investment

And then the seventh item. Of course, all of your money is spent in the wrong place if you don't know the return you are getting for it. Just to rehash what I said at the beginning of the conversation, if you buy anything of value: real estate, stock, bond, house – you know your cost basis and you know your profit or loss at any point in time and when you sell it. Your marketing should be just that plain and simple to track. The systems exist out there to do this. We've developed our Zetetics system to do just that: track phone calls, track cases, track consults and track the dollars back into your pocket. We record the calls for you for quality control, making sure your staff is following the proper phone training. There's nothing worse than spending thousands and tens of thousands of dollars on marketing, only to find out that your front desk is fumbling the first phone call. Or even worse yet, something that we see fairly common – I won't say fairly common – we see regularly enough is the phone isn't even being answered at all! Your staff is so tied up answering appointment changes and existing patient calls that when that new patient does call in, the phone doesn't even get answered.

There are tons of ways that you can do things wrong. There are a few ways that you can do things right. Make sure that you're tracking everything so you know exactly what you're getting. If you're having trouble with your phones, we're glad to help. The backline is certainly a very efficient way to streamline your incoming new patient phone calls and separate them from existing patient phone calls and maintenance stuff.

Get started with some tracking. For three phone call tracking lines that can track three different pieces of your marketing – say you're doing a direct mail piece, you have a Yellow Pages ad or a newspaper ad in a magazine – you've got three different marketing pieces – to track three of them, you're talking about less than $100 a month. Any marketing you're spending out there is more than $100 a month, probably more than $1,000 a month. Even TV spots here in Louisville, Kentucky right now are running $200, 300 or 400 a spot, if you get on any kind of package, you're easily spending $3,000-5,000 a month so track it. Know exactly what you're getting! If you are unhappy with your results, don't base it on guesses or conjectures, just look at the report. The report will tell you that you spent "x" money that led to "x" number of phone calls that converted into "x" number of consultations, we presented "x" number of cases, "x" number accepted and all that generated "x" number of dollars into my bank account. That should be as easy as tracking and marketing is these days. It should just be that simple.

I've dumped a lot of information on you here in this podcast. I hope I haven't scared anybody off, but I'd like to offer to you – completely free – our report to help you get your practice on track to finding the patients that YOU want and attracting the patients that YOU want into your practice. It's our **Dental Website Audit** and it can be downloaded right off our website: www.SmartBoxWebMarketing.com. I would encourage you to take a look at it: it's our 40-page report that we have simply laid out exactly what you need to do to be successful with your online marketing. From automated follow-up, prequalification, video, social media, the whole alphabet soup of Pay-Per-Click and SEO and local search and SEM and SMO and all this stuff – all the jargon. It explains it to you in super simple terms what you need to be doing and, more importantly, what areas and what pitfalls to avoid with your online marketing.

That's all for today. The link again: www.DentalWebAudit.com. Check that out and if you have any feedback, I'd love to hear from you. You can email me directly, colin@smartboxweb.com. Colin Receveur here; thanks for watching this edition of the fast thoughts on dental marketing. Keep moving forward.

Chapter 18

Successfully Unifying Your Efforts

Word Count: **1807**
Approximate Time to Read: **4.0 minutes**

By this point, you should have a good idea of how to use social media, Search Engine Optimization, and online video to your advantage. However, you're not quite done yet. You need to know how to bring all of your efforts together to create seamless marketing. This will offer benefits to you and your practice, as well as to your patients and prospective patients.

Bringing It All Together

Bringing all your marketing efforts together makes it all far easier to manage. In addition, you will find it also boosts your results. There are some specific things you need to do in order to successfully do this though.

Integrating your online efforts provides a seamless experience for your readers and visitors. If you do not interconnect all your various online outlets, it can be easy for readers and prospective patients to miss one or more of your locations. For instance, they might locate your website but fail to realize you are also on Facebook; they might find your Facebook page but not realize you are also on Twitter.

The point of this is to encourage interaction on multiple fronts. The more connected you are with existing patients and others, the better your results will be. For example, if the same person connects with you on both Facebook and Twitter, you can benefit from their list of connections on both networks, which are often composed of different people. The same principle applies to your use of LinkedIn, your blog, and anything else you choose to do. The first step in bringing everything together is to create a central hub for all your efforts. But what might this hub be?

A Central Hub for Your Online Efforts

This idea holds quite a bit of value. It allows you to connect everything to a single location much like the center of a spider web. However, you need to choose the right central location. You have two options: your website or your blog. But, which location is the better choice?

Which Location to Choose?

Deciding to use your website or blog as a central hub can be somewhat difficult. There are pros and cons to both with neither option being perfect. Using your website as a central hub can have some advantages particularly if you choose to integrate your blog with your site as opposed to hosting it somewhere else. This all-in-one situation really does provide you with the best central location. However, it might not be the right fit, depending on the feel you have for your website. If you are trying to achieve a high-end professional site or one geared for costly cosmetic dental procedures, having links to your social networks, a Twitter feed, and other integration options might take away from your aesthetics and overall feel.

Using your blog as a central hub is the best option if you choose to go with a separate blog and website. Obviously, you will want to have some elements of your social networking visible on your website (a small "Connect on Facebook" icon, for instance), but you'll find the casual nature of a blog is a better fit for the way social networking operates.

Why is this? Consider the Twitter feed widget – it's designed to be installed in a sidebar of your blog and highlight recent tweets. Depending on the design of your website, this might take away from the overall value. However, in a blog, it's right at home.

In terms of social media integration, another reason you might want to focus on your blog more heavily than your website is because your blog will be updated more frequently. Your website is going to be relatively static but your blog will be updated weekly, meaning you will have more visitors on your blog – regular readers, new readers, etc. By connecting your blog to all your social networking efforts, you ensure both current and new readers can connect with you. This is the best way to maximize the value of social networking and social media.

Yet, another reason for focusing on your blog exists: giving your users the power to share your content – this is interactivity at its finest. By encouraging your readers and visitors to share your content with their own connections and followers, you are able to boost your traffic, market recognition, and even gain new connections and followers for yourself.

How Do You Connect Your Efforts?

Understanding how to connect your various online presences is vital. There are a few ways you can do this but they're not all of equal value. It's actually best you use a combination of different methods to ensure the best connectivity throughout. Here are some specific ways to this broken down by component type (location):

Facebook: You can use Facebook as an anchor point for almost anything including your blog or website. Your business page has an information section where you can put the address of your blog (or your website, if you so choose). You can put more than one URL on the page if you like, though placing too many will confuse your readers.

Another excellent option for Facebook is to connect your feed to your blog. This will allow your blog posts to pull double duty as updates on your Facebook page, encouraging further interaction with your friends and followers. As a note, it's also best that you fill out the profile information completely, including a picture of you or your office. This helps you appear more legitimate – spammers tend to have no picture and little or no profile information. Set yourself apart from these unsavory individuals by proving you are on the up and up.

Twitter: Much like Facebook, Twitter has a profile information page you need to fill out completely. Unlike Facebook, Twitter's page is incredibly short; however, there is a place to put your website or blog address – make sure you fill this in. This encourages people viewing your profile to click the link and visit the destination page.

Another way you can use Twitter to connect your activities is by tweeting when you update your blog. There are widgets that can automate this process for you, or you can schedule tweets through a third party application like TweetDeck, Su.pr, or HootSuite.

If you choose to tweet updates on your blog, do so on a limited basis. In general, try not to do promotional tweets more than once every couple of hours. An ideal format might be to schedule tweets four times per day – once in the morning, once in the afternoon, once in the evening, and then again before midnight. This helps to ensure all your followers have a chance to see your tweet, no matter what time they use the network but doesn't give you the appearance of being a spammer. Of course, you still need to use Twitter correctly by interacting with others and retweeting other people.

LinkedIn: Like all the other social networks, LinkedIn has a profile section where you can display your desired URL as well as a range of professional and personal information. Again, make sure you fill out this section as completely as possible and make sure you upload a picture. However, because LinkedIn is for professionals, you will receive a lower amount of traffic from this network than through Twitter or Facebook. This does not mean it's not worth your time, though. The quality of the relationships you can build here is considerable and well worth your time.

Your Blog: You will need to take some special steps to connect your various social network presences to your blog. The best way to do this is to have a "Connect With Us" section on the main page of your blog. It's best to locate this at the top of a side bar – placing it lower on the page reduces the chance your readers will see it. Within this section, you should have icons representing the various social networks you use. You'll find a number of WordPress widgets that can do this for you. All you will need to do is add your Twitter, Facebook, and LinkedIn URLs to the widget. A reader can simply click the button and be taken to your page on the corresponding social network. This is a great way to encourage your readers to interact with you on other platforms.

As mentioned previously, you can also place a Twitter feed widget on your blog. This is a good idea because it not only lets your readers know you are active on Twitter but gives them a preview of what your tweets might be (and can help them realize you are not a spammer). Finally, you can also give your readers the power to share your content through social bookmarking sites as well as on their own social network feeds.

Give Your Users the Power to Share

Harnessing the power of your visitors to boost your visibility online will also require you empower them – giving them the ability to share your content. You can do this in a number of different ways, as well. Why is this important? When you provide sharing tools for your blog readers, you encourage them to help you promote your practice without adding any additional cost or work for yourself. Simply put, it's a tremendous way to increase your market saturation without increasing your marketing costs.

How do you know your readers will take the initiative to promote on your behalf? This is where informative, quality posts come into play. If you have solid, viable, useful posts on your blog, you usually don't have to do much more to make your readers want to share with others. However, if your posts lack value or real information, don't expect to reap any rewards here. This raises the question of how you are supposed to actually empower your readers to share your content. You can install a "Tweet This" button at the top or bottom of each post – you will find several automated widgets that can do this for you. You can do the same thing with a Facebook "Like" icon. Both Twitter and Facebook buttons allow your readers to share the post on their own timelines, encouraging others to click the link and read your post. In addition to a link to the post, those receiving your readers' updates will also be able to "follow" or "like" your practice, depending on the social network in question.

In addition to Twitter and Facebook icons, you can also add social media buttons to your blog posts. Social bookmarking sites like Reddit, StumbleUpon, Del.icio.us, and Digg can help you generate the reputation you want as well as boost your web traffic. A number of widgets give you the means to integrate various social bookmarking links into each post on your website, all of which can be easily customized to your specific needs.

Chapter 19
The Power of Video

Word Count: **5711**
Approximate Time to Read: **12.7 minutes**

*"Websites with video are **53 times more likely** to have a first page ranking on Google.*

"Google bought YouTube for 1.65 billion dollars, which to you and I means they want more hits on YouTube videos, so they rank them higher in listings. I interviewed the highest producing solo dentist in the country and one of the things he is doing is taking his TV commercials and putting them on YouTube, as well as on his website. Of course, that boosts his ranking on Google."

~ Woody Oakes

"Well Colin, you know when we first spoke, we had a website going down and I'd been noticing the amount of video that's on different websites – not necessarily ours – and I wanted to get involved with that. How many YouTube things go out every day? Seventy thousand or some crazy number like that? That's what people want. I wanted to be able to do that on my own terms. I didn't want all stock videos. They're okay, I'm not against them but if you have your own patients doing that, it's a lot more believable. I remembered talking with you a few years ago when your father and I were in James' group and then you started to do some web work and things like that. James recommended you so I thought that maybe I'd take a look at that. Also, placement on Google and things like that and other search engines, that interested me. Who can do that – who can handle that and watch over that? I thought you folks would be the people to do it."

~ John K. Argeros, D.M.D.

"Well our website that we had before, patients were going to look at it but it just didn't give them enough incentive to call us. We just weren't getting much feedback from it. The analytics we got, patients were going to that site looking at it for a few seconds but then it didn't seem like the phone calls were coming.

"Second biggest problem: I guess people that would come in,

*they didn't know us, if they had a big case, **you can't throw a $10,000-$20,000 case at somebody that just walks in the door – there's no trust factor there. It frustrated us that we didn't communicate to them the values we have here so we figured if, before they ever walk through the door, if they knew us and trusted us, the bigger cases would be much faster to close.***

*"I talked about doing the website and you said, 'You need video,' and said you could come here – we wouldn't have to fly out to your place. You could bring a crew in here and set up, give us a day, and just told us what kind of patients were good to bring in that we'd done different procedures on. **It was easy and has proved helpful in earning our patients' trust."***

~ Thomas L. Phillips, Jr. D.D.S., Implant Dentist in Fort Worth, Texas

"Taping and presenting testimonials from the patients and from the staff makes a tremendous difference in a way that the marketing is done today because the patient is the person to be trusted and to listen to.

"When the patient tells you he or she had a very good experience: satisfied with the work, very happy, the potential patient – the potential lead listens and that plays an important role in making a decision whether or not to call the office."

~Saj Jivraj, D.D.S., M.S.Ed.

Why Video?

As a dentist, you have exceptional training and skills. Though the range of skills and the focus of each dentist will always vary, every dentist is a professional. This can often make things a little tough for the modern dentist who has to be at the top of their game, offering all of the newest techniques or treatments, providing excellent customer service, and also competing with the other practitioners in their area.

For some, competing for new patients may be only a small matter if the general region has a large market for dental work, but it can be an intense situation when the market is more saturated with practitioners. The dilemma for the dentist is how to go about enhancing their clinical skills while also learning about, mastering, and executing the marketing systems they need to use in order to keep a steady stream of new patients coming through their door.

No matter what niche in dentistry you have whether it be cosmetics, general family dentistry, oral surgery, sedation or implants or whether you are marketing to the affluent or PPOs and HMOs, you can augment your offline external marketing efforts, validate your place in the market, and set yourself up as the expert in your local area using the web and video marketing.

Today's patient is exponentially more educated and aware of their options than they were 10 or even 5 years ago. Google and other search engines have allowed your patients to research not only the clinical options available but also, which local dentists provide these options for them. To get a prospective patient into your office and to the point of opening their wallets, you need at least "three cups of tea" with them. The National Sales Executive Association released a case study that found 90% of all sales are closed on the 4th-12th contact you have with a prospect. Your newspaper ad could be the first contact, your website the second, your free report and autoresponders another; with social media and your videos, you might get them to their fourth (or more) cup of tea before they ever walk through the door of your dental practice.

This section will teach you about the benefits of video marketing for dentists. It will focus primarily on the use of embedded videos in places like websites and blogs and explain the value of a video series on a site like YouTube. You will learn how using videos or links to the videos in social networking sites will serve as the best form of online marketing available! You will discover the world's leading search engine, Google, gives videos tremendous value. You will see you can direct a lot of effort and energy into the text appearing on websites, blogs, and social media but will quickly discover how videos are going to generate a measurably larger amount of validity to your site. This can lead to a higher position for your site when someone searches for your chosen search terms or keywords.

What makes videos such a wise area in which to invest serious amounts of time and energy is that they are now appearing at the top of search engine results – **right at the top of the first page.** The great part about video marketing is the simple fact it doesn't end with the SEO. For example, if you make a very informative, useful, or timely video about some facet of dentistry, it is likely to appear in many different places, be forwarded across social networks, and generally get your office phone ringing with inquiries from those who watched the videos.

What We'll Cover

In order to get a very clear understanding of how video marketing is going to really increase the number of calls you get to your dental practice, we need to understand how some of the different pieces of the marketing campaign work.

First, we have to look at the subject known as SEO or Search Engine Optimization. This shows you how to identify the keywords to use in your various online materials in order to rank highly in search engine results. We'll be sure to go over the steps necessary for choosing the best keywords for your needs. For example, if you are a dentist offering smile makeovers and you want to compete with someone in a neighboring town, we will show you how local SEO terminology should be used to optimize your videos. We will then determine, which of the keywords are the most logical in terms of the results they'll generate for dental practices and the videos made to support them. Next, we will consider videos and how the search engines weigh them in regards to their keywords. We are going to dedicate a lot of attention to how to really build your online image through savvy use of videos.

Whether you ask patients to make testimonials or whether you show your true expertise through the creation of topic videos, you will be amazed at the way these enhance your reputation and build a good image. Finally, we'll look at the other ways you can use your developing video expertise. Whether you want to make screensavers patients can download from your homepage or keep a nice stream of informational video footage running in the waiting room, we'll address the value of every option. So, let's begin the process of learning all about video marketing and how it is going to strengthen and increase your dental practice!

SEO for Video

What does optimize actually mean? Before we head into the formal description of the meaning of optimization, let's be sure you understand what the results of a fully optimized video could mean. When you have posted your videos to your website, blog, social networking sites, and video sharing sites, it will:

1. **Boost the rank of the website in SERP** – The various descriptors used in the video tags, titles, etc. will apply to the keyword usage throughout the whole site. So, optimizing your videos with the

most powerful keywords and then using excellent text in the website pages will have the proverbial "one-two punch" necessary to boost website rank in most search results.

2. **Boost the rank of the video in Google search results** – Google is already known for incorporating video results on the first page of search engine results. If your video is optimized to the strongest degree possible, it will tend to appear as one of the few video clips that have relevance to the search terms entered by a consumer.

3. **Boost the rank of the video in site-specific searches** – When people are looking for videos at sites like YouTube or Vimeo, they have to enter search terms. If you have properly optimized your videos when posting them on these sites, it is likely they will rank well in those search results too.

Naturally, all this means you have to understand the most appropriate way to optimize; this is done during the uploading process. Whether it includes the HTML tags your webmaster enters, the spaces left blank by the video sharing and video syndicating websites, or the tags in your blog, as far as any video file is concerned, you will usually have the option of:

- Drafting a description
- Selecting a category
- Providing a title
- Creating tags that apply to it when it is embedded in a website, posted at a video website like YouTube or used in a blog

These options vary according to the site where the item is posted, but it is a good idea to stick with the same tags, titles, and descriptions at all times and for all sites. They don't have to be the exact same in terms of word order (unless a two- to four-word phrase is counted as a keyword), they just need to use the same sets of terms and words. This will allow search engines to view the video in the same way wherever it happens to be found and to continue to push up the ranking.

We have already learned text content in the body of a website is not viewed in the same manner as things like titles and tags. This means your optimized video might show up in a few dozen places and although it uses the same keywords, titles, and tags at each location, the search engine will give each instance high ranking value. If it were a matter of text content using repetitive keywords, the search engine algorithms would consider this a form of duplication and keyword "stuffage" and penalize the ranking.

Once you determine the right keywords and phrases to use in your SEO campaigns, you will have to apply them to your videos in a similar way. This creates the optimal results in terms of where the video shows up on the "site specific" searches as well as the broader global search engines. Thus, videos with optimized titles and descriptions will place well in the YouTube SERPs as well as the Google SERPs.

Optimizing Videos for Best Results

Because it is most likely going to be YouTube where you begin to post your uploaded videos, we will use their protocol to describe the optimization process. Though other sites may function a bit differently, most are going to provide you with many of the same requirements and options.

Currently, when you register for a YouTube account and request to upload a video, the screen asks you to complete the following fields:

- **Title** – A blank field that allows you to enter a creative title using the keywords you want to optimize for. Be sure; however, your title makes sense and is appealing to those searching for videos with your subject matter; for example, "A Brief Introduction to Dental Implants – Getting a New Smile."

- **Description** – Another blank field you will type a strong and accurate explanation of the contents of the clip. Again, you can use your keywords to their best advantage. For example, "A video explaining dental implants and how they are used for a new smile or a smile makeover."

- **Tags** (Suggested tags appear once you begin typing) – In this space, you can use your entire list of keywords, if desired. The suggested list pops up as soon as you start typing, making it easy for you to add them to your list by just clicking on the words. This is a good idea if you want to attract the most viewers for your videos because it will connect your video to many related searches.

- **Category** – This consists of a drop-down list containing the categories the videos are divided into. Currently, the list includes:

- ◆ Autos and Vehicles
- ◆ Comedy
- ◆ Education
- ◆ Entertainment
- ◆ Film and Animation
- ◆ Gaming
- ◆ How-to and Style
- ◆ Music
- ◆ News and Politics
- ◆ Nonprofit and Activism
- ◆ People and Blogs
- ◆ Pets and Animals
- ◆ Science and Technology
- ◆ Sports
- ◆ Travel and Events

So where does dentistry belong in such a list? It depends upon the issue being addressed in the clip but dental processes tend to appear in the science and technology, while other subjects can easily fall under education, how-to and style, and news and politics. Simply choose your category in a way that maximizes the amount of attention the video will receive.

- **Privacy** – Choose from "Private," "Unlisted," or "Public." The "Public" view is clearly the one you will want to use for all your dental videos.

- **Channel Information** – Don't overlook this portion! It is the one direct way to get viewers right to your website thanks to the option for including URL addresses and links. You can include your site, your blog, or any page on your site that is particularly relevant to the subject matter of the video.

The other video sharing sites currently in use by many dental professionals and millions of other web users include:

- **Vimeo** – Vimeo.com
- **Daily Motion** – DailyMotion.com

- **Yahoo!** – Video.Yahoo.com
- **Metacafe** – Metacafe.com

There are many other video sites but these are the top five in terms of visitation and usage. They are all guaranteed to provide the kind of relevant and interested traffic you will need to get people visiting your site or calling your office – if you take the time to optimize them accordingly. Remember, optimization is going to apply to the videos you post to your own website and blogs as well. In a moment, we will consider building video libraries, using syndication, and backlinks but for now, you should keep in mind all these places generate the same kind of results from optimized video information.

Keyword Tactics: Text Vs. Video

Something to always keep in mind about optimizing your videos is that website owners are not penalized by search engines for repetition in terms of keyword usage. For example, someone with a website that seems to have repetitive text ("keyword stuffing") is going to be penalized by the search engine spiders and given a lower spot on the SERP. The site with the keywords appearing repeatedly in video tags and details is REWARDED for this and gets a higher rank in the SERP.

This means videos instantly provide you with the means of using your keywords in a "natural" manner while also helping to avoid the most common SEO dilemma – keyword stuffing!

Consider this example of keyword stuffing: "If you are looking for dental implants in the tri-state area, come to Dr. Receveur where his expertise with dental implants will allow you to get the brightest and straightest smile possible through the use of dental implants." Horrible, right? Unfortunately, this is exactly what you will find on a lot of dental websites because they are relying on "artificial" keyword usage. This means they want their percentage of keywords to run high in order to positively affect their position on the SERPs, but they leave their customers disappointed by the poor quality of the text. This is the surest way to alienate visitors to the site and to make a terrible first impression.

So, you can do natural keyword usage and artificial keyword usage. Which is the right approach for a dental website? It is not only the videos that require appropriate keyword application but the website too. A dental office is going to be concerned with the content as much as the

SERP so it is going to be best to use the keywords in a natural manner. Because you will be applying keywords to videos you will be posting in a very liberal manner, you are going to be able to keep the text content of the page to a very high level of value for your visitors.

This approach is going to create two results: first, you will have very readable and useful text at the site. This is bound to generate positive results and a lot more traffic when people pass on the details via things like Facebook "Likes," Google "+1s," etc. Secondly, this approach is going to consistently boost the SERP of the site because the keywords are going to appear with each posting of the videos too.

Google, YouTube, and More SERPs

By now, you understand clearly the ways to work around the difficulties of the keyword issue in the SERPs through the use of videos. Just consider the following:

- Google displays a list of YouTube video results at the top of almost every SERP. This list uses thumbnails or small icons that can actually play the video directly in the page of results.

- Videos using optimized keywords in the best ways (such as in titles, descriptions, meta tags, and more) appear in other SERPs too, such as those generated at Bing and Yahoo!.

- Videos that have the highest rankings in the individual video websites (such as the search results through YouTube's engine) have a higher ranking in the SERPs.

- Videos optimized after the keywords are determined are known to perform better in the SERPs.

What all of this adds up to is the simple fact that you might be able to get your website the kind of attention and visibility you want from well implemented video marketing tactics. In a few moments, we will explore the value of "video syndication services" but before moving past this subject, we should consider a few more items. For example, we have not yet touched on the best subjects for a dental office video library!

Using Video SEO to Dominate - A Review

Let's review what all we've covered in this section. You have learned all about SEO and SERP and why the Internet is an essential tool for a dental practice in the modern era. You have also had an introduction to keywords and how to develop powerful keyword lists to use for your video marketing and general SEO efforts, boosting your website's position in search engine results as well as your videos' positions in the SERPs for video sites and general web searches.

We covered how keyword stuffing is obsolete with the combination of "natural" keyword usage on your website and well optimized videos to get the best rank. We then covered how to optimize all of the available fields for videos and how to properly categorize them.

The discovery was made that videos are taken into consideration under a large range of different factors over a website's text content and that this can actually work in your favor by placing your website's videos higher on the page of search results than websites that ranked higher in the actual SERP.

Video SEO Cheat Sheet

How To Make Your Videos #1 On Google

Getting your dental videos to show up #1 on Google might be the best kept secret on the web. Well, actually it isn't a secret at all. It just takes a little time, attention to detail, and of course, great content that will engage your viewers! Here's how you do it:

Step 1: Choosing Your Keywords

The first step is to select the keywords that you want to optimize for, but choose carefully! You want to choose keywords that people are searching for but also have low competition. Getting your video to the #1 spot on Google for a keyword like "dentist" just isn't going to happen. These "short-tail keywords" are a waste of time to try to rank for – your prospects aren't qualified and the competition is insane. The opposite of this, "long-tail keywords," are phrases like "dental implants new albany indiana" where the prospect searching has greatly narrowed the scope of what they are searching for. Focus on finding these to build your video's views!

We suggest using Google's Sandbox Keyword Tool to help with this. If you don't know how to use it, just Google it and the first result will help you through how to use the tool. You want to focus your search on long-tail keywords that have some search traffic, but also have low competition.

Once you find your long-tail keywords, go to YouTube and search to see how many videos you are competing against. If the number there is low, then you have a winner!

Step 2: Optimizing Your Video

Create the script for your video based around your selected long-tail keywords. Be sure to include lots of great information about your topic! You can have the best optimized video in the world, but if the video is garbage then no one is going to watch it. Be sure to use your long-tail keyword at the beginning, middle, and end of the video script.

Upload your video to YouTube and be sure to optimize your video before the upload completes. This will have you off to the races fast!

Here's our secret formula for video optimization on YouTube:

Title: Long-tail keyword

Description: http://www.yourwebsite.com followed by your video script. Note: It is very important that the video and the video script have your long-tail keyword at the beginning, middle, and end!

Tags: Long-tail keyword, your name, your business, your industry, two related search terms

Category: Select one closest to you. That's it! If you've selected a good long-tail keyword, just sit back and watch your video explode to the top of Google. You can repeat this process for each topic you want to rank highly for on Google and YouTube.

The Patient Attraction Podcast
Episode 001: The One About Dominating The Web With Video

Hello and welcome to the first video podcast of 2012. I'm your host, Colin Receveur. In today's episode, we're going to discuss how successful dentists are leveraging video in their marketing. I'm going to be pulling back the curtains to give you the secrets of what we're doing with our best clients. As a free gift to those with a high-level of interest, everyone who stays until the end of the podcast is going to get a free copy of my latest book, *How Really Smart Dentists are Leveraging their Marketing to Dominate the Web.*

You may notice this is a new blog format for the weekly updates. Starting January 2012, we will be doing video blogs; you may have heard them be called vlogs, podcasts, video podcasts, vodcasts ... I simply call them "a guy talking into the camera on the drive into work." We've actually got a shoot at the studio today so this is going to be pretty short and sweet because I don't have a lot of time to talk. I'm heading to San Diego Friday for a week ... pretty excited. The weather is much nicer than this 20 degree crap. A little wine tasting, going to have to drop into the zoo – I haven't been since I was a kid – and we're shooting some video as well for some clients.

Why Listen to Me?

If you haven't listened in before, I'm Colin Receveur, speaker, author, invited columnist for the Profitable Dentist, DentalTown, and founder of SmartBox Web Marketing where we, simply put, get dentists more qualified patients in the niches they have advanced clinical training. The purpose of these podcasts is to educate you about dental marketing so you can make an informed decision about what's best for you and your practice in this new dental economy. So here's what we're going to cover – five important topics dentists want to know about video:

1. Why Video Just Works (When Done Right)
2. Why Video is So Powerful
3. What to Put in Your Videos
4. How to Optimize Your Videos (SEO)
5. Where and How to Leverage Your Videos

Now onto the good stuff! Starting with the first topic …

1. Why Does Video Work?

We hear from doctors often that they "tried video" or they "did a website" and they got nothing. Well first off, as with any marketing, there's more ways to do it wrong than right. You can't just throw up a video shot in your operatory with your Christmas camera and expect people to want to watch it and call you. It's the same for websites. **Bad lighting, shaky camera, poor quality, too clinical – lots of reasons and ways to do it wrong.** There are two things that successful video marketing campaigns do:

1. Use high quality and compelling content to inform and educate

2. Use syndication and optimization to be seen and get found

You have to design your videos based on what your patients want to know. What answers do they want? What are they searching for? Ask your non-dental friends and survey your patients. Patient/client surveys are EXTREMELY powerful and give you the exact information you're looking for. A lot of guys are put off by the intimidation factor or the unknown factor and don't do these surveys but these are invaluable ways to find out information.

2. Why is Video such a Powerful Tool?

Let's start with some simple statistics to get you an idea of how many videos are being watched online:

● In the past 30 days, 82.5% of US has watched a video online.

● YouTube is the #2 largest Search Engine – #1 is Google.

● 60% of searchers (in 2009) would rather watch a video than read information.

Video is powerful because it establishes trust – it puts your face to your name. It allows you to reach out to your prospects and literally speak directly to them. Only 14% of the US trusts advertisements right now. You need to be doing everything you can to gain your prospects' attention AND trust. Video brings warmth and a personal experience to a text-based boring website, and we all know people do business with people they like.

3. What to Put in Your Videos

The #1 thing is to tell them what to do – a call to action! It's the same mistakes many website owners make: they have no CTA on their sites. You must have a CTA on your videos. Offer a free book like we are, free coupon code at the end, a free teeth whitening – some kind of incentive for users to stay.

Answer their questions first, then become their expert. We see many dentists with videos and websites that talk all about them, how great they are, their qualifications, their education, and they offer a menu of their services – but they never address the questions the patients have! You've got to talk to your patients' needs. All your background has an important place to build your rapport, but FIRST you have to grab their attention and help them with THEIR problem. Then, if you do that, they will want to find out more about you and THEN you will become an expert in their eyes.

Uneducated and uninformed patients don't buy. By elevating their awareness and arming them with lots of info, they become a better consumer of dentistry and the dental services you offer. People are looking for choices, options and what's possible. And they aren't going to call you after the first time they find your website, especially not the big cases. It takes 4-18 months to convert the large cases; you need to be feeding them lots of information. But don't dump information on them – drip, drip, drip small pieces they can digest. Info dumps are a waste of everyone's time. Answer their relevant concerns, send them information as they request and can digest it, and you'll be their hero.

One thought – one video, short and sweet, answer their question. The videos we have success with are 30-90 seconds each, covering a range of topics, because patients have lots of questions. Look at your FAQs or keep track of what your patients are asking during consults. Why are you different? Why should they choose you? That's what you want videos on.

4. How to Optimize Videos

Well optimized videos are 53 times more likely to get a first page ranking on Google than your website. Videos now show above organic listings at the top of the first page of search results. There are a handful of aspects you need to keep in mind when optimizing your videos:

- **Title** – it needs to be compelling and relevant. Your visitor should know what they are clicking on and be intrigued to learn more.

- **Description** – stay under 200-250 words. You can't transcribe your video, you don't have enough space for that. Summarize your content if the video is too long and be sure to use your keywords.

- **Tags** – used to further describe your video. Keep the number of tags short: don't use 20+ tags on your videos, preferably 5-10 very relevant words or phrases are best. Be sure you're using your keywords here too.

- **Category** – mostly missed on YouTube, use a category for further optimization. I like to use either Education or Health Care.

- **Syndicate your video** – build backlinks into your website. The more places your video can be found, the more YOU will be found. Distribute your videos to dozens of video websites like FaceBook, link on Twitter, Vimeo, Metacafe, YouTube, and dozens more, linking back to your website with each one. This adds SEO value to your videos and website.

5. Where and How to use Your Videos

- **On your website** – replace your text FAQ page and answer questions with video.

- **On YouTube** – Google now shows optimized YouTube videos above the organic rankings right at the top of the search result page.

- **Mobile video** – huge growing marketing right now – I hope you're taking advantage and have a mobile website too.

- **Social media** – Facebook, Twitter … all have many more uses than just YouTube. Video needs to be everywhere.

The Five Takeaways from this Episode

1. **Why Video Just Works** – how video builds trust in an age of distrust amongst advertising.

2. **Why Video is So Powerful** – the stats behind this shift in how information is being delivered online and why time is of the essence for you to take advantage of it.

3. **What to Put in Your Videos** – what you need to talk about to get your patients listening.

4. **How to Optimize Your Videos (SEO)** – how to get your videos found at the top of Google.

5. **Where and How to Leverage Your Videos** – using your videos to their maximum potential to get seen online.

Get a copy of my book shipped to you

As promised, there's a link at the bottom of this video where you can request a free copy of my latest book.

This 72-page book is chocked full of everything you need to know to dominate your local area and get the lion's share of new patients, and it's free to everyone that listened in today. Simply go to the URL below and we'll ship a printed copy to you.

As always, the fast-movers and early adopters will take the lion's share of new patients. The fundamental shift in how information is delivered that we experienced 5-10 years ago with websites is happening again now with video. Those sitting on the fence, playing it safe, are going to be watching their competition reap the profits. I hope your 2012 is everything you want it to be, take care and I'll see you in two weeks when I get back from San Diego with the next episode.

http://Link.SmartBoxWeb.com/jan12

Chapter 20

Crushing Your Competition with Video

Word Count: **1962**
Approximate Time to Read: **4.4 minutes**

Now is the time to take a look at the list of possible subjects for your videos. By no means is this going to be the most comprehensive list imaginable, but it will provide the "backbone" to a very effective series of videos. All you need to do is consider the subjects that most people might "Google." Combine this list with your area of expertise and the services you wish to market and you have the basis for a good library of online videos.

What Can a Dentist Make Videos About?

Your goal with your finished video should be to appear at the top of the video section on the first SERP for any search. Consider the following:

Let's say you want to know all about teeth whitening in your area. You use Google to find the listings for dentists offering the service in your area. In the listings, however, there is a section showing a bunch of thumbnails for videos about teeth whitening. Do you think you would still click on the regular text results in Google if you could be watching video clips instead? Most people prefer to see some examples of the procedures or treatments they might receive. If you put up optimized videos for all your services, it is quite likely you will get a call from the viewer.

What other concepts should be used for your dental video marketing efforts? Some of the most common include:

- **Orthodontics** - These might cover anything from how they are fitted to the benefits of straight teeth.
- **Teeth whitening techniques** – From take-home kits to in-office laser treatments, this is a good subject for a video series.
- **The benefits of dental hygiene** – Cover subjects like gingivitis, cleanings, and routine checkups.

- **Crowns and bridges** – Show patients how these can be used for a smile makeover as well as for general repair work.

- **Smile makeovers** – This could include bits from many different videos or could be an entire narrative in itself.

- **Veneers** – Many people would greatly appreciate a detailed video about veneers as a means of making their smile more attractive.

- **Implants** – This is a fascinating and contemporary subject that could easily make an entire series covering the different solutions and techniques available.

- **Explanation videos** – A detailed video explanation showing patients the results of different treatments. You may want to get permission from patients to film these.

- **Training videos** – Create videos for your staff members to use.

- **Highlights** – Whether you host an annual seminar, make a weekly "spotlight" video on a current issue, or address questions emailed in to your site, this sort of video keeps your content fresh and interesting.

It is easy to see how a set of videos is going to provide a dentist with a nice array of keywords that will work together to guide potential customers to the site. The videos, however, will also save the dentist and/or the staff from answering the same questions. They can guide someone to view the video directly from the website library, send a link to the video in an appointment confirmation email, or stream videos in the treatment rooms while patients wait.

The videos are also a fantastic way to encourage a patient to consider more than just a single treatment or procedure. For instance, while someone is waiting for their teeth whitening treatment, they can be shown a video of the take-home kits and cleaning systems available through the office. They might also watch videos of invisible braces, crowns, and more cosmetic dental procedures.

Naturally, this also means a dental practice that makes a point of frequently using the videos will soon develop a large collection of them. While all of them will tend to remain active on sites like YouTube or the dental practitioner's own website, it is important to remember the videos are still working for the SEO campaign at the same time. We look at the ways of using your developing video library to improve your position in the SERPs a bit later.

Other Uses for Killer Video

Whether you have paid someone to make the videos or tackled it as a DIY project, you have invested time and energy (as well as money) into the issue. This means you really want to get all that you possibly can from the videos. We already pointed out you shouldn't just archive them to YouTube and your website and let them sit there, gathering dust.

Instead, you should put on your proverbial thinking cap and continually find ways of repurposing or re-releasing each of the videos you have made available. We have found that you can easily put them to use in:

- Blogs
- Video FAQs
- Waiting Room TV Rolls
- TV Commercials
- Screensavers
- Mobile Devices

We will look at each of these possible venues briefly in order to determine the best ways to use your optimized videos to make them the most beneficial!

Blogs

The power of a good blog is incredible, as has been mentioned. A dental professional can offer an amazing range of information and detail in their blog. One of the most profoundly popular things to do with any blog is to embed videos into each entry. We already mentioned this is known as a "vlog," which makes it easier than ever to disperse a video in a simple way through social networking links, subscriptions, and more.

What we haven't mentioned is you can use a video on your blog, your website, AND many video sharing sites and yet, the search engines won't view this as duplicate content. We already know the keywords, descriptions, tags, and categories used for videos are not considered duplicate to anything else and will only increase the rank in the SERP, but we did not mention that blogs with embedded videos can use them as often as they like.

So let's say you decide to offer an annual blog on veneers. You choose to do so around the time that proms and weddings start to occur with the most frequency – the months of May or June. If you feel you haven't made a video that is better than the one you used for the previous year, you can safely embed that video into your blog without being penalized by the search engines for this duplication! This means you might have the same video in your blogroll many times over, and yet still enjoy the benefits of the keywords. You have to also consider "relationship building" that we focused on earlier. The blog is one of the most personalized ways to communicate with patients and colleagues making it a great way to really connect with everyone on a more sincere level. For example, what feels more sincere: an open letter on the homepage of a website or the direct communication possible only through pages of a blog? Clearly, if you are hoping to speak directly to your patients or peers, it will be most effectively done through the blog.

Consider this example: the importance of dental hygiene. You can put videos and pages on your site about the need for a good routine of dental care, but you will find you get a lot more reaction from people if you create a blog post about the worst case of gingivitis you have dealt with or how gum disease can lead to other health problems. People are apt to read the blogs because they are not direct commercial appeals. If you are savvy enough to rely mostly on videos to do the talking, you will begin to see the videos being shared and your message being spread through the many new links and backlinks created. Don't forget, you'll be able to measure success by the number of calls too!

Create a Video FAQ

Though we already covered this topic, let's revisit it quickly. Whether you do this once a week, month, or every six months, a Video FAQ is a great way to introduce yourself and/or your staff to clients and potential clients. It lets people get a good feel for your personality and to become comfortable with you long before they are seated in your chair. Doing a frequent video FAQ is a great way to remain as responsive as possible with your patients and to enhance the contents of your video library. For example, you can just do a straight out Q&A, but you might want to create a theme around one of the answers; this might be after you get a question about someone's gums, allowing you to lead the conversation to gum disease or plaque treatments.

When you make a video response to questions, you can fill the

---

title, description, and tags with all of the relevant keywords as well. This is just another opportunity for you to improve your rank in the SERPs and to get your videos ahead of your competition's on a consistent basis.

Waiting Room TV Roll

When you make a video that is long enough to be broken into a series, it may be a good candidate for your waiting room TV roll. Most modern practices make a quiet and encouraging program available on their television in the waiting area. Many use purchased videos that are commercials for the services available through their offices or they accept promotional pieces from manufacturers. This is why you will hear "ask your dentist about ... " at the end of each film.

Why let someone else do the talking when you can use some of your totally customized and pre-existing commercials instead? It is very easy to create a simple DVD of your favorite clips, just be sure you show nothing with a graphic or disturbing nature. Though someone may want to know all about implants, another person may not want to see anything to do with blood, gums, or drilling prior to their visit with you.

TV Commercials

You can also use these same videos as television spots with local affiliates. Naturally, this means you have to have made high-quality films. But if you did spend the time and money to create good videos for your marketing tactics, it is perfectly acceptable to have them run on the local television stations too!

Computer Screensavers

Because you are working to get the attention of patients and fellow dentists, you may want to use some of your video stills or short clips as computer screensavers. For example, why not work with a graphic designer to convert parts of your videos into screensavers that would appeal to both groups? Consider that you may have made a lot of testimonials that show smiling, happy people: these make good screensavers for almost any setting. You could also do a screensaver of before and after images that can run on the computers in treatment rooms at any dental center. Think about the types of images dental practices would use and simply put together a nice arrangement of those images as taken from the footage you have on hand. This is a very low-cost product that will also get your name and contact details out into the world as well!

Mobile Devices

You will want people to be able to access your website from their mobile devices. This means the site has to have a second version available for their use but this doesn't mean the videos must be dismissed. Instead, you should consult with your webmaster or IT professional to find out, which of the video widgets is necessary for someone to begin streaming the video content you have available through their mobile device. It is really that simple. Someone can use their phone to bring up one of your videos to show someone else how you might provide them with a much-needed dental solution.

Chapter 21

Three Methods to Explode Your Rankings

Word Count: **2766**
Approximate Time to Read: **6.1 minutes**

Creating a Video Library

One of the most interesting things you can do with your dental videos is to build an online library of them on your website. Before just creating a "videos" section, however, remember you don't want to condense all of the terms and keywords down to a single page or location. For instance, if you put every single video on one page, it would look (to the search engine spiders) like you had fewer keywords at work. Instead, you should:

- **Create a User-Friendly Library** – Think like a visitor to your site. How would visitors use the pages? What sort of organization would the videos require to be effective?

- **Organize the Library** – Just like a regular library uses different categories and codes, you should divide your videos into logical groupings and then make individual segments or pages for them.

- **Insert a TOC** – A table of contents linking to the video library is one of the wisest choices you can make. It lets you use keywords in the titles of the links and also lets you benefit from the keywords in the various tags and titles connected to the video. You might also consider dividing your TOC by topic and/or keywords as well.

- **Make No Guesswork** – Your visitors should not have to guess what topics the segments or videos cover. Be sure your descriptions and titles are very clear and contain your chosen keywords or you run the risk of a visitor getting frustrated and navigating away from the page. Plus, by including keyword-heavy descriptions, you increase your SEO.

- **Play with a Click** – You may not realize it but most web users hate when a video link navigates them away from their original page.

To avoid this frustration, simply have your videos play directly on the page (this is a common thing with places like Facebook where you'll notice a video begins playing right in the "News Feed" screen). Though we have not yet discussed the concept of "conversion," keeping the visitor on your page is a lot more valuable than sending them to Vimeo or YouTube to see your video.

- **Break the Videos Up** – Very few people want to view a ten-minute film about teeth whitening, so why not break up your movie into several logical segments? This lets the viewer know they are not stuck with a lengthy film about whiter teeth and also creates more videos with subsequent keywords! Most video experts suggest a video should run no longer than five minutes in total time span.

You might quickly develop an enormous library of videos. Although they will always help with SEO, you don't want to just sit back and rest on this collection as it is – you want to constantly make it work for you. This is done by using the videos in your weekly or monthly blog updates, your social networking sites, and in video syndication campaigns. Using these tactics means you can constantly reuse or recycle the videos you have made by incorporating them into articles, comments, or releases that point the reader back to your website and/or video library. This keeps your SERP rank as high as possible and also ensures the video's strength (in terms of its rank) is continually increasing too.

Building Backlinks

Google says it views a backlink "from page A to page B as a vote, by page A, for page B." Basically, when you take advantage of the options for channel information or links in your videos, you are creating backlinks, which are fundamentally links coming from your videos and pointing back to your website. The implications to SEO are pretty obvious but that is not where the benefits of backlinks end. For one thing, when you have a lot of backlinks at work, it will make it easier than ever for a potential client to find you simply because your material is really "out there" and readily available. If you have incorporated alternative and relevant tags and keywords into the optimization, this makes such a thing even more common.

Good backlink policies ensure you get a true boost to your SERP location. It helps to consider that search engines are able to recognize a lot of things we wouldn't think they would. For example, we already know spiders (or web crawlers) that do all the indexing that make web searchers possible will often quickly identify instances of keyword stuffing.

Consider Authenticity in Backlinks

Web crawlers can also determine if a site is authentic or if it is lacking in credibility. For example, if you use a site to post a video and a backlink but that site has absolutely no relevance to dentistry or the content of the video, the search engines will actually see that and will usually disqualify it from positively impacting your SERP rank. This means a primary rule is to only seek out backlinks from websites that are relevant to yours – meaning they are clearly **related** to dentistry. You can opt to contact specialists, orthodontists, oral surgeons, and many others but the primary point is to be sure they are connected to the field. When a site is relevant, it is most likely a higher quality. If you haven't already done so, you may want to consider the current page rank of the site you're thinking of backlinking on in order to see if the search engines will give it the kind of value and authenticity required.

You should view your backlink locations in terms of their value. When they are valuable, they boost your rank and when they are not, they can actually decrease your rank. For instance, let's say you use an online forum about beauty to post a video link to your series on fillings. This is not a truly relevant connection but if you had used a forum on oral health for the backlink, the web crawlers would recognize the connection and would quantify that link in your favor.

Lastly, try to apply context to the terms you use in the backlink. A backlink often has a set of terms that actually form the link the web user must "click" to follow the path. This means you have yet another chance to use your optimized keywords as the subject matter of the link, giving you another boost with the search engines! For instance, instead of "Visit Dr. Receveur's site for more information about veneers," you may want to consider something more informative like "Dr. Receveur's current services include dental veneers and other cosmetic options." In this way, you would supply the search engines with the details necessary to put the backlink into the most proper context possible while using some of your keywords. Not only does this ensure the link comes with a higher value, it also means the value will increase your site's ranking too.

One final note on backlinks: if you want to be sure to get this sort of powerful backlinking, you must never purchase the link. Backlink creation is something that should be done only through a collaborative agreement, professional connections, or formal arrangements with other websites and professionals in your industry.

Establishing and Creating Backlinks

This may actually be one of the toughest things to do because it means a lot of interaction and exchanging of ideas and information, but it is a very proven approach to a much higher ranking in the SERP. For example, the most common ways to create backlinks are:

- **Getting listed in directories** – Seek out the directories and make the request to be included in the listing. You can then create your profile and include the backlink you choose.

- **Making posts in forums** – Be sure to join in on forums related directly to your field and to post comments to relevant threads. Do not overdo this sort of thing because the web crawlers can pick up on this trend very quickly and cease giving these links any authenticity.

- **Commenting on relevant blogs** – Again, this is similar to the forums in that the blogs must be relevant and authoritative, and your links must not be posted in a high volume closely together.

- **Using article directories** – Though these sites don't often have a place for video content, you probably already have adequate amounts of text to "give" the article directories in order to get the free backlink at the bottom of each piece you provide.

- **Press Releases** – Just like video syndication services, there are press release services too. You can simply include the backlink that relates to a video in your library. For instance, a press release about a new dental implant service in your office could include the backlink to your video library on the subject.

- **Content Exchange** – Your research will introduce you to sites that may benefit from your content. Offer it to them for free but on the condition that a backlink is incorporated into every posted and optimized video!

You should also know that social networking sites can incorporate a sort of content exchange approach to backlinks. This is done when you post a video on your blog, a "Friend" would click the "Share" option or

---

the "Like" option, resulting in your video or the link to it appearing on their "News Feed." Anyone who sees this can click on it and post it to their space, forward it to a friend, etc. Obviously, this is more than simple backlinking; we investigate it fully in the next section.

Leverage Social Media for Better SERPs

Though we all know about LinkedIn, MySpace, and dozens of other social networking sites, for this exercise we will consider Facebook alone. This is because it is one of the easiest and most dominant of the many social networking sites, and it has an enormous number of tools available for a dental professional looking to do some video marketing! Currently, it is believed there are more than 700 billion people with Facebook pages! Just think what that means to your dental video marketing activities when you make a point to tap into this massive pool of potential patients.

Now let's talk about how to gather data about your contacts. Up to this point, you have been somewhat indirectly communicating with your audience, but now you will have to use the "Friend" gathering system that controls how you communicate on Facebook. This is the same as gathering email addresses or other contact information from patients but can be a bit more time-consuming and labor intensive. Basically, it begins when you create a Facebook page and begin looking for "Friends" and other pages to "Like." This results in a burgeoning network that will enable you to create a very effective presence for your practice.

Consider that you can create a video or blog on your website and then post a link to this on your Facebook page. Everyone who has accepted your Friend request or has become a "Fan" of your practice's page will then see this new post. This automatically begins to drive traffic to your site because anyone who views the video is probably going to have an interest in getting the treatment or procedure done or they may know someone who wants it done and will "Share" this information with them on their page. Can you see where this is going? It is the same as old-fashioned "word of mouth," but on a global basis!

You can also use your dental practice's Facebook page to post updates, news, and any other interesting information. For example, the month of June is when a vast majority of weddings occur. This means you can make a post as simple as "Brides and Grooms get a discount when they book teeth whitening treatments together!" and attach a video about whitening services at your office. People will click on the link to the video, watch it, and follow the steps necessary to book one of the special appointments.

How does this impact your SERP? It is going to boost your rank in the search engines every time someone follows the video back to your website or shares it (or another video) from that point. This means you have to be sure you always make the video sharing options readily available or at least be certain the URL and embed information provided is always correct and functional.

It is extremely simple to use Facebook to network with other people in your profession as well. Don't forget to include training videos as part of your library or online gallery of options – you can also use Facebook to let other dental experts know that your training videos are available for their use. When they visit the link and begin sharing it with colleagues and staff through your site, it increases the number of backlinks and your keywords' popularity across the Internet, thus boosting your rank in the SERPs.

A Quick Look at Twitter

We did say we would limit our in-depth coverage of social networking to Facebook, but we do have to mention Twitter briefly. This is radically different from Facebook because of its "micro" size, but it does offer a dental professional the same sorts of opportunities. You are limited to messages of 140 characters or less, but these can always allow you to share a video with those who are "following" you.

Twitter is just as valuable as a marketing tool as Facebook because of its vast audience and its immediacy. For example, we could use the exact same tactic in Twitter as we did in the example given for Facebook – you can create your account and gather "Followers" while also beginning to "Follow" many others yourself. You then "Tweet" about teeth whitening for bridal parties and include the video you want to use for marketing purposes. The true immediacy of Twitter is a bit more impressive, however, because you can actually converse with patients, colleagues, or other interested people in "real time."

Though Facebook can alert you of posts and messages, Twitter seems to be the method of choice for those who want to enjoy the fastest type of online or mobile communication. This can enable you to answer questions quickly, get instant responses on special pricing or deals, and inform people of news of new services or the like in an instantaneous manner.

You Wanna Stand Out From The Crowd?

You have now looked at almost all of the common approaches to enhance SERP ranking. By this time, we hope you have learned how video marketing combined with SEO techniques can greatly enhance your dental practice. The advantages of a well-implemented program of video optimization and marketing are pretty substantial, including:

- Strong interest from search engines, thanks to the lack of keyword stuffing
- Very readable page content that uses natural keyword tactics due to the keyword content in the video information
- Higher ranking in SERPs due to the availability of video lists appearing before many of the website URLs
- Opportunities for patients, colleagues, and other professionals to share information about your practice and your available treatments with a simple click of their mouse
- Immediate or "real time" communication between your practice and current or potential patients
- Instant communication of new treatments, techniques, payment options, special offers, and services available from your office
- Streamlining the explanation of the treatments you offer because the patient will have already seen your videos online or in the office
- Easy advertising of everything from limited-time offers to special programs such as orthodontic programs for families with a lot of kids.

One great use of video marketing we have not yet touched on is the ability to introduce yourself directly to your potential clients. For example, you can make videos about your ethical policies or the general attitude you have about your work. This can be done through a "Meet Our Staff" video or even through patient testimonials. You can also begin to show your level of advanced skills and reliance on the most modern technologies through the videos as well. This allows you to really **stand**

out from the crowd of dental practices in the area and is going to have substantial value to your practice.

What all this means is with a simple series of videos about the things you do and know best, you could begin to attract attention to your practice like never before. But as the last few points illustrate, you also have to identify yourself as a high-quality provider of dental services. This all comes from building an expert image, which is what we cover in the next chapter.

Chapter 22
Blasting Your Video

Word Count: **5642**
Approximate Time to Read: **12.5 minutes**

*"**Thanks for your professionalism and expertise** over the last two days. Thank the crew as well. I really liked the way you coached and treated our patients/parents. I'm sure we are going to have some 'knock-out' testimonials. Can't wait until it's all up and running.*

"I never met the people I worked with that was doing the SEO on our other website. Talked to them on the phone a lot but never met them in person, and I know you're not here just for a one on one personal visit, but the fact that you're here and that you, personally, are here, which is one thing that impressed me – that you're the guy who runs the show and you're here. You didn't just send your excellent crew along to do the work – you're here. To me, that says a lot and that would be like me showing up at something that my staff could easily take care of but I'm there; people like that.

~ John Calvert, D.D.S.
Sedation Dentist in Austin, Texas

"Last month, my partner and I went down to Louisville, where we did our green screen videos for our webpage and had a wonderful experience. All the prep work and time that has gone in for us to do our office work, as well as our doctor prep work, has been done by Colin and his team and we couldn't be happier.

~ Randy Schmidt, D.D.S., M.S.D.
Orthodontist in Chicagoland

"The lead-in from the time of scheduling this day was very helpful: all the emails, the little coaching points, the steps of what I needed to do was very well-written and easy to follow. Your coaching, as far as how to call them and what to say, was right on the money."

~ David Dinsmore, D.D.S.

Video blasting (or syndication as it's also called) is a system that allows you to take a video and have it instantly distributed to a handful of different video channels that are related or relevant to the subject matter. Currently, the most popular venues for this sort of tactic include:

- Traffic Geyser – TrafficGeyser.com
- TubeMogul – TubeMogul.com
- VideoWildfire – VideoWildfire.com
- Hey!Spread – HeySpread.com

Using these services means the video is sent out to dozens of video-sharing sites after being optimized. The sites are able to guarantee a relevant audience receives the video, ensuring that some responses will be generated through this tactic. What this all really means is that the video is sent to the audience rather than just waiting around for the audience to find the video on their own.

A syndication option also saves you a lot of time; it will "globally" apply keywords to areas such as titles, descriptions, and tags. This means after entering the information once, it is applied to every single video you upload during that one session. If each video takes around 15 minutes to normally load, tag, and send, this translates to a tremendous amount of time saved if you only have to do the entire process once!

Let's just consider this example: you have developed a video series about dental implants with a focus on ceramic options soon to come to the United States. You know this is a topic of interest and relevance to a large audience even though there are nine videos in the series. You go to your syndication site, login, and create the appropriate tags, descriptions, title, and add links (all these details would use duplicate information from the other sites where you have already posted the videos). You then upload each of the videos and have the syndication service apply the data to all of the files. The better sites even divide titles into "volumes" or "parts" when needed.

After hitting the submission button, the videos are immediately distributed to the dozens and dozens of video sharing sites the syndication site has relationships with. That's it! The video can also go to article marketing sites, social bookmarking locations, and even podcasts!

A Word on Syndication Schedules

One word of advice in using the syndication options – use them to release all of the videos at one time. It may be tempting to think you can lure your viewers back to the site by telling them the next video is to be released at a later date, but that is not wise in terms of marketing. The modern world demands instant gratification, especially with commercial concepts. If someone likes what they have just seen and wants to learn more, you must give them immediate access to the next in the series. This is far more likely to lead to a call than if you had asked them to wait for the release of the next video in order to learn a bit more about the process they may already be considering.

The syndication option makes it incredibly easy to send all of the optimized videos in a series out into the public with just a few moments of effort. A lot of website owners also like the branding that goes on when they release videos through syndication. For example, if you just stockpile videos at a place like YouTube and your website, you are not getting your dental practice's name out into the world. When you release a series of videos to around 35 different video sharing sites, the number of patients who are going to see your "brand" is increased exponentially.

You Want to Differentiate Yourself?

Additionally, your brand is automatically going to begin to earn a reputation for its authority and expertise. While you may not be the only person offering the services or treatments depicted in the videos, if you are the only practitioner in your region making high-quality films about the processes, your syndication campaigns will "brand you" as the expert in your region. This may seem like a dubious way to develop your professional image but in today's world, it is marketing that tends to make the reputation and not just good services and care.

Clearly, syndication is a great way to saturate the market with your video content, but it should be used in conjunction with the other tactics we cover in this book.

Be the Expert In Your Area

You might be the best dentist in the entire region, but if you don't project that image, you won't have the reputation that you want. Fortunately, the work you do with video marketing is going to give you the perfect opportunity for creating precisely the image you hope to portray.

Consider that videos can:

- Include patient testimonials with the actual patient in front of the camera to say how they feel about their treatment, results, and their general opinion

- Allow you to show any advanced technologies in your office, your skills, and to discuss all of the treatments you perform – in other words, they can make you look like the expert that you are

- Provide you with a way of formally introducing yourself to your clients and potential patients – you can make a brief bio video, a "Meet the Staff" clip, a film discussing your beliefs in terms of professional ethics and customer service, and more

- Begin to develop relationships with clients – whether this is through your vlog (video blog) responses to emailed questions, clips added to social networking pages, or simply through providing free information to any potential patient who needs it, videos speak directly to a patient in a way that text doesn't

- Truly distinguish you from the rest of the dental professionals in the area – when we discussed the use of video syndication, we mentioned the mass release of videos to other sharing sites would begin to "brand" you as an expert and someone who preferred to use cutting edge technologies. Don't forget this fact as you begin to put together your plans for building an image.

It isn't difficult to see how all of these things will begin to contribute to a strong and positive image in the eyes of your current and potential clients, your colleagues, and other dental professionals with whom you interact. Let's now take a deeper look at the most effective tactics to use when developing your professional image through video marketing.

Using Your Patient Testimonials

You must recognize there is a certain power that comes with an unpaid endorsement from a happy and satisfied customer. This is especially true when you consider how unhappy many people are to have to sit through a dental treatment of almost any kind. You want to harness this power whenever possible; one of the most effective and high-quality approaches to do so is through videos featuring patient testimonials.

Now, before you think a "reel" of one person after another just gushing over your practice is a bit too much, you need to know this is not where we are going with the concept. What you need to do is to follow the organizational protocol recommended in the section about the development of an online library. As you begin planning the creation of videos, you will automatically think of patients who may be the ideal candidates for some "before and after" images and who may also feel happy to speak on camera about their experience. Go ahead and begin contacting patients to see if they want to participate. You will find most are more than happy to do so. Try to include people of all ages and people who have had all different types of treatments. You can then insert these testimonials into your videos as they are being created or as a sort of "closing statement" at the end.

Don't forget, you will need some sort of signed release from everyone who appears on camera. We also don't recommend you pay people for their endorsements as this is not an honest or accurate approach to patient testimonials.

Making the Videos

We felt this was an ideal time to talk about the production of the videos. While some dental professionals will have the budgets to hire professionals to tackle the work, others will have to do this as a DIY venture. Regardless of how it is done, you should remember to put the patient into the most pleasant setting possible. You will want good natural lighting, a quiet background, and a location that is clearly a part of your office. For example, you might put a mother and her two kids outside of the office on a bench or just beneath a shady tree. This would allow viewers to recognize the setting, but it would also provide a flattering piece of footage. Alternately, you could get a patient's permission to film them just after they have had their teeth whitened while they are still in the treatment chair. This is an "immediate" response a lot of people would appreciate seeing due to nervousness over the process.

You will want to also make the transcript of the video available too. This can be done in a number of ways such as through a link or even through the posting of the transcript directly beneath the video on the website page. This will apply to any type of video you make, allowing you to use your keywords as much as possible!

Another way to enhance your image is to come across as a highly knowledgeable expert. Although you want to be known as such a good dentist that your patients are happy to go on camera to state the fact, there is a lot of value to being viewed as a technical expert too. In the next section, we'll look at how easily your videos can make you look like a leading authority.

Videos Make You an Expert

Before we discuss the ways videos can be used to differentiate and enhance your reputation as an expert dentist, we would like you to do a brief Internet exercise. We suggest you go to a few of your competitor's websites: click around on the various tabs and informational areas, and generally give them a good exploration. You will most likely find they are all quite similar and "plain." Most will have nice graphics and photographs, some useful links, and details about the practice. Few; however, are going to have interesting and useful video libraries or enhanced informational opportunities like articles or blogs. In the end, most will feel like great big advertisements.

If you have followed our recommendations, you are already making plans for integrating many of the items mentioned previously into your website in order to enhance your video marketing opportunities and that means you are already one step ahead of the competition. This also means you are setting yourself apart from the rest by offering a website that is much more than just a "commercial." By providing educational and informational videos, you are showing you have such an in-depth level of knowledge that you are confident enough to produce films about the techniques and procedures you do.

Don't forget, your video marketing will always include the creation of professional relationships with other dental specialists or practitioners. This means your articles, blogs, and videos will have substantial value to other professionals in your field as well.

When you make a point of establishing yourself as an expert through the creation of high-quality videos, you are converting your website into a useful resource that is also going to create a ton of business for you. For example, someone might use Google to look for "veneers" in their town or city. At the top of the results, they see your video about the subject – you have optimized the video so well that it is the first in the list. The user will want to click on the video, see all of the useful information you have made available, as well as your complete contact information. They will then call or go online to make an appointment. You have to recognize that it was not just the marketing language and the appeal of the results that "sold" the client on you as a dentist. It was that you presented a good "package" through your use of very well informed and professional video communication.

You Vs. Your Competition

While your competition has the same plain, old, predictable sites, you have one that features all kinds of useful information for patients and fellow professionals – this is the epitome of a good image. Remember; however, you need the content to be clear and well organized. You also have to resist the urge to post videos that are more than five minutes in length because few viewers actually want to watch something for that long. The exception to this is the professional videos you created that might include lectures, footage of procedures, etc. Naturally, these are the types of films that should be broken out into ten-minute segments someone can watch without being committed to an hour's time. We would like to also suggest a good tactic for beating out the competition where video clips are concerned – Thumbnail Optimization.

Thumbnail Optimization

In our example above, we cited the dentists who had optimized their videos so well they appeared first in the search engine results. What if they had strong competition in the results? For example, what if there were some videos that ranked ahead of theirs in the SERP? This is when Thumbnail Optimization is going to become invaluable. Though we already went over the procedure for submitting a file to a site like YouTube, we did not discuss the professional image you projected with your choice of still image that appears in the search engine.

For instance, as your video uploads to YouTube, you will see a series of boxes along the top of the screen. These boxes display clips from your video. You actually have the choice of selecting, which of the clips to be your thumbnail. Go through these images carefully because they can often be one of the main reasons a viewer selects your thumbnail over another. If none of the images are appealing, you may want to ask your video editor (or do this process yourself) to insert a nice graphic with the opening title. The very first image is always going to come from the opening of the video. This can give you the opportunity for choosing precisely the image you want to project for the thumbnail in question. Putting your best foot forward at all times is a good way to be viewed as a modern and up-to-date professional: ensuring even your thumbnail images are of the highest quality possible is a strong step in that direction.

Naturally, you can only retain an enhanced and professional image by continuing to add new materials or updates to your video library and website. This is the reason for creating social networking pages – they give you the feedback and questions essential to the creation of fresh materials. In the next section, we look at building relationships with patients through the use of these materials.

Building Relationships with Prospective Patients

How do you use videos to develop relationships with current and potential patients? Though we have already touched on the power of social networks, blogs, and websites to open up a stream of communication between you and patients or colleagues, we haven't really looked at how you might enhance these relationships through them. One way to easily do this is by creating a video blog (or vlog) that shows you answering the questions you have received that week or over the course of the previous month. Not only does this give you the ability to create new and fresh video material, it also allows you to show your customer service policies in practice as well.

The Importance of Responsiveness

The one thing we have not yet touched on but, which is of vital importance to your image is timely communication or responsiveness. When you get an email or question from a client in response to the materials you have made available (through your videos, website, blog, or articles), you will want to acknowledge it immediately. While autoresponders are convenient and reliable, we suggest you either personalize the text in some way or use a manual system that allows a handwritten response to be emailed back to a client or potential patient within a single business day. This response might be as simple as "Thank you for your question. I will provide you with an answer in my next video update." The point is you have responded and will follow-up with the answer they are seeking. If the question is not technical enough to warrant time on camera, take the few moments necessary to draft an email. If it does warrant some attention, be sure to include it in that month's vlog.

You also have to be sure everyone who submits a question is able to receive notice of the release of the next vlog. For example, check that you have an email address or have that individual as a "Friend" or "Follower" through the social networks. You can then release the video through the different channels we covered previously, letting everyone know a new set of answers about dental practices and techniques is available. This same courteous policy applies to dental professionals too. What you have to recognize about this relationship-building tactic is that it is allowing someone to communicate with you personally. This adds value to the social networking service and also enhances your reputation.

The Power of Relationship Building

Consider how someone will respond when asked about your practice if you take the time to create relationship-building systems like the one described above. For example, let's say someone asks a neighbor if they have a dentist they would recommend for a possible filling. The neighbor being asked for the recommendation is quite likely to think of your practice first when you have been so responsive, so interpersonal, and have provided so many informational videos.

Had you failed to respond in a timely manner or never actually answered their question, the person asked for the recommendation may think of you but not suggest you because you had seemed to ignore them. Giving your practice a responsive reputation along with a very personalized "face" is a way to be sure your video marketing can really engage clients, potential clients, and other professionals. People watch the videos, ask questions, make calls, and you (the "star" of the videos) have responded accordingly.

You have also supplied them with useful, interesting, and relevant materials about the services and techniques they can find at your practice without making them deal with a lot of commercial jargon or advertising language.

Relationships Through Additional Materials

You might also want to offer something like an e-zine (electronic magazine) for clients who subscribe to one of your social networks, blog, or site. This gives you yet another point of contact to use in order to speak to them directly. The magazine might be something you create on your own or a publication available through one of your professional organizations used as a monthly tool for direct communication and the offering of special prices and treatments. For example, your "subscribers only" deals could be as simple as a free cleaning or more complicated such as a free straightening assessment. The point is you are developing a special relationship with those who have responded to you through the channels opened by your video marketing tactics.

If you want to continue to improve your image through direct relationships with clients, be sure to use your videos to promote specials through the social networks, emails, and blog too. For example, you might create a Tweet and a Facebook status update that extends a discounted rate for a specific treatment and include the video that describes the benefits of the work.

Down-Home Real People

You might also keep things on a very friendly level by introducing new members of the staff in a brief video clip posted to the same websites and pages. Did you attend a conference or make a speech at a dental event? Let your "friends" know about this too. Choose a patient of the month, show office celebrations or gatherings, and make clips about some recent successful procedures to keep in touch with clients through the use of video marketing.

The basic gist of this tactic is to create a relationship that is much friendlier and far less cordial between you and your patients or potential clients. By doing so, you are going to continue to build a reputation for being a very knowledgeable, approachable, communicative, and trustworthy professional. This means you will have succeeded in your goal of developing a positive and strong image through your video marketing tactics.

Review

In these last few sections, we have focused on enhancing your brand/image through your video marketing efforts. You have learned:

- Your patients can speak volumes about you (literally) through their video testimonials
- The quality of the videos, as well as their length, is a major issue that can impact your image in a good or bad way

- How your videos will be able to portray you as a very knowledgeable expert in a wide array of dental procedures or techniques

- Videos set you apart from the competition, giving you a leading edge when optimized with keywords and the selection of the best thumbnails

- The power of responsiveness in the modern and most electronic environment

- Your videos let you communicate directly with patients, giving them a sense of importance, value, and trust that is difficult to create in any other manner

- How to develop very strong and mutually beneficial relationships with existing and potential patients as well as other dental professionals through an array of additional materials such as ezines and social networks.

In the midst of all of these facts, we can begin to see what the process of video marketing is all about. It is meant to attract the client or potential client, gain their interest in what you have to offer, and then convert them from a visitor to a caller. Up to this point, you have learned a huge amount about video marketing but we haven't yet put it into the context of conversion. We can do that now because you are familiar with all of the jargon required to discuss the issue.

When you are looking to make your website a place where visitors are almost immediately converted into patients with an appointment, you can use videos to a tremendous degree. Your videos can also be the way they are directed to the site in the first place. We now know about all of the tools that can lead someone to the site including keywords, social networks, articles, and the different video sharing services.

Once they get to the site, it is important they:

- **Find what they need immediately** – We discussed the significance of organization and good links; this is going to always be a priority where conversion is concerned.

- **Get a quick loading site** – When someone has reached a count of five and a website is still loading, they tend to navigate away. Because you will have a large number of videos available, be sure your site is organized in a way that allows it to load quickly with each click (and in all types of browsers).

- **Can read the site easily** – There is nothing worse than a chaotic and poorly arranged site. When you have too many things happening on the homepage, you will lose the customer immediately. Be sure you keep things clean and simple.

- **Enjoy good text** – All of your optimization has led to the creation of a website that can easily use very good textual content without fears of keyword stuffage. Be sure your site contains very valuable text and content, and rely on video optimization to provide the best SERP rank.

The Patient Attraction Podcast

Episode 004: The One About Why Patients Buy (and Why They Don't)

Welcome to the fourth video podcast of 2012. I'm your host, Colin Receveur. In today's episode we're going to cover the all important topic of why your patients aren't buying your services, what makes them buy, and how to get them to pull the trigger and move forward with case acceptance. Quick story about why we chose this topic for this week's podcast – we were at a client's office last week doing a two-day video shoot as part of our Premium package and while watching our testimonials next to the testimonials the doc had previously filmed, the doc commented ours seemed so much more **powerful** than the ones he had previously done.

When we got back to the studio, we analyzed what we had been doing and broke our videos down into their individual elements. In this podcast, we're going to be revealing our "reverse testimonial" formula for taking your patients' testimonials from powerful to superhuman strength.

Why Listen to Me?

If you haven't listened in before, I'm Colin Receveur, speaker, author, invited columnist for Profitable Dentist, DentalTown, Elite doc strategies from Big Case Marketing and Dr. McAnally and head chief at SmartBox Web Marketing where we, simply put, get dentists more qualified patients in the niches they want to promote. The purpose of these podcasts is to educate you about dental marketing so you can make an informed decision about what's best for you and your practice in this new dental economy.

Let's jump into today's topic at hand.

Three Important Topics Dentists Want to Know

1. Why your patients aren't buying your services
2. Getting inside their head: what makes patients pull the trigger?
3. How to overcome their objections-before they object

When you really think about it, one of the best things in life is to get better patients: patients who understand the depth of your work

– patients who aren't haggling about your prices and are more than willing to pay higher prices for better work – patients who understand that you need a life other than work – patients you'd be happy to call your friends.

1. Why Your Patients Aren't Buying Your Services

Once you get your patients into your consult room, they aren't buying for one of two reasons:

1. They aren't a good fit for you and you didn't pre-qualify them or
2. They are a good fit, but you didn't remove the risk and objections they had.

This webinar is going to cover #2. Next week we'll cover pre-qualification and #1 in more detail.

Patients have all kinds of risks when deciding to move forward with treatment …

- Risk of being hurt
- Risk of being overcharged
- Risk of having bad dentistry done in their mouth
- Risk of the unknown …

For your patients to buy you must reduce their risk to **-100**.

2. Getting Inside Their Head: What Makes Them Pull the Trigger

Understanding what triggers your patients to buy is crucial. Two of the biggest triggers in your prospects' minds involving risk are, "Can he really do what he says?" (also known as the case study) and, "If it doesn't go right, will he make it right?" (also known as risk reversal). Remember, negative downside overpowers positive upside every day of the week and twice on Sunday. Your marketing and website must be removing <u>all</u> risk and objections from your prospects' minds. When you remove their risk, their objections fall like a rock.

Most importantly, overcoming risk and objections means doing it BEFORE the patient brings it up! This is seen as empathy to your patients – that you are compassionate to their feelings and also avoids the dreaded "I'm going to think about it" line from ever entering into their brain.

Most dentists avoid objections.

They fear confrontation – causing a hindrance to their case acceptance – hoping the prospect will too. Yeah, right.

Another big reason dentists avoid addressing objections is they haven't thought of the answers in advance. Your prospects and patients have the same set of objections. As you begin addressing them, you'll notice they share the same concerns so make sure you are addressing them before they bring it up. If you don't beat them to the punch, they are putting the brakes on. And addressing objections after they bring them up doesn't build empathy or allow you to easily overcome them.

A very easy way to overcome both the risk and objections is by using powerful testimonials. Testimonials are not just this "nice-to-have thing" on your website and marketing material ... they do a task that's vital to your happiness and success. Properly designed, your testimonials will overcome all the objections and risks your prospects have ... and then (and only then) your prospects will buy from you.

It's not just "how great you are."

Your testimonials must be removing all risk and objections from your prospects' minds. They have to be like the magic mirror I talked about before – get on your patients' side, empathize, identify their concerns, and overcome them. When your prospects look into the mirror, they see themselves. Only then will they buy your services.

Price is an objection to prospects buying but surprisingly not the biggest – actually one of the smallest. Many dentists think by lowering their price they will increase case acceptance but that is rarely the case. Feeling is everything when selling dentistry. They have to feel like you are empathizing with them, that you understand their fear and concerns and you are on their side to overcome them. If you don't, the sale will stall.

3. How to Overcome Their Objections – Before They Object

So how do you accomplish this? Easy peasy! It's called the "reverse testimonial." The problem with most testimonials is they talk about how great things are – that's not how people think. Everyone knows that nothing is perfect; if it sounds too good to be true, it always is.

The reverse testimonial appeals to your prospect's skepticism. By starting the testimonial with a doubt or a problem, you are instantly pulling in your viewer and holding their attention. The problems your patient expresses will appeal to your prospects showing you really do care, you really are as good as they say you are and other people have the fears and objections they also have. It's fits into our brain's natural doubt, and gives a well rounded feeling and balance.

Let me give you an example … "I came to see Dr. Smith to get my new dental implants and he did a great job. There was no pain and now I can chew again. I'm very happy with the work and recommend him to everyone I know."

Vs. … "When I first met with Dr. Smith, I had serious doubts that he could help me chew again and overcome my fears of dentistry dating back to my childhood. I've seen several so-called "specialists" over the years and none had been able to really help me. But after meeting with Dr. Smith, I was impressed and decided to give him a try. Being very fearful, I was amazed that with the sedation, the implant procedure was over before I even realized it had started and now I can chew again. Dr. Smith delivered on everything he promised and more."

The reverse testimonial is the most powerful way to quickly eliminate risk for your prospects. It is all about you, but you're not saying it – someone else is and that makes a huge difference because it's now believable and removes doubt from your prospects' minds.

The testimonial by itself is powerful but the reverse testimonial is superhuman.

That's what we're about here at SmartBox: giving your marketing all kinds of superhuman powers. So that's it for this week's podcast. Don't forget to subscribe below to get next week's video podcast or vodcast and if you need help capturing your patients' words, feel free to give us a call. Until next week, keep moving forward.

Chapter 23
Introducing the Panda

Word Count: **1714**
Approximate Time to Read: **3.8 minutes**

Panda Bears are cute and entertaining, but the Panda update from Google has proven to have a very deceiving name. There is nothing cute and entertaining about this update, particularly if the "bear attack" has moved you down in the SERPs (Search Engine Results Pages). Google's engineers are not trying to make life difficult for dental website owners (or any other website owners, for that matter) but they are trying to improve the experience of most Google users.

Over the past few years, Google's design team has been looking for ways to reduce the rate of useless search engine results. For instance, if your patient Googles something like "dental crowns," they might end up finding a results page full of articles and blogs about dental crowns and dental offices outside of their geographic region. For a long time, this has been an acceptable practice, but Google does not like the effects it has on its users (a.k.a. the people searching). They want quality results and have taken great pains to design Panda to give people such results.

What's This Mean for My Dental Website?

It means that you now have to assess your own website, look at the content, and be sure that it matches Google's standards. That is, if you want traffic to head to your site. Let's face it, **Google gets 70 percent of the world's searches**, so YOU DO want to meet their guidelines. This is not as easy as it might seem, but this guide is going to walk you through the process. In this section, we will explain SEO, the Panda, and how to make it all work for your dental practice!

Google & SEO

Does it surprise you to know that Google has completely changed its algorithm? It shouldn't. Google makes tweaks and changes to it very regularly, releasing hundreds of updates over the past several years, most recently with its Hummingbird update.

However, you would be right to feel a bit panicked about changes that could impact your ranking. The good thing to know is that the changes Google makes tend to be methods of working around those who negatively impact search engine results through sneaky, blackhat, and/or fraudulent tactics.

Though we'll go into these things a bit later, you should know that the black hat and fraudulent tactics include simply copying and pasting the text from a competitor's website (particularly one with a higher rank than yours), stuffing your website with keywords, and also using nonsensical or irrelevant text. We've all stumbled upon sites like this that have managed to appear in the first two pages of Google's search engine results.

If you are worried about updates to the algorithm, you should also take the words of Google itself into consideration:

"Co-founder Larry Page once described the 'perfect search engine' as something that 'understands exactly what you mean and gives you back exactly what you want.' We can't claim that Google delivers on that vision 100 percent today, but we're always working on new technologies aimed at bringing all of Google closer to that ideal."

They are able to do so only by assessing and updating the algorithms, **which is why you are reading this in the first place.** After all, it is one of their latest updates, known as Panda, which has caused a lot of people to become upset at their sudden dip in ranking. Panda, also known as Farmer, was created to identify low-quality pages and sites that may have text relevance to a specific query, but, which may not provide the Google user with the best experience.

Why Such Strange Names?

Farmer was used to describe the update because so many sites are "content farms," which help some companies with SEO campaigns, but are not typically of any value to someone searching for the topics addressed in the articles. The reason that the update also has the code name of Panda is quite simple – it is the name of the Google employee who designed it!

Is Google Leaving Website Owners in Bad Positions?

Yes and no ... let me explain. Google is enforcing a sort of quality control that insists that anyone who wants to claim a top spot in the search results should be a high-quality resource.

Many websites are just "aggregators" or "scrapers" of content and information – they aren't really a resource that helps the person searching. They attain a high search engine ranking by scraping content from other sites and aggregating it onto their site. These are commonly known as "content farms." Panda has done away with all of this. Google also provides a lot of tools for helping website owners tackle the sometimes tricky job of SEO since Panda was released. If you use Google's "SEO Starter Guide," it will show you their idea about the best approaches. These include:

- Using unique titles and tags
- Improving your site structure
- Paying attention to ease of navigation
- Optimizing the content, including anchor text
- Interacting more effectively with web crawlers
- Using promotional and analysis tools properly

An Entire Toolbox

Not only can you read how to do many of these things, but you can also find the different tools that you need to get them done! Google is pointing out that the best way to overcome the Panda updates is to go back to the beginning and do all of the things necessary for traditional SEO – without using all of the workarounds and tricks. If you are a dental professional interested in having a dominant place in the search engine results, you have to consider organic SEO, which is something that occurs naturally and gives you a higher position due to the quality and focus of your website. This would mean that you have spent time identifying the appropriate keywords to use in such places as body text, headings, titles, tags, and more.

Google's Power Tools for SEO

First and foremost is **Google Analytics**, which will measure almost every facet of your website and provides clear solutions for improvements in your SEO campaigns. You can see how people find your site, what they do when they are there, and what happens when they leave – i.e., did they interact with the site in a way that equals a "conversion" such as emailing, signing on for a newsletter, or setting up an appointment?

Then there is advertising and marketing: Google helps website owners get the most out of their efforts through marketing tools like **AdWords**, which will help website owners identify and select the strongest keywords for their ads and content. They have also released an entirely new web browser, **Google Chrome**, which is designed for "speed, simplicity, and security." This is an optimized browser radically different from any other and meant to be fast in terms of performance, updates, and support of new applications.

All of these things are meant to work in a two-way stream. Helping a web user to get the most out of their searches and helping valid website owners to truly optimize and direct the best and most "convertible" traffic to their pages. In a later section, we look at the best tips for overcoming problems relating directly to Panda, but what we want to emphasize now is that basic SEO tactics are the most effective if your site has been hit with the Panda update "bear attack."

Who Does Panda Affect?

Google has not given out any specific or technical details about the Panda update. As already mentioned, it is meant to lower the rank of the low-quality content sites while helping higher quality sites climb in the results.

Google has said that around **12 percent** of all search results have been impacted by the implementation of the Panda. Many of the "content farm" sites, such as the famous Suite101 and Ezine Articles, were hit very hard by the change in the algorithm because of their lack of "authority." Here's a good example: a potential patient may decide to use the web to search for information about implants. If they Google "dental implants," they will be shown results from medical and dental sites, as well as the many "informational sites" because these are places where the keywords appear most.

The Panda update; however, has been designed to address these problems for searchers and to instead, identify when the quality of the content is not as good. Thus, the person who Googles "dental implants" and adds their city or region, is going to get the most relevant and useful listings instead of "content farms."

When Did Panda Take Effect?

You should know that Panda was not "rolled out" all at once, but has been modified even since being released in the United States in February 2011. Since then, it has been updated at least five times, with a global release in August 2011. In the next section, we are going to explain how to find out if you have been "slapped" by the Panda and how this has affected your website. We will be using Google Analytics, a powerful tool for monitoring your website and understanding your traffic.

Google's official statements about Panda have been very consistent. One says:

> "About 2% of U.S. queries are now affected by a reasonable amount, compared with almost 12% of U.S. queries for the original Panda change ... Based on our testing, we've found the algorithm is very accurate at detecting site quality. If you believe your site is high quality and has been impacted by this change, we encourage you to evaluate the different aspects of your site extensively. Google's quality guidelines provide helpful information about how to improve your site. As sites change, our algorithmic rankings will update to reflect that. In addition, you're welcome to post in our Webmaster Help Forums. While we aren't making any manual exceptions, we will consider this feedback as we continue to refine our algorithms."

It is very important to note Google's comment about "evaluating the different aspects of your site extensively." Knowing what aspects of your site are performing well (and, which ones aren't) is critical to SEO post-Panda because Google will demote your entire site's rank for weak content. **Next, let's take a look at your website's analytics and discover how the Panda update has effected you ...**

Chapter 24

How is Panda Affecting You?

Word Count: **1644**
Approximate Time to Read: 3.7 minutes

Step-by-Step Analysis

I have included screenshots to help guide you through this process as you are walking through your analytics pages.

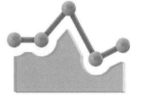

1. The first thing to do is to head to your Google Analytics "My Site."

2. Under "Traffic Sources," click "Sources" then select "All Traffic."

3. Looking toward the bottom of the screen, select Google from the list of search engines to view your "Google-only" traffic.

4. You can now drill deeper into this data by selected a "Secondary dimension." Click "Select" and this reveals a large menu that includes tabs for "Visitors," "Technology," "Traffic Sources," and "Content."

5. From this list, you will want to click "Visitors," then "Country/ Territory." Click "Advanced" then enter "United States" into the filter box because you, as a local dental professional, will want to focus on your appropriate, regional traffic.

6. Click "Apply." What do you see? Is the line across the chart consistent? **Does it show a deep decline in traffic around April of 2011?** If you answered yes to the latter, you have been slapped by the Panda.

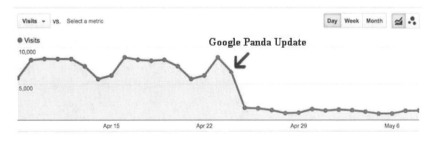

How to See EXACTLY How You Were Affected

If you want to be able to find out if your entire site is the reason behind the decline or if only a few webpages are bringing you down, we suggest using "Advanced Segments" to determine your organic U.S. based Google visits. This will give you far more clarity to analyze what's happening with your site.

This is an advanced section so if you get confused, just skip to the "Interpreting the Data" section and keep reading ...

1. Choose the "Advanced Segments" button on top of the right column, then "+ New Custom Segment."
2. Configure this with:
   a. "Medium" matches exactly "organic"; AND
   b. "Country/Territory" matches exactly "United States"; AND
   c. "Source" contains "Google."
4. Name that segment "Google US organic," then click "Save Segment."
5. The data you get to see will now be for this "segment" of visitors only. This allows you to look at, which of your pages have felt the worst effects of Panda.
6. Go to the "Traffic Sources" tab and select the "Landing Pages" report from under "Search Engine Optimization."
7. By using the filter we just created above, you will now be able to see if the "slap" was sitewide, or if it is specific pages that have declined.
8. Now we just have to use the filter at the bottom of the report to:
   a. Show individual pages, or
   b. Pages that share strings in their URLs, such as FAQ pages that will all have the term "FAQ" in the URL.

With this approach, you will be able to identify the individual pages that may have been affected. The remarkable thing is that Panda works on a mathematical basis. It assigns points (not good points but BAD points) to pages identified as low quality. If your points exceed the accepted

---

"threshold," the algorithm begins to work as a penalty against the site. This translates to a reduction in position in search results. In other words, Google's Panda is saying, "If you don't pay attention to ALL of your pages, we are going to view your entire site as a lower quality." For example, you may have some really excellent, high-quality and truly original pages on your dental site. These cannot; however, offset pages that are not their equal. When you have too many such pages (lower quality), it is going to end up causing a drop in ranking.

Interpreting the Data

You have to isolate the differences between the pages that were hit and those that were not and begin making changes. We suggest that you also make a list of the different kinds of pages you have on the site, i.e., blog posts, forums, high-quality dental articles, low quality "fill," unused categories, quality categories, products, etc. Format this list into a spreadsheet and start adding columns for relevant factors like too many ads, too little content, duplicate content, etc. Next, indicate the number of pages in each category and note any percentage of decline in their "Google U.S. Organic" visits. Determine exactly how much of your site is taken up by the lowest-quality pages by calculating the values for each type of page.

Now you know exactly where to begin improving things!

In the final section, we are going to look at all of the different ways that you can instantly begin recovering from any Panda slaps and boosting your rank in search engine results by conducting SEO work that is going to really **"feed the Panda."**

Panda "Happy" SEO

Remember that Google's management has said: "If you believe you've been impacted by this change, you should evaluate all the content on your site and do your best to improve the overall quality of the pages on your domain."

Removing low-quality pages or moving them to a different domain could help your rankings for the higher-quality content and although that is all well and fine, it isn't necessarily the best approach to getting faster results if your dental website has dropped in ranking since the Panda update. Apart from using the steps in the previous chapter to find out if your entire website (or specific web pages) have been slapped by the Panda update, here's our top nine Panda-fighting tips ...

Our Top Nine Panda Fighting Tips

1. Go back to the basics with classic SEO

● Work on interlinking and backlinks.

● Insert a sitemap that the crawlers will easily read and use for indexing.

● Test any and all links for their quality, and delete valueless links inserted in comments or forums.

● Consider Robots.txt files when you want to prevent crawlers from "counting" a page on your site.

● Ensure your website is compatible with all browsers, loads quickly, and remain fully visible to all search engines. Test on a "text only" browser too!

● Use those ALT and TITLE tags.

● Properly use anchor text in links on a home page, external links, and navigation maps.

● Try to exchange links with relevant professionals and organizations.

2. Write GREAT unique content

● Assess existing text and edit for pages that are "overly optimized." For instance, if a page has "teeth whitening" appearing at a percentage of 5 percent or more, Google might penalize you.

● Yes, you are a dental professional, but make sure that your site's language is more accessible and more "real" for the everyday readers.

● Rely on tools like WordTracker and Keyword Spy to find the best keywords to optimize your particular dental site. Not all keywords are the same and what a competitor is using may not work for you.

● Improve, remove, or block large numbers of pages with duplicate, weak, or almost no content. You can use robots.txt for much of this.

● If you do have a lot of pages with duplicate text, ask your website administrator to add rel=canonical tags to the duplicate pages; this prevents Google from seeing those pages as copies or duplicates.

3. Reduce the bounce rate

- Offer users more when they first enter the site or a landing page. You will want to have relevant (and properly tagged) images and videos along with attractive text. Don't forget about those pages with embedded links to some of your best relevant editorial content.

- Use videos to catch visitors' attention and also to build high-quality backlinks to your site. We will delve further into this in the chapters on video marketing and using YouTube to your advantage.

4. Optimize your site to run FAST

- Panda looks at your website's speed so test the load time of your site on Chrome, IE, and Firefox, among others. Faster load times increase rank.

5. Avoid "black hat" SEO tactics

- If you are copying other sites' content, replace it with better-quality content

- Try removing all or at least some of the questionable pages

6. Don't use template websites

- These were NEVER designed for SEO. Work with a professional to create a website that can be configured for the best SEO performance. A template website will not allow you to feed the Panda!

7. Don't have redundant content on your site

- Create a series of videos or articles that will encourage people to view multiple pages on the site and allow you to use headings, tags, content, and materials that make the Panda happy.

- Build brand awareness wherever you can. This means offering only unique content that is regularly updated and spread out through acceptable channels such as social media, blogs, and classic SEO tactics.

8. Use Google Webmaster Tools

- Submit sitemaps: ALWAYS try to include video sitemaps when possible and use Google's recommended approach for best results.

- Check for errors using Google's tools.
- Increase crawl rate. Crawl rate refers to the speed of Googlebot's requests during the crawl process. Increasing the rate will not have any effect on how often the site is crawled or how deeply. To change the crawl rate:
  - ◆ On the Webmaster Tools home page, click the site you want.
  - ◆ Under "Site Configuration," click "Settings." Then in the "Crawl Rate" section, select the option you want.
- Checkout your site links using Google's tools. Demote as needed.

9. Use Google Website Optimizer

- Google's Website Optimizer is an easy-to-use tool for testing site content that delivers actionable results. It asks you to follow a simple step-by-step process that allows you to create an "experiment" indicating the effectiveness of any website page and also measures how any changes will impact that page.
- Use the tutorial to learn how to test each page of your dental website.

BONUS: Lots of Facebook pages are at the top of Google! Have your Facebook page well-optimized. A successful modern dentist will always be one who promotes website content on social media including Twitter and Facebook. Launching a link-building campaign for your Facebook Business page is a proven tactic to increasing it's ranking in the search engines.

Chapter 25

Information Marketing for Dentists: Part One

Word Count: **3505**
Approximate Time to Read: **7.8 minutes**

Up to this point, you may have been thinking, "This is all great but when am I going to find the time to do all this?!" Marketing your dental practice is tough – you have a tremendous number of things already on your plate. From patient care to investigating new services to provide, your day is full. When you throw marketing on top of that, things can get very stressful, very quickly. In addition, you don't want to come off as a marketer – you want to build trust and foster relationships, not "SELL, SELL, SELL!" There's a way to do just that.

Think Like a Publisher to Educate and Entice

Information marketing provides you with the means to both entice and educate patients. By thinking like a publisher and providing educational, informative material (in a wide range of formats), you build your reputation, offer something of immense value to your patients at no cost, and build strong relationships.

How do you start thinking like a publisher? What does a busy dentist do to embark on an information-marketing program? You'll find some simple, effective solutions that allow you to publish a broad range of content, create engaging stories and gather new ideas to entice and educate your patients.

Articles – Establishing Credibility with an Information Storehouse

While article directories might be useless today thanks to Google's Panda and Penguin updates, that doesn't mean that article writing doesn't offer any benefits. In fact, you can use these to build your site's Page Rank and authority very easily. A few simple tips can help you do just that:

- Make sure your articles are both information and keyword rich. This guarantees that they offer value to real human readers (those prospective patients you're after) as well as search engine spiders (the bots you need to attract to boost page rank and site authority).

- SEO scoring tools (like Yoast for WordPress-based sites) allow you to easily determine just how strong your optimization efforts are and where improvements need to be made. Effective SEO scoring solutions enhance your ROI by ensuring that each article published on your site has maximum impact (without reducing readability or quality for human beings).

- Take the answers your articles provide and put them in a FAQ page. For Internet users searching for simple, fast answers, FAQ pages are ideal options. Not only that, but they are naturally optimized for your target keywords (hint: the answers and services your patients need are usually the keywords you want to target).

- Make your articles shareable. The easier it is for your readers to pass your content to their friends and family, the better your results will be. Simple, effective plugins give you the ability to place social network-specific sharing buttons on the top or bottom of every article on your site.

- Host them on your site. Build an information section where your patients and prospective patients can come to learn more about their topics of interest. By using your articles on your site and contextually linking from those pages to other pages in your site, you build your authority further.

- Make sure you're original. The days when you could reuse content are long gone. We live in a post-Panda world, and that means you need to have original content created specifically for your website. If you can't write articles yourself, and don't have a staff member capable of doing so, hire a freelance writer to take care of it. Original content is vital.

Blog Away – Build Trust and Give Your Practice a Human Face

Blogging gives you tremendous power and capabilities. It also gives you the means to put a human face on your dental practice – your face can be created by writing informative, original blog posts in your voice. Of course, there are some tips for blogging:

- Images and infographics are vital. Plain text is just boring. Internet users love visual media, and you have a tremendous source of images right at your fingertips. Use real images to show before and after shots of patients' teeth, what happens without the right dental care and more. Infographics can be immensely useful as well, and they're also highly shareable.

- Have a plan in place before you start. No matter how enticing your blog posts might be, you can't succeed if you don't have a plan for regular updates. Your plan should be roughed out from the beginning, but leave room for modifications based on what's most popular with your blog readers. Your plan should also be tied into your SEO strategy.

- Again, SEO scoring is imperative. A range of free plugins can help (again, Yoast for WordPress is a prime example, though not the only one out there). However, make sure you don't overdo your keyword use. Opt for a natural keyword density within your blog posts (that's usually something like one use per 100 words of text in the post, plus in the post title).

- Interact with other blogs that share hot topics with your own. By interacting (commenting) on other blogs related to yours or within user forums, you can build a reputation for expertise and providing quality information, and also build backlinks to your own site. To avoid creating the appearance that you're a spammer, though, offer real suggestions and answers to questions. Put a link in your signature or tagline; don't just slap it into the comment field.

Case Studies – Prove the Solution to Your Patients' Problems

Case studies provide significant amounts of information about how your treatments and services have benefited previous patients. They allow you to highlight what the original problem or condition was, what treatment option was performed and then demonstrate how the problem was solved. They're simple, effective and powerful – it's real data involving real people for prospective patients. Case studies offer:

- A direct connection with your patients: they see someone just like them, with their problems, and how you were able to change their situation. That immediate connection is essential. It allows you to instantly get inside your patients' heads and speak to them directly.

- Tell your patients what your services will provide: the concluding portion of a case study is a bit like predicting the future, and tells your patients what they can expect. That not only educates them, but it can provide some significant relief from fear and worry.

- Tell your patients they're not alone: case studies assure your patients that they're not alone in their fears, their worries, or the only one suffering from a particular dental condition. There are others out there, and your practice helped them.

- Build a story: with case studies, you build an evocative true story that is at once honest and direct. This helps you earn trust and build your reputation. It's another way that you can connect directly with your audience, instantly overcoming their worries that you're "just trying to sell them."

White Papers – Highlight, Inform and Educate

White papers are nothing new. However, that doesn't mean they're not powerful solutions to your information marketing needs. White papers offer the ability to highlight a problem, demonstrate a solution and then show your patients how that problem is solved. And they do all this without active selling involved. To make the most of their impact:

- Break up the text with graphics. A good design and layout with plenty of graphics will offer bite-sized chunks of information, plenty of whitespace for your readers and provide substantial visual interest to keep them reading.

- Explain what not to do in your white papers. By giving your patients information about steps they should not take, you further bolster your expertise and reputation.

- Avoid jargon and language that the average person will not understand or appreciate. While some technical language will be unavoidable, tone your white papers down and use layman's terms whenever possible. You should also add an element of storytelling to the papers to grab your readers' attention.

- Solve a problem that matters to your readers. The entire point of a white paper is to show how a problem can be solved (preferably using your dental practice). Make sure the problem you're solving matters to your readers, and then show them how to solve it.

POD Books – Cement Your Authority

What's more authoritative than a book? By creating books and then printing them on demand (or allowing patients to order them on an on-demand basis), you build expertise and authority, provide substantial quality information and more. Why POD, though? POD stands for print on demand, and that gives you immense cost control without having to sacrifice quality. The advantages of POD books include:

- No need to stock your books – POD books require a 48-hour turnaround window. During that short period, they're printed, shipped and delivered. That means you don't have to worry about keeping a stockroom full of books, and reduces your costs immensely. Because they're printed on demand rather than in batches, you (and your readers) save money.

- Because your books will have an ISBN, they're registered at the Library of Congress and are searchable via the ISBN through a number of different websites. You can list your books for sale on Amazon and use the ISBN, or through Kobo, iTunes/iBooks, Barnes & Noble and many other online booksellers. However, that doesn't mean they'll be stocked on store shelves – readers can order from the website, or have a physical bookstore order the books based on the ISBN.

- Your book will be searchable online, which gives you authority within search engines, but providing valuable information in physical book form also allows you to build credibility with your patients and prospective patients. Of course, that means you need to do your job and incorporate the appropriate keywords into the content of the book. There's good news, though. That's simple to do as long as you stay on topic.

- POD offers low-cost book creation options, allowing you to innovate your marketing with high ROI and low entry cost. The only thing that offers a lower entry cost is eBook creation (which we'll touch on shortly).

- Do your research on POD publishers, though. Not all of them are created equal. Make sure that the company you choose is reputable and offers reasonable pricing. Lulu is a frontrunner in the industry, but there are several other worthwhile options, including Lightning Source and CreateSpace (Amazon's POD arm).

eBooks – Catch the Electronic Wave

You might be one of those individuals who haven't picked up an e-reader yet. However, you should understand that the eBook craze isn't a fad – it's here to stay. Consistently, eBooks are trumping print books in the number of units sold and industry growth. You can capitalize on this new market segment by creating eBooks on the fly. The benefits of eBooks for your information marketing plan include:

- They're incredibly easy to make. Write the book, create a cover and upload – those are the three main steps. You can also sell them on your own site, or go through Amazon, B&N, Kobo or any number of other eBook sales platforms. Not only does that mean your patients can browse for your book through sites like Amazon, but they can find them directly through their e-readers as well. Of course, you can offer it as a free download (or a paid download) from your site or blog as well. Online bookseller sites to consider include:
  - ◆ Amazon
  - ◆ Barnes & Noble
  - ◆ Kobo
  - ◆ Apple iBooks
  - ◆ Smashwords (useful for distribution to other sites, as well)
  - ◆ Diesel
  - ◆ Sony Reader Store

However, Amazon is THE powerhouse here. In addition, if you decide to enroll in KDP Select (you go exclusive to Amazon), you can offer your book for free for several days out of each enrollment period.

- They offer built-in SEO benefits if they're not locked behind a firewall. Google Books is an excellent example of this – they consistently turn up in natural search results based on their content. This provides you with additional optimization without any additional costs or steps involved.

- Contextual links in eBooks give direct access to your site. It's easy to create contextual links or other types of links (a list of resources, for example). E-readers have built-in web browsers, and a simple tap of the finger is all it takes to transfer your reader from the pages of the book to your dental practice's website or blog.

- They improve your branding efforts without forcing you into direct selling. Like blogs, eBooks are excellent places to build your brand using your own voice. Moreover, they allow you to enhance your reputation and branding efforts without the need for overt selling of your dental services.

eNewsletters – Building Trust through Updates and Announcements

Newsletters have long been a tool in the traditional marketing toolkit. You can use eNewsletters the same way, and deliver a message right to patients and prospective patients' inboxes. Not convinced that an electronic newsletter is a viable tool? Here are some tips:

- They allow you to share valuable information about services, techniques and dental products that your patients and prospective patients are already interested in. What's more, there's no need to sell here – just give them good information.

- You can include special offers intermixed with the regular information very easily, without becoming a spammer.

- Using a newsletter platform gives you the means to track how effective your campaign is. Most platforms out there (think MailChimp and AWeber) let you see the number of emails opened, the number of links clicked and other data.

- Keep your patients and prospective patients in the loop up to the minute. If you'll be running a special on a particular dental service or a combination of services for a limited time, newsletters let you alert your audience several weeks out, and then in shorter increments until the promotion debuts. It lets you spike and then maintain interest.

The Patient Attraction Podcast

Welcome to this week's episode of the SmartBox Web Marketing Podcast. I'm your host, Colin Receveur. In today's episode we're going to show you how successful dentists are pre-qualifying all their patients and also, we're going to be unveiling the secrets of how we turn dentists into superheroes.

Why Listen to Me?

If you haven't listened in before, I'm Colin Receveur, speaker, author, invited columnist for Profitable Dentist, DentalTown, Elite doc strategies from Big Case Marketing and Dr. McAnally and head chief at SmartBox Web Marketing where we, simply put, get dentists more qualified patients in the niches they want to promote. The purpose of these podcasts is to educate you about dental marketing so you can make an informed decision about what's best for you and your practice in this new dental economy.

Being an expert, or a superhero, in your niche doesn't come easily. But when implemented, it has a powerful effect on your prospects making you the only choice in their mind to go to. I know, this might sound too good to be true but give me 90 seconds of your time and I'm going to give you all the information so you'll be able to decide for yourself ....

We're going to cover three important topics:

- How to pre-qualify all your patients and eliminate the "tire kickers" and dead ends that don't accept treatment
- How to create your marketing to show you as the expert in your niche and attain superhero status
- The BEEF: seven ways you MUST be marketing your practice to survive

I know many dentists when they hear us talking about "pre-qualifying" are thinking financially but it's much more than that. Of course in this new economy, finding patients with money to spend is a big focus, but prequalification covers much more than that.

Let me tell you a quick story about a dentist I know in California. We'll call him Dr. Smith. I've known Dr. Smith for about four years now and one of his biggest complaints in his implant-focused practice is that all the time, patients are coming in for consults that have no clue what's going on!

He has told me on several occasions that on average, of the 55 implant consults he schedules every month, at least half of them expect their insurance to pay 100% of it. That's over 25 consults a month that are a complete waste of time. You figure in the cost of the doctor's time, office and staff time … not to mention the cost of lost opportunity, and you're really eating into your bottom line.

Prequalification is how we help our clients avoid this. We help dentists make sure their patient's expectations match the dentist's focus. This eliminates tire kickers and dead end consults that have no chance of moving forward with case acceptance.

So How Do You Prequalify Your Patients?

Let me start off by telling you how you don't do it. You don't just run an ad in the newspaper and expect your patients to be educated consumers of your dentistry. To educate your patients, it takes time – time most doctors don't want to spend on marketing. That's why we've developed seven completely automated ways to prequalify your prospects and make you the expert in your niche or as we like to call it, the superhero in your local market. Here's how we do it:

Well first, let me say that a website is great. It allows you to give an enormous amount of information to your prospects. But there's a rub: every doctor has a website in today's world. So how do you differentiate yourself? I talked at length in a previous podcast about video and how you can leverage video to really stand out and showcase your talents and expertise. But that's still solely on the web and as great as online marketing is, there's still other great avenues out there on which to be seen.

I want to tell you a story. ***Let's Imagine you needed heart surgery.*** You searched the internet and found a heart surgeon specialist that you think looked reputable. On his website, he offered you a 10-page free report to show you what options might be available to you. At the end of his free report, there was a link to buy his new book and DVD, which contained even more information about how he could help you. You bought them both, and when they came in the mail, you and your wife/husband watched it together.

You went back to his website for more information and signed up for a teleseminar and webinar that he offered. You and your spouse absorbed all the information he gave out and took notes. After the webinar, you gave him your email address so he could send you his monthly newsletter. After a few weeks of further research, you got his newsletter, which told you about current happenings and also advertised an in-office seminar where you can meet the doctor and have a free 15-minute consultation.

WOW!

By the time you walk in the door for his seminar, you're already 110% sold. You already know what it costs. You already know how he can fix you. You already know all your options. You already know he's DA MAN. You just need to know how to make out the check.

Now, I know I just dumped a ton of information on you and I'm sure this all seems very intimidating: webinars, seminars, books, dvds, reports … but let me tell you, we help our dentist clients with all these things day in and day out. **We have the technology and systems developed to make this happen for you.** And honestly, they are not that expensive to put together when you have the right systems in place.

These marketing methods are what our best dentist clients are using right now to kill it in their practices. Don't get me wrong, a website and videos are critical to success but the doctors that are on the cutting edge of marketing and producing the big numbers are embracing these new technologies to reach an even broader audience. By putting your name EVERYWHERE, by having these many, many cups of tea (like I talk about in my book), you build trust and credibility and you achieve **EXPERT** status or as we like to call it, **you become a superhero**. Think back to the heart surgeon: who else would you possibly want to choose after that?

The only real takeaways from this episode are seven marketing mediums you must embrace:

- Webinars
- Teleseminars
- Autoresponders
- In-office Seminars
- Books
- Free Reports
- DVDs

Speaking of DVDs, for everyone that stayed on the podcast today, I have a special offer for you to get my latest DVD, "The Secrets of Dental Niche Marketing." We've sold hundreds of copies of it at $197, but today and only through this special link, I am offering it for only $7. www.DentalNicheMarketing.com Learn the secrets of how to attract, prequalify, and close the cases with patients in the dental niches you have advanced clinical training.

That's all for today. See you guys next week and keep moving forward.

Chapter 26

Information Marketing for Dental Offices: Part Two

Word Count: **8444**
Approximate Time to Read: **18.8 minutes**

Socialize to Educate and Entice

Let's take information marketing a step further. If you enjoy socializing on and off the job, consider using this very natural part about you as a means to supply educational information in a very relaxed atmosphere. Here are some easy ways to introduce you and your practice to prospective patients and gain credibility just by being yourself and sharing your expertise in social-friendly formats.

Going Social with Research – Find Out What Matters to Your Audience

Social media marketing has been touted as the best way to build a community for your practice. That's true. However, many dentists overlook one of the key capabilities offered by social networking sites – the ability to research and find out what really matters to your audience by learning what they're actively talking about.

Virtually every social network in existence provides search and research tools that will allow you to delve down into what's actively being talked about, highlighted or shared that pertains to you, your practice or your offerings.

YouTube, Twitter, Facebook, Flickr, LinkedIn and most other platforms can be searched easily through their built-in tools. You'll also find tools like BlogSearch.Google.com that let you dig into blog post topics and comments. BlogPulse.com is a similar tool. Social media sharing sites like Delicious.com, Reddit.com and StumbleUpon.com can also be used to research and find out what's being talked about, why and how you can provide additional information to your audience on subjects that matter to them.

Build a Tip and Advice Center

Your patients need tips and advice on dental care and oral health. They need more than just a quick-access FAQ, though. Building a tip and advice center on your website can do wonders for your online visibility, but it also provides you with the means to give your patients important information, educate them on proper oral health and cleaning, and further your branding efforts as well.

On top of that, you have the opportunity for further SEO by incorporating important keywords and phrases into the answers and advice provided here. How does it work? Here's a brief glimpse:

- Eliminate any type of promotion by providing straight advice and tips for your patients and prospective patients. Not only will your audience appreciate the lack of direct selling, but you'll lighten your own stress load as well. Your tip and advice center should contain only accurate information with no promotional hype at all.

- Provide real, necessary information that offers immediate value to your patients and prospective patients. In addition, because you're providing that information without a catch (no sales pitch), you build your reputation and enhance your brand as well.

- Internal links and keywords within your tips and advice center support your SEO efforts, and encourage search engine spiders to follow the links and index the corresponding pages on your website. Make sure you use contextual linking practices, though. Link a specific condition name or term to the appropriate corresponding page on your website, or Google will reduce your ranking.

- By using accurate keywords within your tips and advice section (service names, condition types, etc.), you boost your site's visibility and page rank with Google. This is actually an excellent way to build in additional on-page optimization and encourage spiders to index the new content.

- You can implement widgets within the section to help you track ROI, click-through rates and determine what content is getting the most attention so you can tailor your other content accordingly. Based on that information, you can expand those areas that see the most traffic and increase the value that you offer your patients.

- You can easily determine how many people click through your tips and advice center to your practice's website and then make an appointment (become a patient). This provides you with essential information about your return on investment, as well as the effectiveness of your activities.

Building Microsites – Highly Focused and Maximum Conversion

You might not have given much thought to microsites. After all, you have your website and (hopefully) a blog. What do you need with another site? What do you need with multiple additional sites? Actually, microsites offer some powerful benefits. If you're not familiar with them, they're simple – they're single sites, devoted to just one topic or need, and offer no distractions for your visitors. Here's what microsites can offer you:

- No distractions for your visitors: while your practice's website can be a tremendously valuable resource, it can also be distracting. Microsites are devoted to a specific topic, providing your visitors with the information they want and need, and nothing they don't.

- Experiment to find out what works and what doesn't. You can experiment with headline styles and wording, with content types and graphic styles. Experimentation is the key to developing a site style and content range that really works.

- Microsites also allow you to create a vibrant online community and create conversation around topics that matter to your patients and to your practice.

Slidedecks – Develop Thought Leadership and Branding

Everyone wants to be a real authority and thought leader in their industry. For dental professionals, slidedecks provide one of the most innovative ways of doing just that. If you're not familiar with slidedecks, they're pretty much exactly what they sound like. They hearken back to slideshows of yesteryear, but are hosted online in the virtual environment. They can contain anything, from a discussion of proper brushing and flossing techniques to the importance of treating gingivitis immediately. Slidedecks offer:

- Multiple hosting opportunities: slidedecks can be shared on a plethora of different sites, like SlideRocket and AuthorStream. These communities provide more than just a virtual home for your decks, though. They allow users to rate and share your content, spreading the word for you.

- Brand the slides: you can use slidedecks as a branding tool very easily by building your brand directly into the presentation without any selling at all.

- Build the desire to learn more: slidedecks can be very informative, but they can also be used to create the desire to find out more about the services, treatments and procedures that you offer in your practice.

Webinars – Short, Punchy and Powerful

Webinars can be very powerful tools for marketing your practice and educating your patients. Not only that, but they provide a customizable length and format so you can offer short, conclusive educational lessons on topics that matter most to your audience. Of course, you'll have to do things the right way in order to entice your audience and then keep their attention once you have it. Make sure that you:

- Keep it short: make sure your webinars are short and tightly focused. You don't want a rambling, incoherent slog through banality. Rather, you want to create a tightly focused lesson that hones in on exactly what your patients need to know about the topic of the webinar.

- Know what matters: what matters most to your patients and prospective patients? Is it pediatric dentistry? Is it general oral health? Is it teeth whitening? Is it something else? The key to a successful webinar is to laser target the topics that matter most to your audience, so that you can build a lesson around it.

- Introduce new information: it's important that you supply your audience with new ideas and new concepts. For instance, your audience is undoubtedly familiar with metal braces, but do they know about Invisalign? Show them a new concept that will solve their problem, and educate them on the solution – don't sell.

- Challenge their assumptions and behaviors: it's important that you bring something new to your webinar, and that you break them out of their old ways of thinking. For instance, a pediatric dentist could do that by highlighting the need for a child's first dental appointment by the age of one. Give them something new to think about, or a new way of viewing the world.

- Promote your webinar: Remember earlier when we talked about promoting things using eNewsletters? This is a perfect example – you can promote your webinar very easily several weeks out, then a week before, and finally the day before you launch it. Doing so will help get your audience excited about it and boost attendance.

- Incentivize your webinar: if you're really looking for a way to bolster attendance, offer an incentive. Perhaps you can offer 50% off their next procedure, or a free teeth cleaning for attending. The right incentive will offer value to your audience, though, not just to your practice.

Podcasts – Host Your Own Radio Show and Educate Your Audience

Podcasts are hot right now, and have been for some time. If you're not sure what a podcast is, it's essentially an online radio show starring you. They're hosted on sites like iTunes and through Android podcast apps (as well as being accessible via your website, blog, Facebook page and other options), and provide you with a format in which to offer rich, vital information to your audience. That's not all they offer, though. You'll also find that they:

- Let you interview other authorities in the industry, including oral surgeons, other authors, scientists and more – you can give your audience breaking information on the topics that matter to them.

- Turn interviews into podcast episodes using free software: programs like Skype give you the means to conduct multi-person interviews and then transform those interviews into podcast episodes.

- Build your brand into your podcast. You can easily build your brand into your episodes without having to sell anything overtly.

- Get the crowd involved in distribution: you can offer incentives to those who share your podcast and spread the word on your behalf. Those incentives can be almost anything, from discounted services to a personalized "shout out" on the podcast itself.

Video Marketing – Massive ROI and Enormous Visibility

Video marketing has been around for some time now, and if you're not using it to promote your practice, you're missing one of the most powerful tools available to you. Video marketing offers tremendous ROI, and it's highly visible through natural search results. Google loves video, and your patients and prospective patients will too. Here are a few vital pieces of information on video marketing for your dental practice:

- Videos tell stories. Stories have immediate impact on your audience. Videos also offer considerably higher engagement than static images do, bringing your viewers into the story, rather than leaving them as passive bystanders. If you're looking for information marketing techniques that offer the highest in terms of ROI, this is it.

- You don't need to be a pro, or have professional equipment to start with video marketing. While production quality is important, it's more important that you tell the right story. What story, though? Actually, you can tell anything you want – highlight a particular procedure from beginning to end. Show what happens when dental problems are left uncorrected. Show how painless and simple a procedure or technique is – the sky's the limit here, really.

- Keep viewer engagement by creating a hook – that hook might be the ultimate answer to their needs, their desire to find out how a procedure works, the ultimate benefits of laser whitening, or something else entirely. By hooking your viewers from the beginning, you cement their attention and draw them in for the duration.

- Record the video yourself – don't hire an actor. You are your practice's most important asset, and likely a better storyteller than a paid actor who'll need a script. Be yourself. Give value. Offer real information and show real results and repercussions in your videos. Your viewers want and deserve authenticity and you can use video marketing to give them exactly that.

In Summation

It's time to stop thinking of marketing like a businessperson. It's time to start thinking like a publisher. Create content. Educate your audience. Produce content in a diverse range of formats and then spread it around the Internet. Create content products that educate and inform – move direct selling to the back burner.

Success through education and information can be easily achieved, and you don't have to worry that you're turning your patients and prospective patients off with your sales spiel. Information marketing is THE key to dental practice success.

Toothache Niche Marketing Secrets

with Colin Receveur & Yar Zuk

Colin Receveur: Hello everyone. This is Colin Receveur from SmartBox Web Marketing. On today's call we've got Dr. Yar Zuk, the crazy celebrity tooth-collecting marketing expert that you might have heard about John Lennon's tooth last year. I met Dr. Yar last year at the Profitable Dentist conference down in Destin, Florida, with Woody Oakes. We hooked up and we've been doing some cool things together with toothache marketing and putting our brains together and giving dentists some real tools to pull in the kind of patients they're looking for to keep their schedules full and build up their practice. So, Yar, are you with me on the line here?

Yar: I'm here. How are you doing?

Colin: I'm doing great. Thanks for hopping on with me.

Yar: Oh, it's great. This is fun.

Colin: So what is it that got you into the toothache market? How did that come about?

Yar: Well, in 1987 I moved to this little city in central Alberta and bought a practice with my classmate. It was a mall practice, which was kind of cool at the time. It was a big fad. Malls were getting dental practices all over the place. We were open early to late, and we just noticed a lot of people would come to see us for toothaches, and we'd get lots of new patients too. But the people would just generally look at us as a place to go when they needed help. So it became a critical part of our billings and I decided to exploit that and definitely brand ourselves as the place to go for urgent care.

Colin: That's cool. Some of the people on the line tonight might know that you are the guy that bought John Lennon's tooth.

Yar: Yeah. That was just over a year ago now. When I saw that little ad about the upcoming auction of John Lennon's tooth, I knew it was a massive marketing vehicle. It was odd, really crazy and stupid to spend a lot of money on a tooth. But I'd just sold a satellite clinic and had the money in the bank, so I needed a new project. I thought, "Well, let's see what I can do with this tooth." Over the last year, we've had just loads and loads of fun with it. There's been TV programs and lots and lots of publicity. I'm heading to New York City to go on a TV show in a week or two. We've got a couple of charity events. So it's just been a blast. If someone is interested in that kind of stuff, they can go to www.JohnLennonTooth.com and see all the wild publicity that came with that.

Colin: So how did that tooth come about? Did somebody steal it or did a dentist legitimately pull it out of his mouth?

Yar: Yeah, I think the story is he probably went to the local dentist and brought the tooth home and gave it to his housekeeper as a souvenir for her daughter and they kept it in the family. The housekeeper also had one of Julian Lennon's baby teeth too that she probably swapped out a little British Pound for or whatever. So that came along with the deal.

So it was in the family for all this time and they just finally decided to sell it. It's kind of nice that the old lady is still alive. I think she's just over 90 now. But yeah, I'm sure it's kind of nice to get a little bonus because I'm sure the housekeeper, even though it's for a celebrity, they don't always make that much money. So I'm sure the money was needed by the family.

Colin: That's cool.

Yar: I filled out a Guinness application. I'm sure there's a Guinness record every time you do something weird with it, like I put it into a pendant. It's traveling the UK right now raising awareness for mouth cancer. The BBC has picked it up and like 17 different dentists are keeping it for about a week or so. They get local newspaper press and they are dressing up like Beatles. It's, again, for a good cause. I mean John Lennon was a big smoker. He probably influenced some people to smoke. So I think this is payback that his little tooth is just an odd gimmick to attract attention for a needy cause – or a worthy cause, I should say. But yeah, we're having lots of fun.

It also goes along really good with the toothache theme, right, because I don't just market toothaches for my dental office. We've kind of segmented into different areas and that's, again, something we can talk about some more.

Colin: So tell me, what do you do to position toothache marketing? How is that different than, traditionally, how a dentist might market themselves?

Yar: I think the average dentist just basically comes up with some kind of cool logo and their name and they just think that they can just be busy and see everybody and do everything. But for us, like right now I'm wearing a baseball cap with Titleist on the top of it. So if I wear Titleist hats and I walked around town, people would think I'm a golfer, right?

So if you want to be something, you have to kind of dress and act the part. So for us that meant … I drew a little cartoon character with this woman's face, and we developed a whole marketing brand. We came up with a mascot so he can run around and dance around at parades, using the logo all over the place in newspapers and marketing on bus benches, and magnets and pens. With the pen, it just basically says "Toothache." We inject all kinds of little bits of this logo into our marketing. It doesn't have my name on it, for example. It has the office name on it. When we set up the second clinic, we kind of based it totally on the toothache brand. We took the outside signage – the glass that faces a corner intersection – and we put giant orange lettering with the word "Toothache" with a question mark on it. We just get tons and tons of people seeing it every day. You can't drive by it without seeing that.

So the number one reason people want to go to the dentist is usually something is wrong so it's definitely been neglected. So the average dentist who just basically doesn't show that they're interested in a certain segment is basically known for nothing then, right?

Colin: It is. You fall into the masses and …

Yar: You're just another dentist.

Colin: Just another guy in the crowd; no differentiation.

Yar: Yeah, it's been very important for us.

Colin: What kind of marketing and packaging systems do you do with your toothache practices?

Yar: Well, we offer kind of an area exclusive. If a dentist that is in a certain city that is smaller, we could say, "Well you could use our marketing that we've developed and tested on an exclusive basis." So it's not like if you sign up for Invisalign and then your competitor signs up for Invisalign, then you are going to see the same ads in the newspaper and on websites. So this is a unique way to brand yourself.

I just think it's time that dentists step out of the masses and try to be a little unique. I know they're usually a little scared but if you are just another Joe, then you are just going to be in the crowd. If you want to be shining and be in the spotlight, even though you might be shy like I am, you sometimes have to just step out and lay it down and say, "Hey, I'm going to focus on this." Most people have been going after being a cosmetic dentist whether that meant just saying that they were or maybe doing whitening or taking a lot of veneer courses. But I think in this economy, the toothache is just the ground level. You are going to scoop up a lot more patients. If you are trying to do full-mouth makeovers, to me, in this market, it's a tough choice to be that cosmetic dentist. So I think you can't go wrong with this kind of a market.

We offer a lot of those development pieces that are already done. You just customize it with your own information. And for the website part of it, that's what we've got you to help us with.

Colin: Part of what we do with a lot of the websites that we're building for your guys and for our dentist clients is back to that differentiation. Every dentist has a website these days. A lot of websites have three or four, ten, fifteen websites in some cases. But if you are just that dentist that just has a website and looks the same as everybody else you know – patients have to have a reason to call you. They have to like you. People do business with people they like.

We put a lot of video on websites: make you likeable, make you personable. I see the same stuff you are talking about – shy dentists that don't want to get in front of the camera, or maybe they were in front of the camera before and had an inexperienced interviewer or somebody that didn't do a very good job and they got a terrible result out of it, and now they are kind of gun shy to it.

Yar: Yeah, it's kind of nice to be able to have someone to help them and get a second chance at it because it is something that most of us aren't used to: talking into a camera and being comfortable. But if you really believe you are helping someone and can look at it that way, I think it takes away some of that weird feeling that maybe you are trying to show off or something. But you just have to get out there and lay it on the line.

For me, a lot of times I use my dental assistant to talk about my other niche or whatever. So it's kind of nice. I can step back and let her be the "woman of the hour" kind of thing. But it's probably best if a dentist can just get in there because staff can change. If you ended up building up a staff member and your competitor steals her, that would be kind of spooky.

Colin: [laughs] Yeah, definitely.

Yar: While we're on the website section, to me I think it's good to have a main website, just a general one like typical dentists have, but I would recommend developing totally separate stand-alone websites to work on the specific niche that the dentist is trying to exploit.

So if it's toothache, then have it as a very prominent feature. With us, since we sold off this second clinic just last year, I've kind of agreed to let them use the toothache brand more prominently than mine. My main office still has a little bit of that theme, but I'm sitting back and letting them kind of enjoy that niche for now.

It also lends itself, for example – toothaches, we get it down to even wisdom teeth. So we might have a bus bench that says wisdom teeth. There's nothing wrong with even doing a website dedicated to wisdom teeth. Even though you are not a surgeon, I think there have been records where general dentists become very good at surgery and that cross references with the toothache, because a lot of times people are calling in with an infected wisdom tooth. So if you can solve their problem, it also spins out into possible sedation ideas. So it's very fun.

Colin: We do a lot of that same tactic with the GPs and docs with some clinical training that are wanting to take on those cases. Being found in Google for searches like "periodontist" and "oral surgeon." While you are not marketing on your own websites that you are a periodontist or an oral surgeon or that you can do these specialized procedures, being found in those searches is certainly somewhere you want to be. So, broadening your base and getting found in all those different keyword terms is very important as well.

Yar: Oh yeah. I'm sure it is. I'm not up on that part of it, but that's your specialty, so that's good to have.

Colin: How many different niches are you branding yourself in, Yar?

Yar: Well, with my whole practice, we have about six dentists. So for myself personally, I work on my own high speed braces niche. So I'm the guy that does Fastbraces or braces a little faster than most people in town. I combine orthodontics and cosmetic dentistry. My other partner,

---

he does maybe more veneers and bridges and works with an implant doctor, so there's that niche. There's the general ortho that my other partner does. He's not an orthodontist but he does a lot of ortho. He also does snoring, so there's another niche.

Then there's the toothache niche I just, again, use as a general draw, and it helps to get the new associates busy. And then it's just a family dentistry niche, as people want to know, "Okay, can I bring my kids there?" So we kind of, depending on the ad, and a lot of times I'm just using radio ads to talk about this. So if it's about me, I usually use high speed braces and the trademark and my own name and number. If it's toothache, it could be insurance: "We accept insurance. We're open late." That kind of thing. And then we use the Bower Dental name.

So even though it's the same office, I just do a little bit of a tweak to separate us a little bit so it doesn't sound like we're doing all these things at once. That's a common mistake. Most ads say, "Well we do this, this, this, and this." "Well, if you do all these things, you are really not that good at it," is what people often think. So I just want to be known for my little service and the other doctors, I don't necessarily brand them as viciously as I do myself but it definitely keeps a steady stream of different types of people coming in.

Colin: So, Yar, what are you doing with radio to promote the toothache niche?

Yar: Well what we've done, and again, I'm helping this second clinic specifically focus on toothache marketing, is I come up with a radio ad. In this case I came up with a radio ad to compliment a bus bench. So the bus bench caption is "Wisdom teeth?" Or "Wisdom tooth?" or whatever. And the same logo with the swollen face and that kind of thing.

So then I drafted a wisdom tooth pain radio ad. We tested it and the office spent something like $3,000 running it over three months. They ended up getting $30,000 worth of treatment out of it. Obviously, people are always going to need wisdom teeth taken care of, right? It's just one of those perpetual things that rather than hopping onto different ideas, I think it's better for an office to focus on toothaches, wisdom teeth and broken teeth – just keep with the whole theme. The return on investment is pretty damn amazing. I mean, to spend $3,000 over three months might sound like a lot to the average dentist, but if you do an extra $30,000 worth of work, it just only makes sense. If you increase your spending in that area, you may or may not get any more patients, but you could also track how it goes, and then from using one radio station, then you could go to another radio station. And you are usually going to find a different market.

Colin: I just had a light bulb come on in my head about what you are doing differently. I mean this is just bread and butter dentistry, essentially.

Yar: Oh yeah.

Colin: A lot of dentists focus on what they do. They do crowns, and bridges, and fillings, and partials, and dentures. They do all of these clinical procedures. But you are not marketing the procedures you do. You are marketing the pain that your patients experience. You are marketing broken teeth, missing teeth, ugly teeth – things that hit home with your patients. Whereas all the other dentists that are looking for this bread and butter dentistry are talking about the tools they use to fix it. Well, patients don't care about the tools. Patients don't care about fillings, and crowns, and bridges. Patients care about spaces, broken teeth, and pain.

Yar: They've got a problem. I guess if you can just relate to them on a basic level: "What's your problem? If you've got this problem, then I'm the guy to call." That's exactly right. It's simple, but unfortunately dentists have to think a little more simply, more on a grassroots level, to actually relate to the actual patient. Because we are all reading those fancy journals and talking about these terms that no one else is going to understand, and that is one of the issues, is that dentists don't relate well to the public. So getting down to what their issues are. That's a great point.

Colin: You mentioned the high speed braces that you are doing. What are you doing to accelerate the treatment time on that?

Yar: Well, like most of the shorter term braces programs, I'm looking at mostly trying to look at aesthetic improvements and not necessarily all the same improvements an orthodontist would do that would take longer. And so, I'm offering treatment in a shorter time for less cost. And the thing that I can do that most orthodontists can't do is I can combine composite bonding with the treatment. So I will take on extremely messed up mouths that are all worn down and I'll rebuild them using full mouth reconstructive techniques and then combine some ortho to join it together. I'm competing with an orthodontist that would work with the prosthodontist. So you can imagine getting two specialists together, the cost would be enormous. So I can do some pretty amazing things at just a mere fraction of what they would charge.

And a lot of times, orthodontists are not trained to do … they don't feel comfortable with composite bonding to deal with wear. So they are fiddling and fussing with how to get the brackets in the right place. To me, it's much more of an advantage to be able to bond ahead of time, re-tip the teeth, or even do it during treatment. A lot of times, the orthodontist has to wait until afterwards because they don't know how to work with the general dentist who has maybe not taken the courses.

So anyway, when you can combine a few different techniques and loosen the rules a little bit, you are not quite as regimented that you necessarily have to follow all these little sequences of wires, people are just thrilled to get the braces on and off. They don't necessarily want to be textbook. So I'm having a blast with that.

Colin: And is that a system that any docs can learn how to do?

Yar: Yeah. Right now, I mean you could take an ortho course. You could take one of the shorter term courses – take courses from Frank Spear or John Kois for full mouth reconstruction. And if you can do all that and put it together, you've got the same kind of training I can do. And you are going to kick other people's asses if they're just taking a one-day or two-day course. I mean, the orthodontist is looking down at all these GPs that do a quick course, and for good reason. They are going to try to do everything they can with simplest of treatment. And there is a gray zone where you have to kind of learn a little bit more.

So the training is out there. I don't necessarily teach the training. I just say if you want to learn the courses and use the techniques, I wrote a book called "High Speed Braces" on Blurb, so people can check that out or go to HighSpeedBracesInstitute.com for a little more information. But I think it's the most conservative way to do cosmetic dentistry these days. It just takes a little bit of training.

Colin: You've written several books. How many are you up to now?

Yar: Well, I'm probably up to 10 or 12. This last weekend I pumped out a book. I'm not feeling the greatest. I've had a little bit of the flu but my daughter is in dental assisting school right now. She's going to get done in a few months so I decided to write her a book on what I think she needs to know to be a good dental assistant in her first year.

So I spilled my guts into a quick book. I put it up on Blurb. It's instantly available. I can print off a copy. I think it's something other dentists should look at if they have a niche that they're working on. Sit down for a weekend and just write down all the information you want about it so that you have your own book. If you have that, a patient is going to sit in your waiting room and think you are the expert. If you want to be the king or queen of your niche, then why not be the expert on it?

Colin: So you set out all your books in your waiting room?

Yar: Well, not all of them. It would look kind of busy. But I do include … like if a patient comes in for a high-speed braces consultation, a lot of times while they are waiting for me to catch up, my assistant will give them one of my books and they'll run through it and they'll say, "Wow. He's the author." They often say, "Well, you are the expert. You wrote the book." And literally, I did write the book. So that helps them just have a little more confidence in me that someone, if all they are doing is handing a person a pamphlet from the company that has nothing to do with you, aside from maybe you taking the course there, it's a different level.

So books are so easy to do these days. With Blurb, you can just type it out in a Word document, upload it on Blurb.com, and then add some photos. Again, I've just had so much fun with them and highly, highly recommend dentists looking at Blurb.

Colin: Wow. That's very cool. I've not heard of Blurb before, but I'm going to make a note here and I'm going to go check it out. We've done a bunch of book writing for our docs and Blurb sounds like it's a very print-on-demand company. You can order just a couple books at a time instead of getting …

Yar: Yeah. To keep it active you have to order one or two books, I think. But you can offer it in all these different formats. And from there, you can take the link and actually upload it onto your website so a person can flip through the pages of your book on your website. And that also, I'm sure, increases your web standing, but that's not really what I know anything about. I built a lot of my own websites and I built a lot of my own little marketing stuff that I do, but I highly recommend some professional websites, but I like the idea of having control myself. But I have a little more motivation than the average person.

Colin: I think so. I don't know many dentists that have written a dozen books and put all the systems together that you have.

Yar: Well, again, they're not great books. I don't waste time editing. Most dentists, again – way too perfect. They'd be embarrassed that another dentist would read it, and I don't really care. If someone doesn't like what I've said, it doesn't matter to me. For the book just to be out there I think is more important.

For example, I wrote a book for dentists on toothache marketing. It doesn't matter if I spelled something wrong. If they are into wanting to know how we made millions of dollars with toothaches, then they are going to overlook these things. I'm not here to show off. I'm just here to share some things.

I wrote a book for high speed braces for dentists, and then I also wrote a book for high speed braces information for patients. So I just speak in layman's terms. I don't use all the fancy words that a specialist would use or whatever. And I think it's important not to get really fancy when you are writing books for patients. I mean, that's a common problem is the dentist will explain things in such technical jargon that an assistant has to spend twice as much time trying to get them to understand what we're talking about.

Colin: We see that a lot on these "Meet the Dentist" pages on doctor websites, where it's filled with the alphabet soup of accreditations and continuing education and all this stuff. Yeah, it looks impressive, but nobody understands it. You have to have a dictionary to figure out what it all is.

Yar: Yeah, keep it real simple. "What's the problem? If you've got a toothache, basically get in here right now. I can help you." Don't go over all the reasons why you have toothaches and don't waste a lot of time. Call the office. If you knocked a tooth out, again, maybe stick it in some milk, coconut milk or something. Get down to the bare essentials.

Same thing with high speed braces. We just say, "Do you have crooked teeth, or spaces, or gaps? Are you concerned about that? Well, here's some examples of what we do." And one of the fun things that we use hooking up to websites is YouTube videos. So we're recording someone getting their braces taken off that day and just how excited they are when they first see themselves in the mirror. And that's just that one chance that you have to capture their excitement.

And again, I don't really care if the treatment looks textbook to an orthodontist or not or if we can even see their teeth that clearly. Most of the time there are shadows and stuff. It's more just the patient's reaction. If the patient is just thrilled and sometimes crying with happiness, then that is what comes across in the video. Again, if you produced it, you'd probably do a whole bunch of takes. By the final one, it would look textbook. But the real emotion, the raw emotion would be lost, because most people aren't real good actors, right?

Colin: Yeah, definitely. I love the YouTube video stuff you are doing. You can put anything in text on a website. You can say you are the best, or the most gentle, or the most pain free, but there's nothing you can do that's going to mimic the investment of putting videos on your website. Your patient videos, yeah, just that raw emotion. There's absolutely nothing that you can ever put that will compete with that, other than just putting video of your patient on your website.

Yar: We've never done it with toothaches, but I think that's another market. The patient, when you see them for a follow-up, you could do a video and just say, "Could you tell us how much you were in pain and how we helped you?" I think you'd get that same sincere response, and I think people really appreciate the help when you get them out of pain. Even if it is sometimes they have a little healing period; it's not like it's always magic. But these people are definitely willing to share their experience on video, and most dentists just don't take advantage of that.

All you need is an iPhone and a consent form; they just sign it. They have to sign the exact use that you are going to use with the confidentiality laws where I am. It would vary, and I think in some places you can't use patient testimonials, and that's just the way it is. If I was there, I'd probably use them anyway until I got in trouble, because if the laws are wrong, I mean if they are too restrictive, I think it's time that dentists stand up and say, "Listen, let's be realistic." Maybe get a few people together and rebel against the old school guys. But that's my thought.

Colin: We've had some guys that are kind of skittish. You know, some of the board laws, Illinois comes to mind. They're kind of funny about testimonials and all that. I've heard from Texas that they are kind of funny. We've got clients in both states that are doing it. Both of them have been contacted by the boards. Neither one of them has had any trouble beyond just the initial contact of, "Hey, this is against the board by laws. You can't do that." And then they reply and say, "Well, this is the Internet. These days everybody is doing it. If I'm not doing it, somebody else is doing it for my office." You know, the patients are out there on the review sites posting reviews – testimonials. It's not something that just because you're not playing the game doesn't mean the game isn't being played. It's just being played without you.

Yar: Yeah. There's ways to get around. Again, I think it's reasonable just to go ahead and do it and not worry about getting a slap on the wrist. You are not going to lose your license, I would think. It would be pretty extreme if you lost your license for showing off a testimonial, if it's a real one. I mean, I could see if it was a fake one or something, that's different. But if you are just telling the truth and someone is happy with your treatment, the laws of the land, I believe, allow freedom of speech. And so, I think, like you are saying, the dentists are doing it. If all they are getting is a little letter then it's worth just going ahead and doing it and don't worry if your competitors complain. That just shows that you are outside the box and you are more likely to be the one that people are going to call.

Colin: I think if your competitors are having the time to complain about you that says something in itself.

Yar: Well, that's what most dentists are actually doing. They spend more time whining about what the other ones are doing than they are actually marketing their own practices. Locally, I'm just a hyper-marketer. It's really hard to stop me. If they say I can't do this, I do something else. I find ways to keep …

I had one psychologically imbalanced dentist. He was obsessed at trying to stop me. So he probably hired someone to try to document every little thing I did, including speaking in the space at, like, The Profitable Dentist. He would print off what I was talking about, and every little move I made he would try to document. He probably only caught a quarter of what I did. But he literally sent it all into the Dental Association. I've got this huge box – it's probably 30 pounds of documentation. I've never opened it, but the Dental Association wanted me to have it. I just haven't even bothered. Maybe there's a citation that I've missed or something. But the bottom line is if dentists are just going to whine about their competitors, that's great. It just gives the main guy more time to rock and roll.

Colin: [laughs] I completely agree with you. My thought is why are they whining? They are whining because you are taking business from them.

Yar: Yeah, there is something they are upset about.

Colin: If you are doing it ethically, telling the truth and not falsifying things … you know, the laws are behind the times with the testimonials and all that stuff. That's just the way of the world these days. Everybody's doing it.

Yar: It's just a sign of jealousy, and it's a good sign. If someone is not jealous of you then you are not trying hard enough. If you are not the top, then you've got to work toward it. Why wouldn't you want to be known for whatever you are doing? It just makes sense, right?

Colin: Definitely. If you are the go-to guy that pops in somebody's mind when their kid falls off the trampoline and cracks their tooth, they're not shopping around when they have a screaming kid that just broke his two front teeth out. They are going to a trusted source or they are going to call a friend who's going to recommend a trusted source. And if you are not on the tip of one of those person's tongues, you just missed that.

Yar: Oh yeah. If your magnet is on their fridge, they're going to say, "Oh my God, there's the toothache guy. Let's get there." And we're open late. Like you said, it's the first inclination: where are they going to go? It may not even be their regular dentist. Their regular dentist is probably golfing and it's the afternoon. And oh, he doesn't pick up his phone.

A lot of dentists do that. They don't even give their home numbers on their machines. They don't have an answering service. So we see these people and a lot of times, they get pissed off at their dentist and they say, "Screw them. We're going to move to you because you were there for us."

Colin: One of the first things we do with new clients is we send them a form that we've put together with tips on what they should and should not be doing. Number two on the list is: have your phones answered live. No matter what, always have a live person answer that phone, because if somebody calls your office and leaves a message … most of the time they won't even leave a message. We hear doctors say all the time, "Well, if people call, we know if they don't leave a message. We get a notification of that." Well maybe, maybe not. People can hang up before the message kicks in and you probably never know about it.

Yar: Oh yeah. We're lucky. Getting a hook into that caller, you are going to reel them in. If you don't get that hook, if it's not a live person, that's exactly right. Most offices aren't going to be open the hours that we are. We're open from eight in the morning until nine at night. So actually, our own staff are getting those calls right then. And after hours, we do have an answering service. But most of the people are going to be calling within that time segment. But even lunches and stuff, we're still getting the lines. The lines are always ringing. They're always getting picked up. We're funneling people in. So just having a live person is going to add up to probably hundreds of thousands of dollars every year for the average dentist.

Colin: If docs want to know more about getting into the toothache niche and how you can help them with that, how can they do that?

Yar: Well, what they could do is they could read the book "Toothache Marketing" that's on Blurb to see if it sounds like something they would want to do. The website KillerToothache.com is our mother site. It's basically a membership site where you can hook up and get little samples of what we do, sort of free e-reports and that kind of thing so you get a little taste of it. But a lot of stuff is in the book anyway.

But what I can do is whenever this is being listened to, I can probably set the book preview on free on Blurb.com so people can flip through the pages and see what we're doing. But again, we built a multi-million dollar practice in a short time. We get associates booked up really quickly. So toothache marketing, that niche is definitely valuable. I don't want anyone else to do it in town. They try to copy what we do, but it's not the same.

So if people are interested, just check out the website. I guess contacting you is another idea. You could pass them on to me and help them a little bit with websites and help with that part of it. But for the general questions, that's cool if they want to hunt me down. I keep kind of busy with all my other projects, but if someone is interested in an area exclusive, then we can talk about it.

Colin: Great. So, Killertoothache.com is the address, or feel free to call the office here: 888-741-1413 and we'll direct them to you or answer any questions that they have. We've been building some cool websites for some of your members these days with the toothache niche, and we've actually got some demo sites available out there in cyberspace. I don't have the websites here on the tip of my tongue.

Yar: Another thing, they could also go to "Toothache Guy" on

Facebook, and then we could probably post some links to your different demo sites, too. toothache guy on Facebook. That will be fun.

Colin: Perfect. Well, I appreciate your time, Dr. Zuk, and look forward to seeing some of the crazy marketing ideas you come up with next. It's always interesting to follow you.

Yar: Thanks a lot. It's been fun.

Colin: Take care.

Yar: You too, Colin. Bye-bye.

Colin: Bye-bye.

Chapter 27

Questions to Ask Your Marketing Firm

Word Count: **13,060**
Approximate Time to Read: **29.0 minutes**

"Being able to pick up the phone and call somebody that you can say, 'Colin, I need some help,' and they pick up the phone, is awesome."

~ Michael P. Abernathy, D.D.S.

"I think there's one other area that they do really well. A lot of people come in, go to a website and they're gone. Well guess what? Problems arise, questions need to be answered – we need to know if we're not getting what we want out of a website, what kind of changes we need to make. It doesn't take a huge investment; it can be added to – it can be incremental.

"He's very responsive! I've called any number of times in the last few months for a little tweak here or a little tweak there, or to change something, or to change the wording and he's always very helpful. **Oftentimes, he makes the changes while we're on the telephone and just says, 'Refresh your page and you'll see the changes.'"**

~Maxwell R. Gotcher

"I've always had to chase my website guys to get something done or try something new. **With SmartBox, I have a discussion and it's done.** *I don't have to keep following up. As a dentist, I'm busy. I've got a practice to run, I've got staff to manage and I've got two young kids at home so I really don't want to be doing the chasing. They listen to me as one of their clients and we work together as a team so that I'm satisfied with the end result."*

~ Saj Jivraj, D.D.S., M.S.Ed.

"A HUGE THANK YOU to Colin Receveur, of SmartBox Web Marketing for his amazing customer service and help and for his

"beyond-the-call-of-duty" assistance."

~ *Charles Payet, D.D.S.*
Dentist in Charlotte, North Carolina

To assist you in auditing your current dental website and marketing firm, we've put together this checklist of 102 critical questions you should be asking. Any reputable marketing firm will give you clear, concise answers to these questions. **Don't get bamboozled!** We wish you all the best during your exploration process. Please contact me at **(888) 741-1413** if you feel you're a good match for our services and want to get started finding the new patients and cases YOU want.

Website Design

Topic: Custom Designed Websites

Explanation: If your website looks like and carries the same message as your competitor, your prospects won't pick either of you. You must differentiate yourself by design and unique message.

Questions to ask:

● Will my website be custom designed?

● Is my new website a templated "cookie cutter" that looks like everyone else's?

● Is it a unique design with compelling content that truly differentiates me?

Topic: Google Friendly Website

Explanation: Many "designers" can make your website look pretty, but if your website isn't built from the ground up with SEO in mind, you'll never be found.

Questions to ask:

● Is my website Google-friendly?

● Do you also offer in-house Search Engine Optimization services?

● Are you confident in your optimization tactics? Do you offer a guarantee?

● Will my website be designed to "look pretty" or is it designed with Google in mind?

- Will you guarantee a top ranking on the search engines?

Topic: Mobile Website

Explanation: Sixty-five percent of local searches came from mobile devices in 2012, Google says. Because of the extremely small screen sizes compared to desktops and laptops, you need to offer a mobile optimized version so your prospects can get your information easily, no matter how they find you.

Questions to ask:

- Will my website have a mobile friendly version built for those searching on smart phones such as iPhones and Androids?
- Will my website have a tablet friendly version built for those searching on iPads and other intermediate-sized screen devices?
- Will my mobile website be optimized to show in the mobile search?

Topic: Rotating Images

Explanation: Rotating stock image banners and even those with actual patient photos are notorious for running off your prospects. While they look pretty and I'm sure your patients compliment the nice photos you have, dozens of studies have proven that they actually drive prospects away.

Question to ask:

- What do you think about putting a rotating image banner on my new website?

Topic: Adobe Flash

Explanation: Google can't read Flash – plain and simple. Anything you build with Flash won't be found in Google. Also, iPhones, iPads, and many other mobile devices are not Flash compatible either. We recommend avoiding Flash entirely for the best compatibility and Search Engine Optimization.

Question to ask:

- Will my dental website have any Adobe Flash on it?

Topic: SEO Capabilities

Explanation: Many marketing firms do not offer access to the "code" of your site to optimize. Consequently, those websites never achieve great rankings on Google and Bing.

Questions to ask:

- Will I have 100% ability to organically optimize my website for the search engines?
- Can I add new tags, code, and other critical SEO elements to my website?

Topic: Website Navigation

Explanation: Too often, the navigation area on websites are identical in color to the background and/or text, practically camouflaging it. Use contrast to make it clear to your prospects where they need to be looking.

- Will my navigation area and links stand out?
- Please show me 5 websites you've done recently.

Topic: Updating Your Website

Explanation: Many marketing firms offer no way for you to update your own website. Some take weeks to make simple changes and will charge you for it.

With our SNAP technology, if you can edit a Word document, now you can update your website too. Don't worry, if you don't want to update it yourself, we can do it for you.

Question to ask:

- Does my new website include a super easy-to-use way to update it myself?

Topic: Contact Information

Explanation: Believe it or not, we see websites every day you can't find the contact information of the office!

Questions to ask:

- Does my phone number and contact info stand out on the front page?
- Please show me five websites you've done recently.

Topic: Clinical Photos

Explanation: Many dentists are excited to show off their clinical skills, but your prospects don't want to know how it's done, they only want to know that you're the dentist for them and you'll do a great job. Before and after pictures are great, but skip the "during." Showing clinical photos will scare off many prospects!

Questions to ask:

- Do you recommend showing step-by-step photos of reconstructions?
- Do you want "clinical" photos to include?

Website Content

Topic: Text Within Images

Explanation: Many web marketing firms take the easy way and embed text within images. Google can't read this and you won't get indexed properly in the search engines. All the text on your website should be actual text, (use the highlight test) styled with proper CSS.

Questions to ask:

- Will you use images to hold the text on my website?
- All the text will be text, not images, right?
- My phone number will be text, not an image, right?

Topic: Repetitive Call-to-Action

Explanation: If you want to emphasize something, you repeat it. If you want your prospects to take note of the next step, make sure you repeat it several times.

Questions to ask:

- Is your Call-to-Action repetitive and relevant to my prospects (the patients I want to attract)?

Topic: Keywords

Explanation: Your keywords are not what you think! You want your website to appear for the keywords that the prospects you want to attract are searching for! If you're marketing for "free x-rays and exam" then "Chicago Dentist" is probably a good keyword. But if you're marketing to deep disability large reconstructive and cosmetic cases, those people will never find you on those keywords. Be sure you research and find out what your patients are searching for, then optimize your marketing for those terms.

- How do you determine what keywords you'll optimize my website for?
- What research do you do on those keywords?
- How many other dental practices that want patients in <my niche> have you worked with?
- How often are you re-evaluating my keyword list?

Topic: Blog Updates

Explanation: If you're going to get a blog, you need to update it regularly. Stagnant blogs lead prospects to believe you've abandoned your website. Keep things fresh and update it with new content regularly.

Questions to ask:

- How often are you updating my blog?
- Are you updating my blog for me, or do I have to?

Topic: Do You Address Your Prospects' Problems, or Do You Talk About Yourself?

Explanation: Checkout the "Wewe" test on our website: http://link. swm.tv/wewe

Questions to ask:

- How will you relay my expertise to my prospects?

- How will my new website answer the questions my prospects are searching for?

Topic: Copyright Date

Explanation: If your website says "Copyright 2008" at the bottom, your visitors (and Google) know your website is stale and hasn't been updated in a while.

Questions to ask:

- How often will you update my website?
- Will the copyright date update automatically every year?

Topic: "Click Here"

Explanation: Google looks at your "anchor text" that you use for links very closely when it's analyzing your site's SEO. Make sure you use relevant, specific words for your links, not just "click here."

Question to ask:

- Will you build my website with the BEST Search Engine Optimization practices in mind?

Topic: Broken Links

Explanation: Broken links can leave your visitors frustrated and lead to Google de-ranking you. It's a sign of a bad, mismanaged website.

Question to ask:

- Will you proof my website for broken links once it's finished?

Topic: Video that Plays Automatically

Explanation: When done right, video that plays automatically is great for the user experience, but it must be relevant to what they want, and they must be able to pause it if they choose.

Questions to ask:

- Can you setup my website to automatically play a video?
- Will my prospects be able to easily pause my video?

Topic: Call To Actions

Explanation: Many dental websites only offer their phone number as a method of contact. While small cases and prospects might immediately contact you, larger cases require contact with "less risk" so they can get to know you first.

Questions to ask:

- Will my website have a CLEAR Call-To-Action other than "call me"?
- Will my website have additional information offers, newsletter signup, webinars, and other "risk-free" ways for my patients to learn more about me?

Topic: Music

Explanation: Some website designers want to play background music. This is proven to chase off your prospects!

Question to ask:

- Do you recommend playing music in the background?

Topic: Vanity Phone Numbers

Explanation: While they appear pretty and easy to remember, this is just shooting yourself in the foot! With click-to-call technology and many searching on mobile phones, plus many calling from new phones that don't have letters on their keypads, vanity numbers are frustrating to type in and detract from your prospects' experience.

Questions to ask:

- Will you be using a vanity number on my website?
- Will you use toll-free (800/855/866/877/888) numbers on my website, or local (my area code) phone numbers?

Topic: TV Commercials on Your Website

Explanation: Your TV commercials are meant to grab a prospect's attention in 30 seconds or less and compel them to call or visit your website. So why would you put a commercial on your website – they've already found you! It detracts from the user experience. Use video that is extremely specific to WHY they are there, that speaks directly to THEIR problems.

Question to ask:

- Will my website have tons of video on it?

Web Marketing

Topic: Spying on Your Competition

Explanation: There are many tools available that allow you to spy on your competition, stealing their keywords and advertising strategies. Why try to reinvent the wheel when you can swipe a successful marketing campaign from someone else?

Questions to ask:

- Can you show me what my competitors are marketing for and what keywords they are optimizing for?

Topic: Domain Name

Explanation: Another critical piece of good SEO: the domain name you choose should reflect your target market. Using specific keywords in your domain name is a surefire way to boost your SEO.

Questions to ask:

- What domain name are you using with my website?
- Are you using keywords in my domain name?

Topic: Robots.txt

Explanation: A critical file to proper SEO, robots.txt tells all the search engines what pages to index and, which not to. Without it, you have no control over, which pages Google grabs (and, which it doesn't).

Question to ask:

- Will you manage my robots.txt file on my website?

Topic: Link Building

Explanation: If you were to compare links to our bodies, links are the "blood" of the Internet. They connect to everything, they carry your prospects from one page or one site to another. They are also the #1 metric that Google examines when determining your rank in the search results.

Questions to ask:

- Are you building links into my website and local search listing?
- Where are you getting these links from?
- Are they coming from highly relevant dental-related websites?

Topic: SEO Capabilities

Explanation: Many marketing firms do not allow you access to edit the "code" of your website to optimize. Consequently, those websites never achieve great rankings on Google and Bing.

Questions to ask:

- Will I have 100% ability to organically optimize my website for the search engines?
- Can I add new tags, code, and other critical SEO elements to my website?

Topic: Press Release

Explanation: Designed to jumpstart your marketing campaign, will you get a press release with your web marketing firm?

Question to ask:

- Are you utilizing press releases with my marketing campaign?

Topic: Video Optimization

Explanation: Google is now putting videos right at the top of the search results. You can claim another top ranking spot by optimizing your videos for the services and locations you serve.

Questions to ask:

- Will my videos be optimized for the services I offer and for my local area?
- Will the title, description, category, tags, and location all be completed on every video?

Topic: Google AdWords Express

Explanation: To be seen everywhere includes the pay-per-click (PPC) area on Google. This is a very high-traffic area of Google that consistently produces solid results in many markets.

Questions to ask:

- Does your marketing plan include an AdWords Express campaign targeted at local searches?
- What size geographic area are you targeting with my ads?

Local Search/Google Places

Topic: Media Content

Explanation: Multimedia on your local place listings is crucial to getting a top ranking.

Question to ask:

- Will you have all 10 images and 5 videos filled up on my local place listings?

Topic: Completed Profile

Explanation: Google will give preference to those listings that have the most content in their listing. Google even shows you the percentage of completeness your local listing is.

Question to ask:

- Will my profile say "100% complete"?

Topic: Have You Added Attributes to Your Listing?

Explanation: Attributes are a powerful way to add extra information to your local listing about specific services you offer and your uniqueness.

Question to ask:

- Will you add attributes to my local listing?

Topic: Claim Your Listing

Explanation: The #1 way that people find local services in their area is with local listings that show up in search results.

Questions to ask:

- Will you claim my local listing and optimize it?

- Will you continuously optimize my local listing?

Topic: Have You Claimed All Duplicates and Properly Managed All Your Local Listings?

Explanation: Duplicate listings are a real pain to manage! If you don't get every one of them (and I've seen a dozen duplicates for a single office), your patients might be finding the wrong profile that could have outdated information and/or be unimpressive.

Questions to ask:

- Will you claim and merge all my duplicate listings?
- Will you monitor Google monthly for additional duplicate listings?

Pre-Qualification

Topic: Patient Education

Explanation: Patient education is paramount to case acceptance. Educated patients are better consumers of the dentistry you offer.

Questions to ask:

- Will my consults come in educated and prepared?
- Will my prospects be thoroughly educated and informed about how I can help them?
- Will they be given all this information in a way they can "consume and digest" or will it be info dumped on them?

Topic: 12 Cups of Tea

Explanation: Your prospects in need of large case reconstructive and cosmetic dentistry will want to absorb information from you multiple times before they decide to have you do their work.

Question to ask:

- Will my website have free reports & books that have been ghost-written for me, webinars, teleseminars, white papers, podcasts, and other forms of information that my prospects can subscribe to to learn more about me (and set me up as "the" expert)?

Topic: Your Human Side

Explanation: Your patients want to see your "human side" before they call you and come into your office. This begins developing the relationship of trust, which is exponentially important as case size increases.

Questions to ask:

- Will you produce custom video for my website?
- Will you produce video that elevates my expertise to attract the patients I want?

Social Media

Topic: Facebook Business Page

Explanation: Being seen everywhere is the key to dominating your area and your niches. It's critical to have a presence on the social networks to "build your tribe."

Questions to ask:

- Will you build a social media presence for me?
- Will you setup a Facebook business page for my practice?

Topic: Twitter Business Page

Explanation: Many business professionals frequent Twitter.

Question to ask:

- Will I have a Twitter business page setup and customized to my practice?

Topic: Social Media Call-to-Action

Explanation: Are you just posting updates and offers to your wall, or have you set up your Facebook page to actually contain a funnel that drives leads?

Question to ask:

- What will be my Call-to-Action on Facebook and Twitter?

Topic: Facebook Configuration

Explanation: If your default tab on Facebook is the wall, you're missing a ton of leads. Create a new page that funnels the traffic to your webpage while offering an incentive for people to follow and like you.

Questions to ask:

- What will my default tab be on Facebook?
- Do you recommend an incentive for my prospects to "Like" and "Follow" me?

Topic: Video Syndication

Explanation: Having videos is just the first step. The second step is people actually watching them. By syndicating your videos to many different websites, more people will find and watch them.

Questions to ask:

- Will my videos be syndicated across the video and social networking websites?
- Will you regularly optimize and syndicate my videos?

Video

Topic: Reverse Testimonials

Explanation: Patient testimonials are great but by using the reverse testimonial technique, you can make your patients' words carry five times the power.

Questions to ask:

- Will I get twenty+ powerful reverse video testimonials and sixty+ custom educational videos for my website?
- Will you come to my office to film the video or is your video "boilerplate"?

Topic: Patient Filming Location

Explanation: Dental chairs often have very negative associations. We recommend filming your patients in a neutral place, such as consult room, waiting room, or somewhere with nothing "clinical."

Question to ask:

- Will any of the patient testimonials be filmed while my patients are in the dental chair?

Topic: Video Optimization

Explanation: Google is now putting videos right at the top of the search results. You can claim another top spot by optimizing your videos for the services you offer and the locations you serve.

Questions to ask:

- Will my videos be optimized for the services I offer and for my area?
- Is the title, description, category, tags, and location all completed on every video?

Topic: Educational Videos

Explanation: Forrester Research found that websites with video are 53 times more likely to have a first-page Google ranking.

Questions to ask:

- Will my website have educational and patient reverse testimonial videos?
- Will my videos be captivating or boring?

Topic: Education-Based Marketing

Explanation: Educated prospects are better consumers of your dentistry and require less time and education during your consultation.

Questions to ask:

- When my patients arrive for a consult, what will be their knowledge level?
- Will I already be "the expert" in their mind, or will I be the "free 2nd opinion"?

Topic : Video Syndication

Explanation: Having videos is just the first step. The second step is people actually watching them. By syndicating your videos to many different websites, more people will find and watch them.

Questions to ask:

- Are my videos being syndicated across the video and social networking websites?
- Will you regularly optimize and syndicate my videos?

Tracking

Topic: Phone Call Tracking

Explanation: Intake form tracking is notoriously unreliable. Can you look in the mirror and tell yourself you know where 100% of your calls and dollars came from?

Questions to ask:

- Will I get an industry leading phone call tracking system that can tell me how many phone calls, consults, case acceptances, and exact dollar amounts I generated from all your marketing?
- Will my new patient phone calls be recorded so I can monitor my staff's phone skills and training?

Topic: Website Heat and Click Mapping

Explanation: Knowing exactly where you prospects are reading and looking on your website is extremely valuable because it allows you to position your best offers where people look the most.

Question to ask:

- Do you have the technology to do eye-tracking and heat map analytics on my website?

Topic: Google Analytics

Explanation: Google Analytics provides all the detailed statistics about your website that will help you keep producing results.

Question to ask:

- Will you install Google Analytics to track my website's traffic?

Topic: Google Webmaster Tools

Explanation: Google Webmaster Tools (GWT) offers critical data that Analytics does not about your website such as errors, diagnostics, sitemaps, and search query data. To keep your website in tip-top shape, you must have it installed.

Question to ask:

- Will you install Google Webmaster Tools to see more detailed information about my website?

Monitoring

Topic: Weekly/Monthly Strategy Calls

Explanation: We include actual face-to-face and dedicated phone time with you – the doctor – to develop and maximize your marketing strategy.

Questions to ask:

- Are you reviewing my stats and results weekly and monthly?
- Will you include time to tailor my marketing to my uniqueness?
- Will you check in on my success regularly?
- Will you provide me with ROI tracking forms to show you exactly how my marketing is performing every month?

Topic: Communication, Simplified.

Explanation: Have you worked with web marketing firms before that tried to talk to you in a foreign language? We understand the value of communication that you can relate to and understand. If you want the "nitty gritty" technical talk, we can give it to you, but if you just want to do dentistry, we can will explain it all to you with words and analogies you can easily understand.

Questions to ask:

- Will you talk to me in a language I can clearly understand?

Topic: Results Guaranteed

Explanation: If you're using a web marketing firm, are they guaranteeing their results?

Questions to ask:

- What guarantee, if any, do you include with my website?

- Does your guarantee wager a portion of your fees on my success?
- Will you check in on my success regularly?
- Will you provide me with ROI tracking forms to show you exactly how my marketing is performing every month?

Being Everywhere on the Internet

With Colin Receveur & Dr. James McAnally

James: Up next we're going to have Colin Receveur with, "Being Everywhere on the Internet." Like it or not, 35% of large elective cases show up or don't show up via your practice website and all the things you are doing online. For regular dentistry, the majority of those searching for "just a dentist" are doing that research online. No matter how you dice it, while certainly not a cure-all magic marketing bullet, every practice must have and incorporate the web as part of that marketing puzzle. There are several big questions seldom raised when discussing websites and online marketing for dentists and other service professionals. Number one: does this expert know anything about selling a cash-based service like dentistry? And number two: if this expert has something that really works, are they going to turn around and sell it to my competitors in my local market?

This is a pretty big secret … it's not so much a secret amongst those of us who are in the know but the reality is, especially with Google and how websites are ranked, there's a limitation to how many of that exact same ranking strategy can be deployed in a local market before it doesn't work anymore.

These are certainly two questions that came to the forefront of my mind over the last two years as we were searching for someone to be a web expert for our members. Our next speaker, Colin Receveur, has an intimate background of our profession, courtesy of his very successful father who happens to have a top performing practice and is also one of our Elite program members. In fact, he develops and provides our turnkey sites for Elite program members themselves, and also provides limited availability web services for advanced clinicians outside of that program. Of course, that means we don't sell it to every dentist on the block.

Colin started his own IT company eight years ago – which is 72 years in Internet time so don't let his youthful looks fool you. He owns a slew of certifications with Google, Microsoft, Cisco – they all come with little important letters after them. More important than those letters is his intimate knowledge of what we're up to as dentists and his ability to tie all the pieces together on the web. The fact that he gets it is why he has rapidly become known as a Google God for service professionals.

Yes, online technology is allowing us to leverage our time, effort, money, and energy to be in more places at once that we previously ever imagined: in front of our patients, our prospective patients and staying ahead of competitors. That's exactly why I asked Colin to put together his presentation to discuss just that: "Being Everywhere on the Internet." Colin, take it away.

Colin: Thanks James. I'd just like to start off and see how many people, by a show of hands, actually have a website for their practice already? And how many of you are using video or autoresponders or some of the more advanced tactics that we've seen James talk about? Very good, very good.

Thanks for having me, James. Who uses the web? The web is constantly evolving. 82%, Neilsen reports, go to the web to find local services in their area these days. That's over the Yellow Pages, over the newspaper and other traditional advertising mediums that have been used in the past.

Of those who search the web, Neilsen reports that 84% of people go to Google more so than Bing, Yahoo, other search engines that are available on the Internet.

Web marketing is simply the practice of enhancing your visibility on the Internet. Putting a website out there is kind of like putting a billboard up in the middle of nowhere. You want to make sure that your website is found and found by the people that are going to convert into patients for you.

This is an example of a search engine result page from Google. The red highlighted is going to be your Pay-Per-Click rankings: your Google AdWords. The green is the local listings and the blue is the organic results. The organic – when you hear people speak of getting to the top of Google – the organic is where they are trying to up-rank themselves into. A typical search engine result page, when done properly, could look like this. This is actually Dr. Receveur's found with a search for "New Albany dentures," which is our hometown. You can see sponsored listings, local isting, and then using many sites, taking advantage of the top three organic results here.

You'll also notice an example of a bad AdWords campaign right here. This guy is in Ohio and he is paying to show an ad for Louisville, Kentucky. That's wasted money. For instance, if we were to click on this advertisement here, that dentist would be charged a dollar, $2, $5 for that click for somebody that's potentially 500 miles away and has no possibility to convert into a patient.

Internet real estate – your domain names, your www dot coms: in 2004 there were 35 million domains registered with about 24,500 being newly registered per day. In 2008 there was 177 million total registered with about 73,000 new domains registered every day. 2009 is believed to be the peak, if you will, of new registrations but that doesn't mean the pool is decreasing. Kind of like the oil fields – you can only extract so much yet, one per second is being newly registered. Kind of like the old saying of the western gold rush: they aren't making any more land. There's only so many variations of your name out there on the Internet and so many dot coms to buy and once they're all taken, they're all gone.

Web marketing has become the new gold rush, if you will. The Yellow Pages has been in a steady decline; last year the Yellow Pages printed 540 million books – the "user friendlies" – all their physical books that they printed. In comparison, Google registered 1.1 trillion searches for local businesses last year. In 2009, 1.57 trillion searches: a huge increase – a 50% increase between '08 and '09 for local business searches. That accounts for people going online and searching for dentists, plumbers – everything across the board.

A lot of people here might not realize or understand how web marketing works. It's no different, really, than any other advertising medium. It's a matter of getting your traffic; this is achieved through Search Engine Optimization and through your Google AdWords. You have to get people to your site just the same as you have to get people to see your billboard or getting people to see your advertisement in the newspaper. You have to have people looking at it in order to convert them into patients. And when you do, that puts money in your pocket and as we surveyed here earlier, everybody would like to make more money.

An example of the traffic, as I said, is Search Engine Optimization – the natural organic listings. When people talk about getting to the top rankings of Google, that's what they're talking about doing. You can also do it through the paid listings, search engine marketing through your AdWords where it's a bidding war to get up to the top. I'm going to show you nine free tools and three AdWords tools that you can use to accomplish this. There will be a handout in the packet, so I'm going to go through these free tools very quickly and we can discuss them more later.

How SEO works: somebody goes on the Internet – they chipped a tooth or they had a crown fall off and they realize, "Hey, I need to find somebody that does dentistry." So they go online, which Nielsen says 82% of people go online to find that service, and they go to Google.com. They type in "'your local town' dentist" or "'your local town' dentures": maybe their denture doesn't fit anymore.

Search Engine Optimization is simply the method to connect their search term to your website. It's a way to make your website appear above your competition so that person finds your website, finds your phone number and calls you when they need that dental work done.

One of the tactics is through keyword research: finding out what keywords they are searching for when they are ready to make that purchase. One of the big complaints I hear is people with AdWords campaigns, and they say, "Well, I tried it, but I was paying $15, $20, or $30 a click and it's not being profitable." There's many different factors that go into that huge sum you are paying for every click. There is a thing called "quality score" and finding out, which keywords people actually buy on.

You don't want to advertise for every keyword out on the Internet. Somebody searching for "dentist" in Google, they might want to know who is Elmer Fudd's dentist. They might want to know how to get into dentistry school. Those are all phrases that if you just bid on the word "dentist," your advertisement is going to show up for and you are paying for clicks on those if somebody were to click on them. So you want to limit the scope of the keywords that your advertising on. Spiders browse your website and they report back to Google and index what keywords are found on your website so that when somebody searches, Google knows how to display you.

Any search engine's job is to take their visitor – their customer – and deliver them a website and not have them come back for another search. If I go to search on Google and I search for "plumber" and I come back to Google and search again, Google looks at that as they did a bad job the first time. I wasn't satisfied, so they probably need to tweak that result, find out what I looked at the second time and make it a better optimized process to deliver local, relevant results to people.

The keyword packing in the past – if you ever went to a website and it was all gibberish, it said "dentures" 10,000 times on it and it had just a bunch of gibberish and it seemed like they were trying to say "dentures"

100 times over, and over, and over – that's called keyword packing. Back in the early 2000s, that was one tactic that a lot of websites used to kind of cheat their way up the scales. Google has done away with that algorithm.

On your pages, you want to make sure you have a 500-word minimum. Google likes to reward unique and quality content. If you have a very cookie-cutter site with the same content as 500 other people on the Internet, Google is not going to give you the same kind of ranking advantage that they would give you if you wrote all the content yourself. One great example is for a heating and air company that I manage their Pay-Per-Click campaign. When we sat down and analyzed during the initial meeting, we found two phrases: "AC blows hot" versus "AC blowing hot." Two phrases that random people go in and search for on Google wouldn't seem that different to most people.

Who thinks that "AC blows hot" might be a more profitable keyword to search on? "AC blowing hot"? The only difference is one word. But something in the sight of people searching leads people that – when they say blowing, maybe that's your AC is blowing hot air on you versus your buddy calls you and says, "Hey, my AC blows hot air. What should I do?" That just goes to show you that people that type in "AC blowing hot" are more likely to buy your services.

Search engine faux pas: things not to do/things that can get you blacklisted and/or removed from the search engine rankings

Not all of these will get you removed but they are all practices that won't help you advance online.

Google has trouble reading Flash and Shockwave.

A lot of websites I see are very animated. Their whole site is a big whiz-bang whirl. Those are very cool, don't get me wrong – they are very neat to look at but Google can't read them. They can't index them and see what you are saying on there. And oftentimes, when you have a site like that, your visitor gets so caught up in the animation and the graphics they're not doing what you want them to do, which is to call you, to give you their email address so you can market to them down the road or contact you in some other manner.

Image-only pages where you just have one big image for the whole page

Some more technical things: image maps, frames, password protected pages. Adobe PDF document – Google has recently released a lot more support for so those are becoming more accepted nowadays. Dynamic pages and dropdown menus … that's more of a technical aspect but things that Google doesn't index quite as well versus using other methods.

Helpful Tools

The #1 free tool, and these aren't in order of significance, just the first one I'm going to show you is **Google's Wonder Wheel**. To find it, after you do a search on Google, click on the "show options" button right here and then you'll find the Wonder Wheel link down here in the bottom corner. This will give you a good idea of relevant keywords to what you've searched for: other terms that other people are searching for that you might want to look into. And if you are looking into it to advertise, other keywords that you might want to look into advertising under.

SEO Book's Rank Checker is a great tool to see where you rank in the search engines.

XML Sitemaps – Google likes to know where all your pages are – a sitemap is like a roadmap to your site. You submit it to Google and it tells Google what every page on your site is so that it can find those pages and index them.

Google's Webmaster Tools are a great way to look at query searches that are coming across your site and see other traffic and statistics that are coming in. They'll also show you any errors they find on your site.

KeywordDensity.com will give you the number of times a keyword is used on your site. I spoke before about keyword packing and trying to pack all those keywords into your site to be found better – which is a bad tactic because they will penalize you. However, you do want to use a normal conversational tone of keywords in your text.

If you would normally talk to somebody and talk about dentures, implants, or whatever niche you are talking about, that's the same tone you want to use in your website. Don't try to use the words too much or Google will catch onto that. They use automated algorithms, as well as they do personal, manual checking of certain websites randomly.

Yahoo Site Explorer is a great tool for looking at inbound links: other pages that link to your site. Other pages that link to your site are an important component of Search Engine Optimization. There's two parts: your on-page, which is your actual website/things you can change about your website that will help your ranking and then there's other people and how they relate to your site, which is also an important component. A great example of this is George Bush.

In the 2008 presidential election, some of the Democrats thought it would be funny and they launched an Internet campaign, and they put a link to George Bush's profile on the Whitehouse.com website. And the little link text said "miserable failure." They launched this link on millions and millions of sites. If anybody went to Google and typed in "miserable failure," the #1 result was George W. Bush and it actually carried over into Obama's profile that replaced his when he won the election. So other sites and how they link to yours are a very important component of where you rank when people search for you.

Search engine marketing, the paid aspects of your advertising campaign/the ads on the side. What is search engine marketing? It's the art of serving ads – very directed, targeted ads to people that are searching for you in your area.

Search Engine Optimization – the organic – is very different from what I'm about to show you here. Google AdWords: Google provides one of the many Pay-Per-Click options. Yahoo has a Pay-Per-Click service. Bing has a Pay-Per-Click service. Overture, which was in the early 2000 days, was kind of the originator of all this.

It's a way to reach your customers at the precise moment they are looking for your products and services on the Internet. You are not paying just to put your ad up. You are only paying when a user clicks on your advertisement. So you can display it a million times and if one user clicks on it, you are only paying for that one click.

Kipling, in 2008, reported that online advertising generates three times as much revenue as printed advertising. As I said before, your ads advertising on Google, 82% go online to find local services, and 84% of those people use Google. So by advertising on Google, you are taking the majority share of all the people that are searching for a local service. And Google's catchy phrase: "It Ads Up" for Google AdWords.

Keyword bidding. AdWords is basically a bidding war. In the early days, it was strictly a bidding war. Somebody could make a chainsaw advertisement appear for somebody looking to buy a set of dentures. Google realized that that's not in their best interest because they are delivering non-relevant results to that person searching.

So they've introduced other things, namely one called **Quality Score.** If you have a Google AdWords account, you might notice that one of your columns on that page is Quality Score. This times your bid factors where you are placed on that page.

So I've been in situations where a new customer might have a very bad Quality Score and Google will not allow them to overbid their next placement – they can't bid enough to get into the higher position on Google. So Quality Score is a very important component of your AdWords campaign. And Google will slap you with a tax: the Google Slap, as it's called.: if you have a bad Quality Score, they charge you more per click and that's your penalty for what Google deems not being relevant.

An example of this … **there are three different ways you can bid on keywords. A "broad match,"** such as if you bid on the term "best dentist," you will show up for these three search terms here. Your advertisement will show up for all three of those search terms. Only one of those three you would really want to be bidding on. The other two are completely irrelevant. You don't want to pay for an advertisement for somebody that's looking on how to become a dentist. We're all here looking to expand dental practice and provide services – you are not looking to be a dental school.

A **"phrase match"** is narrowing it down by putting that inside quotes. What this means is that phrase has to appear somewhere in the query. So, this is a great way to narrow it down, but it's still not foolproof because somebody could add words before or after that search term that make your website irrelevant.

And the most exact way is **an "exact match."** What you bid on is exactly the only results that your ad will show for. So if you put it in brackets and you say, I only want to bid on 'best dentist,' I want to pay $3 a click maximum for [best dentist]." Your advertisement is only going to show when somebody searches for that – nothing before, nothing after.

And then there's also **negative keywords.** For instance, I know in Ron's case, there is a New Albany, Ohio, as well as a New Albany, Indiana. So, Ohio is one of our negative keywords because we don't want our ads showing for somebody that's searching for Ohio. That's completely irrelevant.

How to Tweak Your AdWords

Relevance, relevance, relevance. You have to be relevant. Google will penalize you. You'll pay a whole lot of money if you aren't. Research your competitors and grow your list. You'd be surprised how many misspellings produce and are profitable.

In your ad groups, you notice somebody searching for "dentures." This is another big common faux pas I see with AdWords. When somebody is searching for "dentures," you don't want to deliver them an advertisement about sedation. If somebody is searching for "fear," you don't want to show them implants. You want to give them very tight, relevant results. You do this through creating tight groups of advertisements. A lot of AdWords campaigns simply have a big list of keywords and a bunch of advertisements, and they all just get jumbled together and spit out every, which way. Split test your advertisements. In traditional advertising terms, let's say you had a 10,000 person mailing list. You split that 10,000 down the middle, creating two 5,000 person mailing lists. You send a different direct mail card to each one and see the results.

Same thing online. We can split test advertisements and see, which one produces better. It's done in real-time, randomly, one and one, one by one. Eventually you find out. Same with the "AC blows" versus "AC blowing." One word changes in your advertisements can produce the same results. You'll see a one word change in your headline or your text will create another half percent conversion rate. And common metrics are impressions – how many times somebody sees it, which you are not being charged on. You are only charged when they click – how many times somebody clicks. The rate in which people click is the division of impressions by clicks: your cost per click and then your conversion rates.

You can also do geographical targeting, which is a major component. You don't want to be advertising all across the country for your dental services. You want to be marketing in a 50 or 100 mile radius.

The next free tool is **Google's own keyword tool.** This will find relevant keywords for your campaign. It will even scour your website and partially do the work for you: analyze your website and generate a keyword list. This is the area where you can actually plug in your website and generate that keyword list. Just put your website in there and it will analyze it and spit out a list of keywords that it recommends.

Keyword Spy is a fantastic tool if you have other people in your area that are AdWords advertising. Keyword Spy allows you to see what they are bidding on, how much they are bidding, and all of their advertisements in one central area. It's basically kind of stealing their information. Actually, we pay for it when they've already spent the money to research it.

Google's Local Business Center: the local listings. On the right, you have the paid. On the bottom, you have the organic. The local listings are a little green cloud – that's what this is right here. It will actually show your name and address. And this backend provides you will all the statistics on that – how many people looked at it. We've talked about how you get people to your website through your Search Engine Optimization and through your AdWords. Now we're going to talk about how you convert those people into patients because just sending people to your website and finding out how many hits you got on your website doesn't really put any dollars in your pocket. If you are not converting them into calls, you are just another advertisement – another website out there on the Internet.

Conversion is done through drip marketing, autoresponders, social networking, and video. I'll show you a free tool that we use to do this. We provide the autoresponder or drip marketing with every website we do. It's a critical part.

Once you pay for that click, you pay that $3, $4, or however many dollars you pay to get that person to your website, you want to keep them. If it's a big case, if they are spending 20 or 30 or $50,000, chances are they are not going to find your website and decide you are the one right there on the spot. It's going to be a one, two or six month process of looking around and shopping.

So when that person comes to your website, you want to grab their information. And you want to send them an email every couple weeks for the next year about random stuff – not a sales pitch. If they are interested in dentures, send them some simple denture tips and simple health related tips – anything just to put your name back in front of them. Show them you're still there. Send them patient testimonials: video emails in your drip marketing like Ron was talking about earlier. We can coordinate this with offline marketing as well. In this preconfigured automatic sequence, when that patient puts their email into your website, they get a preconfigured sequence of a year, completely hands-off.

In that sequence, you can also configure to send them a postcard in the mail to just kind of sum up … maybe they are not an email person. Maybe they are more a postal mail/snail mail kinda guy – you can coordinate with offline marketing. And you want to do multiple sequencing: one for dentures, one for implants. Again, you want to be very relevant. If they are looking for denture help, don't send them stuff about being scared of the dentist and how you can calm their fears. In this new digital age and especially the younger generations in the future, as they grow up and become more into the big case arena, are very instant gratification centered. They want what they want right now and they don't want to see anything irrelevant. Automating offline fulfillment, mailers and DVDs – all things you can do through our system.

Social networking is kind of the same concept as drip marketing. Somebody goes to your website, you want to make them your friend or they want to make you their friend. Same concept. You want to stay in touch with them down the road. Send them a Facebook message. Send out a broadcast. Get them to join your Facebook page. It's not likely to give you much ranking in search engines to give you a higher rank, but you will retain those people that go to your website.

Facebook actually bounces between #2 and #3 with YouTube as top Internet sites. Google is the #1 site, Facebook #2, YouTube is #3, Blogger is the #7 website on the Internet, so on and so forth. But those are some popular social media sites that you definitely want to make sure your name is on.

This is a free tool that I use: **Hello Text**. There are many of them out there. This is my favorite. It allows you to update all your social networks in one click. So instead of going to 10 different websites here that are listed, you set up an account with Hello Text and you go to Hello Text only, you type something in the status box and it propagates it to all your sites at once. Very simple administration. It's a free service. All these are free tools so far.

Video on the Web

I can't talk enough about how important video on the web is. YouTube gets 200,000 new videos posted daily. And in the past 10 weeks, more new video has been added to YouTube than all major news networks have produced since 1948. That accounts for about 20 hours of new video every minute. About 1.2 billion videos watched per day and YouTube is #3; like I said, it bounces around with Facebook for the #2/#3 position.

Tracking Your Results

I've shown you how to get the traffic to your site – how to convert that traffic into patients. Now what you want to do is make sure you know what's going on. If you are not tracking what's going on, you don't really know if it's working, if it's not working, or really what you are getting. I'll show you two great tools to do that with.

Phone conversion tracking: you want to track the search results. Not only do you want to track hits and clicks, you want to track phone calls. Chris will talk a ton about this tomorrow but recording the phone calls for quality assurance is a great way to make sure that your staff is doing what you want it to do. Just because you get those hits and clicks and you get the phone calls, if you are not continuing that sales process, you are not going to see the results from all your hard work.

With the phone tracking that Big Case uses, you can hear a whisper in your ear when that lead calls. So if you put a special trackable phone number in a Yellow Pages advertisement or in a newspaper advertisement, somebody sees that advertisement and they call one of the doctors here that used it, when your front office staff answers the phone, they hear, "Yellow Pages" or "newspaper" whispered in their ear before the call is connected. So if you want to cue up a special script to that advertisement – some kind of special you are running – it gives them a little bit of advance notice what they're getting into.

Call recordings: you can use these anywhere. You can do local or toll-free numbers, depending on what kind of image you want to relay. Google reports that 63% of consumers complete a sale offline. Keep in mind that statistics take into account the Amazon.com's, the TigerDirect.com's, all of the very product-oriented sales as well. They don't have a statistic for only service oriented sales online. That number would probably be close to 100%. But even people that are ordering little widgets off the Internet like to complete the sale by phone.

This is an example of the call tracking, kind of what you can see from the results. You can see the different campaigns over here. You can see how many of your calls were answered, how many went to voicemail, how many were hang-ups: a hang-up is before the call is actually connected to your staff. And then by day of the week here, call status per day and by hour. You can see that 4 PM and the morning are hot hours for phone calls from these advertisements. You can also see who is calling you: see the name, their number, the phone number that it forwarded to, your office line, time, duration, and answer.

And this leads us to our next free tool: **Google Analytics**. Google Analytics will tell you everything you need to know and everything you never wanted to know about your website. They'll tell you more than you'll ever be able to comprehend. They provide too much information, in a lot of cases. But it's great because you can see exactly what's happening on your website and tweak the parts that aren't performing.

One of the … I don't want to say a drawback but one of the missing links in the past has been that you had your web marketing and everybody can see exactly what's happening on the web and then you have your phone tracking over here, and you can tell that a phone call came from a specific advertisement but you can't interlink the two. For instance: somebody searches, they go to your website, they see your trackable 800 number and they pick up the phone and call you. You can see somebody searched and you can see somebody called you from that advertisement, but you can't see what the person that called you searched for. I've developed a system that can link the two. So when somebody calls your office, you can see what that person searched for and where they came from online before they called your office – kind of the missing link between the two worlds.

And to review just all the topics we covered, I'll open up the floor to questions at this time.

Call-in Questions

Man: I didn't get where you got the whisper and the telephone call.

Colin: What it does, it's a seamless transition. You are provided with a special number that forwards through the Big Case systems. It forwards to your office line so there's no extra hardware that you need.

Man: I got that part. So that's coming from Big Case Marketing.

Colin: Correct. Yeah, the whisper is simply something before the call is connected. Just a little tone in your ear so you know where the call is coming from – what advertisement.

Man: One of the things that I have difficulty in my practice doing – and we do record all phone calls coming in – and we have a different number for all the TV, and all the radio, and the print ads that we do, and a different number for the Internet.

Our #1 number called is the Internet, so much so that we're thinking of removing the Internet from the recorded because so many calls come from there that aren't necessarily related to the marketing. The question is, do you have a system of being able to figure out how the person who heard the TV commercial but didn't call from the TV commercial, then went to the website, as we're trying to do with the TV commercial – do you have a way of tying those two together? If so, how?

Colin: Absolutely. What you can do is, for instance, I use Ron as my example all the time because he's the dummy. Let's say your website is BestOhioDentist.com. You can also purchase BestOhioDentist.net, put that website in your advertisement and set up a special tracking code on it so that only people that go to that .net address, the only place that web address is seen is in your advertisement. So anybody that goes to that address you know is directly from your advertisement. Does that make sense? It's more of a technical thing, but it's very easy to set up.

Man: Could you discuss the totality of web marketing, how the fact that a good keyword, for example, may not mean very much if you don't have video on it; how the video and the website and all of it all works together to give you the best economy.

Colin: Sure. I get a lot of questions for people that just want to do AdWords or they just want to do Search Engine Optimization. My answer is sure, you can do piecemeal. But what happens then is you send a lot of traffic to your website, but people get to your website and they go, "Well, this guy is the same as everybody else," or, "He's okay." Or guys that do the video and they don't do the search engine marketing and the Search Engine Optimization, they don't get any traffic to convert.

You could have the greatest website in the world but if people aren't seeing it, you can't get any patients from it. By the same token, you can send all the traffic in the world to your website but if it doesn't convince people that they need to call you and make that next step: tell people what they need to do – you're not going to convert any patients. So it's the "whole pie" approach to things. You have to get the people and send them to the site, and you also have to have the videos to convert them. The video is a huge growing sector, as I showed you with the statistics, on getting people to call you after they get to your website.

Man: In regards to Facebook, Twitter, Blogger, and whatnot, have you ever found any success with specifically advertising on Facebook on the right-hand side? Secondly, how do you get Twitter, Blogger, and whatnot to really help build up your organic searches?

Colin Receveur

Colin: That's a great question. In the past, I haven't seen a whole lot of success from Facebook advertising. With that said, the fastest growing segment of Facebook right now is the 55- to 65-year-old female. I know my mom just got an account on there. I think as time progresses, you are going to see the older generation get onto the Facebooks – the social networks, and that's going to become a more powerful medium, where, in the past, it was mostly the 20s guys/30s. But it's progressing into the next age groups.

Man: How important is the integration of things into your website construction in relation to Search Engine Optimization? For instance, I'm sitting here, I have a website that I've had for some years. If I wanted to use these strategies, so to speak, do I have to rewrite the website and reconstruct this thing from the ground up in order to, let's say, tag it properly? Or can you work with existing websites that have already been written or do they just float in general because they haven't been constructed properly?

Colin: There's different answers to that. There's the coding: the part you don't see on the website that's very important to how you get ranked. And that part can be changed, really, without any change to the look. Think of just putting a different engine in the car. You are changing the engine, it might go faster, but it all looks the same. The look of your website, it really depends. Some websites that I see are just not designed well: they are confusing, they don't have clearly defined navigation areas or good content organization. So, a lot of times you have to redo the website. Otherwise, the person is going to go to the page and go, "Wow. I'm confused. Where do I click? What do I do?" You know, you've got 100 things that are bolded and there's not a clear indication of what to do.

Man: Which ties into the relevance issue that you were talking about.

Colin: Exactly. There was a study done, I think it was Comscore that did this study: a user, when they go to your website, you have 20 milliseconds. They make their decision on your website within 20 milliseconds. That seems crazy. They did a study where they flashed web pages in front of people for different amounts of time. They found that the user's decision at 20 milliseconds and the user's decision at two seconds was nearly identical. So that first impression really counts with your website.

Man: Colin, is it true that if you constantly update your website, add more content – more news, then Google will pick you up faster or sooner than anybody else?

Colin: I don't know that they'll pick you up faster or sooner but they will give you more ranking. Changing your content, adding unique content all the time, turning it over, having a blog; a blog is a great simple way to do it. And don't be scared by the word. I see a lot of people that hear that four letter word and they get weak in the knees. But it's nothing more than typing a Word document and hitting submit and there's your article on the Internet. So yeah, a blog is a great way to do that.

Man: Second question is to add whisper to your phone call, do we have to call our local phone company to set it up? How does that whisper happen?

Colin: It's set up through Larry, and he can do all the details and all that for you on how that works but it's separate from your local phone company.

Woman: I noticed that there's a lot of practices that have more than one website. Do you recommend that? Is it better to get a whole lot of websites out there? Will you produce more?

Colin: You want quality first. But, quantity with quality is better than having one quality website. Mini sites are a great way to dominate your rankings. Using mini sites are a great way to take the first half page of your listings. If you go back to your hotel room, try searching for "New Albany dentures implants." You'll find that Dr. Receveur's websites – he has seven of them, three of which we just recently launched in a new geographical area – but four of those sites that have been existing for several years take up the first half page of the results when you search for that.

Woman: So if you basically do implants, or cosmetic dentistry, or even just general dentistry, should you put them on different websites?

Colin: Yes. Using niche sites is something that I strongly recommend. This site here, New Albany Implants, it's his implant site. This is Indiana Smiles, his main site. There's a Columbus, Ohio, guy here, which is irrelevant. But if you go down below – I couldn't include it because of space constraints – but there's also New Albany Dentures and New Albany Sedation that appear down here below. Depending on what you search, they come up in different rankings. But yes, quantity with quality is a fantastic way to basically dominate the search engine result page: SERP for short.

Man: What kind of pagerank can we expect? I've been doing all this work on my website and I never got past three.

Colin: Are you talking about up in the little Google toolbar where it says three out of ten?

Man: Yeah.

Colin: That was great back in the early 2000s. PageRank played a very important part in the actual ranking on this search engine result page. Nowadays, they don't give so much weight to it so I would look more at. If you remember the free tool I gave you, the Rank Checker, take a look at that and focus more on your rank there because that's going to give you a better idea of where you appear for different search queries. Your actual page rank that Google provides just doesn't hold a lot of weight anymore. That page rank is based on inbound links and as I told you with the White House, George Bush's thing, they have taken weight off of that so people can't abuse it.

Man: Another question. In the analytics, I've been watching the average time someone spends on the website. I notice it's climbing and I'm happy for that. But I don't know whether my numbers are any good. In 2009, we went from about a minute, 37 seconds, we're up to a minute, 51 seconds. So that's improving, but are these people having five minutes and my site is underperforming, or are they all at 16 seconds and mine is great? I don't have any idea.

Colin: Are you doing any kind of phone tracking?

Man: We do some phone tracking, but I don't have that whisper. I heard that and went, "Wow, that's fantastic." We do so many different things to get people to our website. We know they've come from the website but we don't know whether it was organic, SEO or AdWords. Or sometimes, people just type your name in and it comes up and they say website, even though they heard somebody say it. So we've had a tough time tracking. I think that whisper is going to help a lot. But I can't answer that exactly.

Colin: There's many answers to it. Once those people get to your website, obviously the time they spend on the site isn't as important as what they do. You could have 15 second average times, but if they come to your site and give you their email address, or they come to your site and call you immediately, that's a whole lot better than having even a 10 minute visit time on your site.

So I would look at making sure you capture their email address. With Dr. Receveur's sites, I have several different locations as you scroll down the page continually asking and asking for their email address. "I'll give you a free report. I'll tell you the nine biggest secrets of dentures. What's your biggest fear? We can solve it." And ask for their email address, because they get thrown into that sequence. You hit them automatically for a year down the road and convert them. So I would make sure that you are looking into the follow-up metrics.

Man: You mentioned the first impression look of the website – that first 20 milliseconds. Do you have examples of a certain type of look to the website, ones that work and ones that don't work so well?

Colin: I don't have any here on my presentation with me. I'd be glad to show you some examples afterwards. We can go find an Internet PC. They've got a lobby with wireless. But yes, there are some standardized looks. I use, I don't want to say a template, but I do use the same kind of look and feel on most websites I do for dentists because I've tested it over the years. I did Dr. Receveur's first website in '97. By today's standards, it would be a blooper. But yeah, there are some standardized looks, feels, and colors that I use.

Man: Colin, is there a difference between websites that want to garner patients versus websites that want to educate patients that may have already come to see you?

Colin: You get the Wikipedia – the overflowing amounts of information from it?

Man: Well, in other words, my goal in a website, rather than just to get people that pick implant dentistry, would be a person I've seen and I say, "I want him or her to go onto the website to learn more or to see more about what we do."

Colin: Definitely you want to educate your patients. But I've found that putting, for instance, some before and after pictures and telling them too much about the clinical side of the procedure – how you do an implant – turns off a lot of patients. So, yes you want to educate them but don't over educate them to where you tell them that you're going to be drilling in their jaw. Maybe they are scared to death of drills – something to that effect. But yeah, you definitely want to educate them, but keep it in a sales sense, moving down the end of the funnel.

I just did a new educational type seminar with Dr. Ron. We filmed him. It's a 19-minute deal. It's going to be used in-office to where he gets that patient in from the website as a lead, they go into the consult room, he plays this presentation, and then he goes in and talks to them. So they get their complete education about everything after they've already responded. They're in the office. So you make sure you don't scare them away too soon.

Man: I had one other question that I need to ask. In my area, when you type in "implant," the first one that comes up is the $825 dental implant. That's #1 no matter what you put in. I don't know how they got there, but they got there. My question is, is that an approach? In other words, whatever else you are going to read that's already there, but that's what got them there is the $825 implant.

Colin: I'd put some prices in on the advertisements for consultations – to kind of qualify them – if they are coming in for a big case and you put down that you charge $147 for a one hour consult or whatever you do. I don't know that I would put up prices of actual procedures. But sometimes a qualifier for a consultation price can kind of scare away some of the deadbeats that are looking just for a freebie or a handout. I know James does the research study. Putting a price qualifier on that is a great way to scare away people that might just be coming in because they think it's free.

Woman: On your homepage, that's what Google immediately sees when they go and they spider, right?

Colin: Correct.

Woman: Say you have the animation at the top – the first quarter of your homepage. You don't have any content. When you were talking about the word packing, is it not useful to have the hidden text behind it? Even though the patient doesn't see it physically on the website, it's still behind there.

Colin: The hidden text stuff is kind of the same thing … it's different from word packing. I don't want to say Google doesn't give any weight to it, but that's a tactic that's been used for 10 years. People that do hidden text to make the words rank them up, Google knows the trick and they have it into their algorithms to avoid it.

Google is not looking at your page – they are looking at the code i the page. There's ways to make, in the code, your text appear before the video, but on the display, your video before the text. So instead of using hidden text, that would be what I recommend. It's a completely technical thing that the user doesn't see at all. But that's how I would look at doing that.

Woman: And do you recommend any website developers?

Colin: That's why I'm here.

There's a lot of guys. There's other competitors that do what we do. The one thing that I would tell you is ask them for their results. A lot of companies will tell you what they do, but they won't show you what they did. Any of you are welcome to pull up Ron's, or in a private consultation, I'd be glad to show you some other clients that I've worked with and what kind of rankings and results I've shown for them.

Woman: You do recommend a more individualized … I know I've researched other dentists, obviously, and looked at their websites online. I've come across several that are almost exactly the same except for the colors; even the content. It's just kind of a generic … a lot of verbiage, a lot of words. There's a lot of content, but it's the same exact content. So how much does that hurt?

Colin: Google doesn't release their exact algorithm. They don't tell you if you do *this* they are going to derank you five positions. So it's kind of a guess and check. But they do tell you generalities. They will tell you that non-unique content is bad. They will derank you for that. So you want to be unique. You want to update the content. But as far as exact numbers, unfortunately that's one of their proprietary things. None of the search engines say exactly what figures where.

Man: You had mentioned different sites – one for implants, one for sedation, one for dentures. I understand the importance of it. Now, what if you are in more than one geographic area? Is it better to put different addresses on those websites? Or how do you go from one location and optimizing into another geographic area?

Colin: You can certainly put multiple addresses on one website if you want. I recommend that you split them up and make one address per website. The niche sites, like here, New Albany Implants, that's location specific – New Albany – and procedure specific – implants. The other three sites that I mentioned for Dr. Receveur that we launched were for Louisville, Kentucky. New Albany is simply a suburb of Louisville. So

the other sites are www.LouisvilleKentuckyDentalImplants.com, www.
LouisvilleKentuckyDentures.com, etc. So yeah, location and procedure
specific is a great way to take over these rankings down here.

With the AdWords, you can specify different geographic areas. By
putting different keywords in your domain names – different keywords
on the pages, you can go after different geographic areas in the organic
rankings as well.

Take Action Now!

"I'm looking to put all my competition out of business."

~ Raleigh Pioch, D.D.S

*"He has online technologies allowing us to leverage our time, effort, money and energy to be in more places at once than we've previously ever imagined: in front of our patients, our prospective patients, and to stay ahead of competitors. **The reality is, if your market is available, whether it be for a website that he could produce or for analyzing your local marketing situation for your online marketing, you'd be crazy not to grab it before another doctor does because someone will take it.** So again, get going with Colin. You'll be glad you did."*

~ James McAnally, D.D.S.

*"SmartBox Web Marketing designed and created my website. They did it very quickly and the results were excellent. They used many of my ideas and suggested many more that have made it turn out much better than I expected! **I'll keep on working with them and highly recommend anyone to do the same.** Thank you very much, Colin!"*

~ Andoni Guisasola, D.D.S.

*"I had talked to a few other companies and just called them up and they wanted you to do a lot more research and some just didn't seem to gel as well. They said we'll do this part of it: we can do your website but we don't do the SEO or you have to do your own Facebook. When you kind of explained that you covered it all, that's what I want – that's who I'm looking for. And then you said you were going to do Pay-Per-Clicks, do Facebook, **coordinate everything under one roof** so that's what I was looking for. You said I could be as involved as much as I wanted or you could take over it and just run with it."*

~ Thomas L. Phillips, Jr. D.D.S.

*"If you are looking for someone to build a new website for your dental office, I personally recommend Colin. Given how much I already know, **it is clear to me that he knows his stuff, and I am confident that you will be pleased with his work.**"*

~ Charles Payet, D.D.S.

olin Receveur   355

*"'Hold for line one for sales, hold for line two for support with software,' – it's just not like that. **It's an individual who actually comes from a dental field** (has a little genetics going in there from Dad being a dentist,) so it's a huge, huge difference. We highly recommend them. You've got nothing to lose; all you have to do is give them a call. **All you have to do is look them up on the Internet and let them show you what they can do for you.**"*

~ Michael P. Abernathy, D.D.S.

"I would definitely refer anyone to try this out; it was great."

~ J.D. Murray, D.D.S.

"If your market is available, you'd be crazy not to grab it before another doctor does."

~ James McAnally, D.D.S.

Reference, Resources and Terms

Drip Marketing Resources and Glossary of Terms

SmartBox Web TV

Video training resources for smart dentists

http://SmartBoxWeb.tv

SmartBox Article Library

How-to articles and training covering all aspects of web marketing

http://SmartBoxWebMarketing.com/article/

The Patient Attraction Podcast

Our daily podcast that we post to weekly with the latest in web marketing

http://www.smartboxwebmarketing.com/itunes-podcast-webinars/

Get Infusionsoft

Making your marketing happen automatically!

http://InfusionsoftForDentists.com

HootSuite

Social media dashboard – plan and organize your social media instantly

http://HootSuite.com

Glossary of Terms

Bit.ly - URL shortening and redirection service that allows you to easily share and track how many people click on your links

Blog - A type of website where articles are posted by an author and displayed, typically in reverse chronological order to people browsing

Google Shortlink - Shorten, share and track your shortened URL

Hashtag - A type of identifier used with Twitter allowing you to categorize and assign a topic of interest to an update you are making

Immediate Buyer - A person who is ready to make a buying decision in the next 30 days

Landing Page (Lead Capture Page, Squeeze Page) - A single web page that is shown in response to an advertisement – typically will display very directed sales copy that is an extension of the advertisement, targeted specifically at what the prospect is interested in

Lead (Prospect) - A person who proactively reaches out to your office

PageRank - An algorithm invented and named after Google's founder, Larry Page, that assigned a numerical value to a webpage for the purpose of measuring it's importance

Referral Source - The person who recommends or refers a prospect to you

Risk-Free Offer - Provides a path for a prospect to contact you in a non-threatening way to get more information about your services

RSS - A method of sharing your blog or news updates with your readers, also known as a "web feed"

Sales Pipeline (Funnel) - The process your prospects go through on their way to becoming a paying patient

Search Engine - A website, such as Google, Bing, or Yahoo, designed to index and categorize the Internet's information into an easy to use database to help a searcher find what they are looking for

Search Engine Marketing (SEM) - The form of Internet marketing that promotes your website through the use of paid advertisements, one example being Google AdWords

Search Engine Optimization (SEO) - The process of improving the visibility of a website or web page via the natural (organic) search results

Social Bookmarking - A method for users to store and share bookmarks of their favorite websites with their friends online

Social Media - The web-based and mobile technologies that turn communication into an interactive dialog, allowing for the exchange of user-created content and social interactions

Social Media Marketing (SMM) - Also called Social Media Optimization or SMO, the targeted marketing through social media and networks – viral marketing campaigns fall under this category

Social Networking - An online website that focuses on building and nurturing social relations amongst people with common interests or activities

Tags - A term used to help describe or categorize a piece of information, such as a blog or website

Tire Kicker - A person who is looking for more information about your services but is unlikely to follow through with the purchase

Tweet - An update on Twitter

Vlog - Same as a Blog but instead of posting articles, the author posts videos, usually displayed in reverse chronological order

Web 2.0 - The evolution of websites into a user-centered design that allows for sharing, collaboration, and interoperability on the World Wide Web; trademarks of web 2.0 are social networking, blogs, wikis, video sharing, and cloud applications

Web 3.0 - The future of the Internet, relying not only on social interactions and video but also including augmented reality (such as Layar) and geo-social applications (Foursquare, Google+, Facebook Places) that build upon Web 2.0s technologies

Some experts predict Web 3.0 to be the Semantic Web where rather than a search engine being geared toward keywords, it will be geared toward the user experience, taking into metrics like culture, location, or localized jargon when returning search results to the user.